The Rural Church in America
A Century of Writings

GARLAND REFERENCE LIBRARY
OF THE HUMANITIES
(VOL. 1160)

The Rural Church in America
A Century of Writings
A Bibliography

Gary A. Goreham

GARLAND PUBLISHING, INC. • NEW YORK & LONDON
1990

Library of Congress Cataloging-in-Publication Data

Goreham, Gary.
   The rural church in America: a century of writings: a
bibliography / Gary A. Goreham.
      p.   cm. — (Garland reference library of the humanities ; vol.
1160)
   ISBN 0-8240-3439-2 (alk. paper)
   1. Rural churches—United States—Bibliography. 2. United States—
Church history—Bibliography. I. Title. II. Series.
Z7757.U5G6   1990   BV638
016.2773'009173'4—dc20   89–39156
                                                          CIP

Printed on acid-free, 250-year-life paper
Manufactured in the United States of America

Contents

Acknowledgements

This compilation of rural church references could not have been accomplished without the assistance of several people. I wish to thank the staff of the Interlibrary Loan Department at North Dakota State University, Lorretta Mindt and Deb Sayler, for their efforts in securing hundreds of documents over the past three years. Their prompt response and flexible assistance contributed greatly to the production of this book.

In addition, I wish to acknowledge the assistance of the library staffs at Bethel College and Seminary (St. Paul, Minnesota), the College of St. Thomas (St. Paul, Minnesota), Concordia College (Moorhead, Minnesota), Emory University and Candler School of Theology (Atlanta, Georgia), Montreat-Anderson College (Montreat, North Carolina), Seattle Pacific University (Seattle, Washington), the University of Georgia (Athens, Georgia), and the University of Washington (Seattle, Washington).

Many individuals provided documents and suggestions for this book. I wish to thank Gary Farley (Home Mission Board, Southern Baptist Convention), John Holik (University of Missouri, Columbia), Herbert Klem (Bethel Theological Seminary), Marvin Konyha (U.S.D.A.), and Carlton Sollie (Mississippi State University). Mary Lackmann and Cynthia Saar, graduate assistants at North Dakota State University, helped locate many of the older documents. Brenda Ekstrom provided technical assistance with the computer and offered her expertise in editing. Richard Rathge, director of the State Data Center at North Dakota State University, kindly offered moral support as well as computer facilities.

Finally, I wish to thank my wife, Jonna, and daughters, Jessica and Julie Anne, for bearing with me through the course of this project. They patiently visited library after library during our vacation times.

Introduction

Prior to 1920 the majority of Americans lived on farms or in rural communities. As a result, authors who wrote about churches and the people who attended them were, to a large extent, writing about the *rural* church. However by 1980 the population shifted to the point that only one out of every four Americans lived in rural areas. This rural-to-urban population shift has not been without impact on the rural church and what has been written about it.

Authors throughout the past century described how social, economic, and demographic change in rural America affected the church. They discussed ways the church responded or failed to respond. Some lauded the efforts of the rural church to serve the needs of rural people. Others decried its failures. Nearly all wrote with the passion of rural prophets. Their platforms included academic journals and popular magazines, clergy conferences and university reports, academic books and denominational bulletins. A collection of these writings helps us better understand where the rural church has been, where it is, and where it may be going.

The church continues to be a force both in the lives of rural people and in their communities. Thus, most of the larger denominations maintain departments to provide services to rural churches. Many of their seminaries offer coursework on rural ministries. Additionally, social scientists continue to conduct research on rural churches and the religion of rural people. The purpose of this book is to provide those involved with rural churches a historical overview of the rural church as well as references to current writings on the topic. The specific scope and audience of the book is described below.

Scope

The United States is not the only country where rural churches have been studied. In the process of searching for writings on the rural church, documents on the topic were located from nearly every country in Europe. Very few of these were

written in English. Additionally, a host of writings were found
that pertained to missionary efforts in the rural areas of Asia,
Africa, and South America. While these documents would likely
be of value to rural church leaders and researchers, they were
excluded because of space limitations. A collection of these
references would certainly require additional volumes. Thus, this
collection contains only documents pertaining to the rural church
in America written in English.

Although other bibliographies of rural church literature have
been written, most of them provided listings only of then-current
documents. Researchers and denominational leaders typically
make use of current as well as historical writings. A historical
perspective is an asset to many of their studies and decisions.
For example, they may ask what are the similarities between the
church's response to the farm crisis of the 1980s and the
depression of the 1930s or the postwar recovery of the late 1940s
or the activism of the 1960s? Or what ideas for rural ministry
have been successfully used but recently overlooked that could
once again be employed? To answer these kinds of questions, it
is vital to have access to writings over an extended period of
time. As a result, this text went beyond the current writings and
included references to documents from the past century.

The media used to discuss rural churches included books,
journal articles, conference proceedings, papers presented at
professional meetings, governmental reports, land-grant university
reports, denominational publications, theses and dissertations, and
periodical articles. An attempt was made to locate all of the
references to rural churches written over the past century in each
of these media. Inevitably, not all documents in each media were
uncovered. I would be grateful for references to any other
documents not included in this collection.

Some of the writings located were only tangential to the
topic of the rural church. For example, documents were found
that pertained to religion in Appalachia or other regions of the
country, religious groups such as the Amish or the Hutterites,
and agricultural issues. Although a few of these documents are
included, an exhaustive listing of references on these kinds of
topics was not within the scope of this text. Additionally, a body
of literature emerged that pertained to small churches. Although
a substantial number of rural churches are relatively small, the
topics of small churches and rural churches are not necessarily
synonymous. Thus, only those documents about small churches
that pertained also to rural churches are cited.

For the purposes of this bibliography, documents may be
classified into four categories. The first category includes writings
on the rural church authored from a religious perspective.
Second, documents about topics other than the church authored
from a religious perspective were located. The third category
comprised writings about the rural church from a nonreligious

perspective. Finally, documents have been written from a nonreligious perspective about topics other than the rural church. The scope of this text was limited only to the first three categories of documents.

Methodology

The overall method used in collecting the references listed in this book was that of "snowballing." The project began by obtaining rural church writings physically available at the North Dakota State University library. Many of these documents cited other documents. In order to determine the applicability of the second set of documents for inclusion in this book, they were ordered through interlibrary loan. The borrowed documents cited additional writings which were, in turn, obtained through various loan processes, hence the "snowball" methodology. This method was particularly useful for obtaining books and journal articles.

In addition to the books and journal articles immediately available, a bibliographic search of various abstracts and computer listings was conducted. The bibliographic search provided a rich source of journal and periodical articles. After these documents were located, the "snowball" method was employed.

A number of individuals aware of the project provided me with copies of documents they had on hand. These individuals are affiliated with various denominations, universities, or the U.S. Department of Agriculture. They had access to a substantial number of papers presented at professional meetings, conference proceedings, and denominational publications. As with the previous sources of rural church references, the "snowball" method was again used.

In some cases, copies of various documents or complete bibliographic information could not be located. A decision was then made to determine if the document should be excluded or if it should be included with an incomplete citation. The decision to include a document with incomplete bibliographic information was based on my own judgement. In total, nearly 2,200 references were located.

Organization of the Bibliography

The references included in the text were sorted according to their media type. Chapter 1 includes books, pamphlets, and theses. Chapter 2 lists academic journal articles. Government publications and land-grant university reports are included in Chapter 3. Papers delivered at professional meetings and conference proceedings comprise Chapter 4. Chapter 5 contains a list of periodical and newspaper articles. Within each chapter, references were sorted by author and date of publication.

Two indexes were created to assist readers in finding references. The first index lists the authors of the documents. Wherever possible, the author's full name was included in the index. However, the author's name as it was found on the original document or as it was included in the bibliographic source was used in the reference. The second index contains a list of subjects. Where possible, key words were used as given in the bibliographic source or in the document itself. When key words could not be located, they were developed based on my own reading of the documents.

Findings

A reading of the documents included in this bibliography provides a broad overview of the history of rural church concerns as well as an indication of current issues. A number of themes emerged: (1) the impacts that contextual changes have on the rural church; (2) the church's response to these changes; (3) the struggle to define the nature and mission of the rural church; (4) the struggle to develop a theology and philosophy for the rural church, as well as related issues like a theology of agriculture, the land, and rural life; and (5) descriptions of the methods and techniques necessary to accomplish rural ministries. Each of these themes is briefly addressed below.

First, that social, economic, and demographic shifts impact the rural church is not a recently observed phenomenon. As early as the turn of the century, authors viewed industrialization and the resultant population shift to urban areas as the most important cause of decline in rural churches and morals. An anti-urban bias was more than evident! Research conducted from the 1930s through the 1960s consistently found that population shifts and changes in the structure of agriculture related directly to changes in the number of rural churches and church attendees. Nevertheless, the relationship between contextual change and the impact on rural churches may not be as simple as would first appear. Institutional variables such as polity, theology, and congregational leadership interact with contextual factors to alter the impact of contextual change on various types of church groups in rural communities.

Second, the response various authors recommended for the church to take in light of its changing context matched the ideology of the time. The modernist-fundamentalist controversy of the 1920s bifurcated the perceived role of the church in its rural context. One group of authors advocated active involvement in economic and community development, while another group of authors encouraged churches to renew their evangelistic fervor. Although the bifurcation continues to the present, both groups of authors appear to have assimilated some of the other's suggestions. This could be the result of a growth in the number of federated and yoked churches that, despite differing denominational backgrounds, have come together for survival purposes. Additional research is needed to clarify this observation.

Third, just as rural sociologists struggled to define rurality and to delineate rural-urban distinctions, students of the rural church struggled to determine how it is unique from other churches. Some authors opted for a nominal definition. That is, the rural church is rural simply because it happens to be located in a rural setting. On the other hand, other authors believed that there is something qualitatively different about the rural church that differentiates if from all other churches. The later group held that the rural church, because of its distinctiveness is charged with a unique mission. They cited its responsibility for stewardship of natural resources and the environment, responsibility to provide food to the hungry throughout the world, as well as its responsibility to minister to a unique clientele--rural people.

Related to the nature and mission of the rural church was a fourth theme, development of a theology and philosophy of rural church, the land, agriculture, and rural life. At least two groups of authors were observed. One group of authors were, for the most part, affiliated with denominations such as the Mennonites that have traditionally been agriculture based. These authors believed the land to be a sacred trust and held a near-sacramental sense of people's need to be close to the land. In contrast, a second group of authors were more utilitarian in nature. They attempted to develop a theology of the land around increased agricultural production. Their intent was to reduce world hunger and rural poverty.

Fifth, a substantial number of the documents dealt with methods and techniques for administering church activities in a rural setting. These ranged from conducting worship services to enhancing Christian education programs to building youth programs. Since about the mid-1970s most writings appear to be aimed at small church audiences in general rather than specifically at rural church audiences. A change in the structure of some of the nation's larger denominations reflected this shift. Many changed the names and emphases of their departments of town and country churches to departments of small churches.

Other themes from this collection of rural church references will no doubt emerge. It is our hope that this book will be an asset to the research and decision making efforts of those using it, and thus that church life in rural America may be more fulfilling.

Books,
Book Chapters,
and Pamphlets

Books, Book Chapters, and Pamphlets

1. Abell, Troy D.
   1978 "The Holiness-Pentecostal Experience in Southern Appalachia." In John D. Photiadis (ed.), *Religion in Appalachia: Theological, Social, and Psychological Dimensions and Correlates*. Morgantown, W.Va.: West Virginia University. pp. 79-101.

2. Ackerman, Joseph, (ed.).
   1944 *The People, the Land, and the Church*. Chicago, Ill.: The Farm Foundation. 172 pp.

3. Adams, Rachel Swann.
   1961 *The Small Church and Christian Education*. Philadelphia, Pa.: Westminster Press. 75 pp.

4. Agricultural Missions, Inc.
   1930 *The Church and Rural Reconstruction: A Report on Program and Policy for the Years Ahead*. New York, N.Y.: Rural Missions Cooperating Committee, Agricultural Missions, Inc. 30 pp.

5. Agricultural Missions, Inc.
   1945 *The Christian Mission Among Rural People* (second edition). New York, N.Y.: Rural Missions Cooperating Committee, Agricultural Missions, Inc. 211 pp.

6. Agricultural Missions, Inc.
   1957 *Procedures in Rural Reconstruction: A Christian Approach to the Years Ahead*. New York, N.Y.: Agricultural Missions. 32 pp.

7. Alexander, John L., (ed.).
   1914 *The Teens and Rural Life Sunday*. New York, N.Y.: Association Press. 151 pp.

3

8.   Alison, W.H.
     1961   *The Deterioration of Rural Churches in North Missouri.*
            Unpublished Ph.D. dissertation. Kansas City, Mo.: Central
            Baptist Seminary.

9.   Alldredge, Eugene Perry.
     1923   *Georgia Baptist Rural Churches: A Survey.* Nashville, Tenn.:
            Baptist Sunday School Board. 46 pp.

10. Allred, Thurman W.
     1981   *Basic Small Church Administration.* Nashville, Tenn:
            Convention Press. 64 pp.

11. American Lutheran Church.
     1984   *Rural Ministry: An Overview of Concerns and Efforts of the
            American Lutheran Church.* n.p.: Committee on Rural
            Ministry, American Lutheran Church. 29 pp.

12. American Unitarian Association.
     19--   *Religious Work and Opportunities in Country Towns.* Social
            Services Bulletin No. 15. Boston, Mass.: American
            Unitarian Association, Department of Social and Public
            Services.

13. Anderson, Dwight Ezra.
     1940   *Leadership for Rural Life.* New York, N.Y.: Association
            Press. 127 pp.

14. Anderson, Loren E.
     1960   *The Mission of the Church to Rural America.* Unpublished
            B.D. thesis. Chicago, Ill.: North Park Seminary.

15. Andrews, David G.
     1988   *Ministry in the Small Church.* Kansas City, Mo.: Sheed and
            Ward. 120 pp.

16. Ashdown, William.
     1962   *Motivation and Response in Religion: A Report on Religious
            Response, Attitudes and Motivation in Four Southern
            Counties.* Cincinnati, Ohio: Glenmary Missioners.

17. Ashenhurst, James Oliver.
     1910   *The Day of the Country Church.* New York, N.Y.: Funk and
            Wagnalls Company. 208 pp.

18.   Bailey, Liberty Hyde. (chairman).
      1911 *Report of the Commission on Country Life*. New York, N.Y.:
            Van Rees Press. Reprinted in 1944, Chapel Hill, N.Car.:
            University of North Carolina Press.

19.   Bailey, Liberty Hyde.
      1913 *The Country Life Movement in the United States*. New York,
            N.Y.: Macmillan Company. 220 pp.

20.   Bailey, Liberty Hyde.
      1915 *The Holy Earth*. New York, N.Y.: Charles Scribner's Sons.
            124 pp. Reprinted in 1980, New York State College of
            Agriculture and Life Sciences, Cornell University, Ithaca,
            N.Y.

21.   Bailey, Liberty Hyde.
      1927 *The Harvest of the Year to the Tiller of the Soil*. New York,
            N.Y.: Macmillan and Company. 209 pp.

22.   Bailey, James Martin.
      1959 *Windbreaks: Six Stories of the Rural Church in Action*. New
            York, N.Y.: Friendship Press. 111 pp.

23.   Bailey, James Martin.
      1959 *Youth and the Country Church*. New York, N.Y.: Friendship
            Press.

24.   Baker, R.T.
      19-- *Financing the Country Church*. Richmond, Va.: Department
            of Country Church and Sunday School Extension.

25.   Baltz, Frederick.
      1985 *Bible Readings for Farm Living*. Minneapolis, Minn.:
            Augsburg Publishing House. 112 pp.

26.   Baptist State Convention of North Carolina.
      1943 *Rural Baptist Churches of North Carolina*. Raleigh, N.Car.:
            Committee for Study of Rural Churches, Baptist State
            Convention of North Carolina. 56 pp.

27.   Baptist Sunday School Board.
      19-- *100 Successful Country Churches*. Nashville, Tenn.: Baptist
            Sunday School Board.

28.   Barnard, Margaret B.
       19--   *Problems and Opportunities of Country Life.* Social Service
              Series Bulletin No. 33. Boston, Mass.: American Unitarian
              Association, Department of Social and Public Service. 35
              pp.

29.   Barr, Roger Wayne.
       1978   *Ministry in Contemporary Rural America: The Christian
              Message and Land Use--Contextual Evangelism.* Unpublished
              D.Min. thesis. Claremont, Calif.: School of Theology. 113
              pp.

30.   Barry, Alvin Lee.
       19--   *The Preparatory and Continuing Education of the Town and
              Country Pastor.* n.p.

31.   Baumbach, Bernard Claire.
       1951   *The Church as a Vehicle of Community Values in a Changing
              Rural Economy.* Chicago, Ill.: Division of American
              Missions, National Lutheran Council. 88 pp.

32.   Beard, John Augustus.
       1946   *The Story of John Frederic Oberlin.* New York, N.Y.:
              Christian Press Fellowship. Originally published by
              Pilgrim Press. 100 pp.

33.   Becker, Edwin L.
       19--   *The Pastoral Unity Plan.* Indianapolis, Ind.: Department of
              Church Development and Evangelism, United Christian
              Missionary Society. 42 pp.

34.   Becker, Edwin L.
       1950   *Disciples of Christ in Town and Country.* Indianapolis, Ind.:
              Missionary Education Department, United Christian
              Missionary Society. 46 pp.

35.   Becnel, Thomas.
       1980   *Labor, Church, and the Sugar Establishment: Louisiana, 1887-
              1976.* Baton Rouge, La.: Louisiana State University Press.
              276 pp.

36.   Belcher, Richard.
       1959   *Adult Guide on the Church's Mission in Town and Country.*
              New York, N.Y.: Friendship Press. 64 pp.

37.   Belknap, Helen Olive.
       1922   *The Church on the Changing Frontier: A Study of the
              Homesteader and His Church.* New York, N.Y.: George H.
              Doran Company. 143 pp.

38. Bell, David, William Cascini, Harold Kaufman, Arleon Kelley, Leonard McIntire, Robert Ordway, Horace Sills, and Carl Williams.
   1967 *Ecumenical Designs: Imperatives for Action in Non-Metropolitan America.* New York, N.Y.: Steering Committee, National Consultation of Church in Community Life. 186 pp.

39. Bemies, Charles Otto.
   1912 *The Church and the Country Town.* Philadelphia, Penn.: American Baptist Publication Society. 72 pp.

40. Best, Irmgard, (ed.).
   1972 *Appalachians Speak Up.* Berea, Ky.: Berea College Press. 215 pp.

41. Bhagat, Shantilal P.
   1985 *The Family Farm: Can It Be Saved?* Elgin, Ill.: Brethren Press. 74 pp.

42. Blackwell, Gordon William, Lee M. Brooks, and S.H. Hobbs, Jr.
   1949 *Church and Community in the South: Report of the Institute for Research in Social Science of the University of North Carolina for the Committee on Restudy of Religious Education of the Presbyterian Church in the United States.* Richmond, Va.: John Knox Press. 416 pp.

43. Blizzard, Samuel W.
   1955 *The Roles of the Rural Parish Minister.* New York, N.Y.: Religious Education Association

44. Blizzard, Samuel W.
   1956 "The Role of the Rural Minister in Community and Cultural Change." In *New Horizons for Town and Country Churches.* New York, N.Y.: Department of Town and Country, National Council of Churches of Christ in the U.S.A. pp. 26-40.

45. Blume, George Terrill.
   1957 *Spatial and Social Relationships of Rural Churches in Six Selected Areas of Missouri.* Unpublished Ph.D. dissertation. Columbia, Mo.: University of Missouri. 182 pp.

46. Blunk, Henry A.
   1978 *Smaller Church Mission Guide.* Philadelphia, Pa.: Geneva Press. 80 pp.

47. Bockelman, Wilfred.
   1959 *On Good Soil.* New York, N.Y.: Friendship Press. 173 pp.

48.   Bollwinkel, Mark Stewart.
       1979   *The Role of the Pastoral Ministry in Rural Development.*
              Unpublished D.Min. thesis. Claremont, Calif.: School of
              Theology. 86 pp.

49.   Bossi, Stephen E.
       1980   "The Land: Who Shall Control?" In Charles P. Lutz (ed.),
              *Farming the Lord's Land: Christian Perspectives on American
              Agriculture.* Minneapolis, Minn.: Augsburg Publishing
              House. pp. 79-106.

50.   Bovee, David S.
       1986   *The Church and the Land: The National Catholic Rural Life
              Conference and American Society, 1923-1985.* Unpublished
              Ph.D. dissertation. Chicago, Ill.: Department of History,
              University of Chicago. 541 pp.

51.   Boyer, Merle W.
       1965   "The Kerygma and Rural Life." In Jacob M. Meyers, O.
              Reimherr, and H.N. Bream (eds.), *Theological and
              Missionary Studies in Memory of John Aberly.* Gettysburg,
              Pa.: Times and News Publishing Co. pp. 68-80.

52.   Brabham, M.W.
       1922   *The Sunday School at Work in Town and Country.* General
              Sunday School Board, Methodist Episcopal Church,
              South. New York, N.Y.: George H. Doran Co.

53.   Bread for the World Educational Fund.
       1980   *Land and Hunger: A Biblical Worldview.* New York, N.Y.:
              Bread for the World Educational Fund. 30 pp. Reprinted
              in 1982, Washington, D.C.: Bread for the World
              Educational Fund. 31 pp.

54.   Breimyer, Harold F.
       1980   "Energy and Agriculture: A Search for Balance." In
              Charles P. Lutz (ed.), *Farming the Lord's Land: Christian
              Perspectives on American Agriculture.* Minneapolis, Minn.:
              Augsburg Publishing House. pp. 147-164.

55.   Brewer, Earl D.C.
       1947   *The Church at the Crossroads: A Primer for Christian Workers
              in the Small Churches of Town and Country.* New York,
              N.Y. and Nashville, Tenn.: Abingdon-Cokesbury. 128 pp.

56. Brewer, Earl D.C.
    1948 *A Program for the Local Rural Church.* Report of
    Commission 7 of the National Methodist Rural Life
    Conference. New York, N.Y.: Department of Town and
    Country Work, Division of Home Missions and Church
    Extension, Methodist Church. 30 pp.

57. Brewer, Earl D.C.
    1962 "Religion and the Churches." Chapter 14 in Thomas R.
    Ford (ed.), *The Southern Appalachian Region: A Survey.*
    Lexington, Ky.: University of Kentucky Press.

58. Brewer, Earl D.C.
    1962 "Religion in the Changing Highlands." Part II of W.D.
    Weatherford and Earl D.C. Brewer (eds.), *Life and Religion
    in Southern Appalachia.* New York, N.Y.: Friendship Press.

59. Brewer, Earl D.C. and Loyde H. Hartley.
    1978 "Two Dimensions of Appalachian Religion." In John D.
    Photiadis (ed.), *Religion in Appalachia: Theological, Social,
    and Psychological Dimension and Correlates.* Morgantown,
    W.Va.: West Virginia University. pp. 229-254.

60. Brewer, Earl D.C., Theodore H. Runyon, Jr., Barbara B. Pittard,
    and Harold W. McSwain.
    1967 *Protestant Parish: A Case Study of Rural and Urban Parish
    Patterns.* Atlanta, Ga.: Communicative Arts Press. 129 pp.

61. Bricker, Garland Armor.
    1913 *Solving the Country Church Problem.* Cincinnati, Ohio:
    Jennings and Graham; New York, N.Y.: Eaton and Mains.
    296 pp.

62. Bricker, Garland Armor.
    1919 *The Church in Rural America.* Cincinnati, Ohio: Standard
    Publishing Company. 193 pp.

63. Brown, Carolyn C.
    1982 *Developing Christian Education in the Smaller Church.*
    Nashville, Tenn.: Abingdon Press. 96 pp.

64. Brown, Carolyn C.
    1984 *Youth Ministries: Thinking Big With Small
    Groups.* Nashville, Tenn.: Abingdon Press. 96 pp.

65.   Brown, David J., Robert Haskins, and William Swisher.
       1977   *Small Church Project: Final Report.* New York, N.Y.: United
              Church Board for Homeland Ministries. 43 pp.

66.   Brueggemann, Walter.
       1977   *The Land: Place as Gift, Promise, and Challenge in Biblical
              Faith.* Philadelphia, Pa.: Fortress Press. 228 pp.

67.   Brunner, Edmund deSchweinitz.
       1917   *The New Country Church Building.* New York, N.Y.:
              Mission Education Movement of the United States and
              Canada. 141 pp.

68.   Brunner, Edmund deSchweinitz.
       1919   *The Country Church in the New Social Order.* New York,
              N.Y.: Association Press. 164 pp.

69.   Brunner, Edmund deSchweinitz.
       1922   *Church and Community Survey of Pend Oreille County,
              Washington.* New York, N.Y.: George H. Doran Company.
              51 pp.

70.   Brunner, Edmund deSchweinitz.
       1922   *Church and Community Survey of Salem County, New
              Jersey.* New York, N.Y.: George H. Doran Company. 92
              pp.

71.   Brunner, Edmund deSchweinitz.
       1922   *Community and Church Survey of Sedgwick County,
              Kansas.* New York, N.Y.: George H. Doran Company.

72.   Brunner, Edmund deSchweinitz.
       1923   *Church Life in the Rural South: A Study of the Opportunity
              of Protestantism Based Upon Data from Seventy Counties.*
              New York, N.Y: George H. Doran Company. 117 pp.
              Reprinted in 1969, New York, N.Y.: Negro Universities
              Press.

73.   Brunner, Edmund deSchweinitz, (ed.).
       1923   *Churches of Distinction in Town and Country.* New York,
              N.Y: George H. Doran Company. 198 pp.

74.   Brunner, Edmund deSchweinitz.
       1923   *Tested Methods in Town and Country Churches.* New York,
              N.Y.: George H. Doran Company. 173 pp. Reprinted in
              1930, New York, N.Y.: Institute of Social and Religious
              Research.

75. Brunner, Edmund deSchweinitz.
1925 *Surveying Your Community: A Handbook of Method for the Rural Church.* New York, N.Y.: George H. Doran Company. 109 pp.

76. Brunner, Edmund deSchweinitz.
1930 *Industrial Village Churches.* New York, N.Y.: Institute of Social and Religious Research. 193 pp.

77. Brunner, Edmund deSchweinitz.
1934 *The Larger Parish, A Movement or an Enthusiasm?* New York, N.Y.: George H. Doran Company. 95 pp.

78. Brunner, Edmund deSchweinitz and Mary V. Brunner.
1922 *Irrigation and Religion: A Study of Two Prosperous Communities in two California Counties.* New York, N.Y.: George H. Doran Company. 128 pp.

79. Bunge, Harry.
1962 *A Study of the Nebraska Sandhills.* Prepared by request for the Lutheran Study Committee for the Nebraska Sandhills. Chicago, Ill.: Church in Town and Country, National Lutheran Council. 50 pp.

80. Burgess, David.
1952 *The Fellowship of Southern Churchmen, Its History and Promise.* Black Mountain, N.Car.: Fellowship of Southern Churchmen. 8 pp.

81. Burkart, Gary P. and David C. Leege.
1988 *Parish Life in Town and Countryside: The Non-Metropolitan Catholic Church--An Overlooked Giant.* Report No. 13 (October). Notre Dame, Ind.: University of Notre Dame.

82. Butt, Edmund Dargan.
1954 *Preach There Also: A Study of the Town and Country Work of the Episcopal Church.* Evanston, Ill.: Seabury-Western Theological Seminary. 140 pp.

83. Butterfield, Kenyon Leech.
1911 *The Country Church and the Rural Problem: The Carew Lectures at Hartford Theological Seminary, 1909.* Chicago, Ill.: University of Chicago Press. 153 pp.

84. Butterfield, Kenyon Leech.
1923 *A Christian Program for the Rural Community.* New York, N.Y.: George H. Doran Company. 188 pp.

85.   Butterfield, Kenyon Leech.
      1933   *The Christian Enterprise Among Rural People*. Nashville,
             Tenn.: Cokesbury Press. 247 pp.

86.   Butterfield, Kenyon Leech, William J. McKee, and Thomas Jesse
      Jones.
      1928   *Principles and Methods of Christian Work in Rural Areas*.
             New York, N.Y: International Missionary Council. 69 pp.

87.   Byers, David M. and Bernard Quinn.
      1974   *Readings for Town and Country Workers: An Annotated
             Bibliography*. Washington, D.C.: The Glenmary Research
             Center. 128 pp.

88.   Byers, David M. and Bernard Quinn.
      1978   *New Directions for the Rural Church: Case Studies in Area
             Ministry*. Atlanta, Ga.: The Glenmary Research Center
             and New York, N.Y.: Paulist Press. 186 pp.

89.   Cain, Benjamin Harrison.
      1941   *The Church Ministering to Rural Life*. Dayton, Ohio: Home
             Mission and Church Erection Society, Church of the
             United Brethren in Christ. 104 pp.

90.   Cain, Benjamin Harrison.
      1950   *Guidance in Program Planning*. Dayton, Ohio: Department
             of Church Extension, Board of Missions, Evangelical
             United Brethren Church. 104 pp.

91.   Cain, Benjamin Harrison.
      1957   *Strengthening the Program of the Town and Country Church*.
             Dayton, Ohio: Otterbin Press. 56 pp.

92.   Cain, Benjamin Harrison.
      1960   *The Town and Country Pulpit: Sermon Blueprints for Forty
             Special Days*. Anderson, Ind.: Warner Press. 112 pp.

93.   Cain, Benjamin Harrison.
      1970   *From Plow to Pulpit: Memoirs of Benjamin H. Cain--55 Years
             a Pastor, Conference Superintendent, and General Church
             Secretary*. Warsaw, Ind.: n.p. 157 pp.

94.   Carlson, William E.
      1958   *The Rural Church: Is It In Danger?* n.p.

95.   Carothers, J. Edward.
      1970   "Overcoming Cruelty with Love." In Max E. Glenn (ed.),
             Appalachia in Transition. St. Louis, Mo.: Bethany Press. pp.
             82-92.

96. Carr, James McLeod.
    1956 *Bright Future: A New Day for the Town and Country Church*. Richmond, Va.: Board of Church Extension, Presbyterian Church in the U.S.A., John Knox Press. 164 pp.

97. Carr, James McLeod.
    1958 *Glorious Ride: The Story of Henry Woods McLaughlin*. Atlanta, Ga.: Church and Community Press. 156 pp.

98. Carr, James McLeod.
    1960 *Working Together in the Larger Parish*. Atlanta, Ga.: The Church and Community Press. 105 pp.

99. Carr, James McLeod.
    1962 *Our Church Meeting Human Needs*. Birmingham, Ala.: The Progressive Farmer Company. 152 pp.

100. Carroll, Jackson W., (ed.).
     1977 *Small Churches are Beautiful*. San Francisco, Calif.: Harper & Row. 174 pp.

101. Carter, Michael Vaughn.
     1987 "From the 'Hollers' to High Street: A Brief Look at the Appalachian Serpent Handler's Presence in the Urban Midwest." In Robert M. Shurden (ed.), *Faculty Studies 1987*. Jefferson City, Tenn.: Carson-Newman College. pp. 12-22.

102. Carver, Thomas Nixon.
     19-- "Rural Economy as a Factor in the Success of the Church." Social Service Series No. 8. Boston, Mass.: American Unitarian Association. Department of Social and Public Service. 20 pp.

103. Catholic Church.
     1982 "Strangers and Guests: Toward Community in the Heartland". *Bishop's Bulletin Special Supplement*. A document signed by over 70 Catholic bishops in 12 midwestern states on May 1, 1980.

104. Catholic Rural Life Conference.
     1939 *Manifesto on Rural Life*. Milwaukee, Wis.: Bruce Publishing Co. 222 pp.

105. Caudill, Harry M.
     1962 *Night Comes to the Cumberlands: A Biography of a Depressed Area*. Boston, Mass.: Atlantic Monthly Press Book. 394 pp.

106.   Chambers, Martin Reed.
        1948   *Rural Churches in the North Carolina Conference of the
                Methodist Church, 1928-1947: A Study in Trends.* Durham,
                N.Car.: Commission on Town and Country Work,
                Methodist Church. 38 pp.

107.   Chapin, Stuart F.
        1935   *Contemporary American Institutions.* New York, N.Y.:
                Harper and Brothers. 423 pp.

108.   Choate, Norman.
        1971   *Experiments in Town and Country Ministries: Three Case
                Studies.* Washington, D.C.: Center for Applied Research in
                the Apostolate. 29 pp.

109.   Church of the Brethren.
        1974   *This Land: Ours for a Season:* Report of a Study Committee
                on the Church and Agriculture. Elgin, Ill.: World
                Ministries Commission, Church of the Brethren General
                Board. 52 pp.

110.   Clark, Carl Anderson.
        1959   *Rural Churches in Transition.* Nashville, Tenn.: Broadman
                Press. 145 pp.   Reprinted 1970.

111.   Clark, Elmer Talmage.
        1924   *The Rural Church in the South.* Nashville, Tenn. and
                Dallas, Tex.: The Cokesbury Press. 51 pp.

112.   Cleveland, Philip Jerome.
        1960   *Three Churches and a Model T.* Westwood, N.J.: Fleming H.
                Revell Company. 189 pp.

113.   Cleveland, Philip Jerome.
        1962   *It's Bright in My Valley.* Westwood, N.J.: Fleming H.
                Revell Company. 192 pp.

114.   Cobb, A.L.
        1965   *Sect Religion and Social Change in an Isolated Rural
                Community of Southern Appalachia (with) Case Story: Fruit of
                the Land.* Unpublished Ph.D. dissertation.

115.   Cofell, William L.
        1970   "The School and the Church in Changing Rural America."
                In Victor J. Klimoski and Bernard Quinn (eds.), *Church
                and Community: Nonmetropolitan America in Transition.*
                Washington, D.C.: Center for Applied Research in the
                Apostolate. pp. 35-48.

116. Cogswell, James (ed.).
     1974 *The Church and the Rural Poor.* Atlanta, Ga.: John Knox Press. 107 pp.

117. Coles, Robert.
     1971 "God and the Rural Poor." In Robert Coles *Migrants, Sharecroppers, and Mountaineers,* Volume II of *Children of Crisis.* New York, N.Y.: Atlantic-Little, Brown and Co. pp. 281-288.

118. Comfort, Richard O.
     1947 *The Training of Town and Country Ministers in the United States.* Swannanoa, N.Car.: Warren H. Wilson Institute of Rural Church Work.

119. Congregational Christian Church.
     19-- *A Self-Evaluation Scale for Town and Country Churches.* New York, N.Y.: Town and Country Department, Congregational Christian Church.

120. Congregational Christian Churches in the U.S.A.
     1949 *The Church and the Family Farm--A Group Discussion Guide.* New York, N.Y.: Congregational Christian Churches in the U.S.A., Board of Home Missions, Town and Country Department. 15 pp.

121. Conway, Marion H.
     1964 *The Country Parson.* Franklin Springs, Ga.: Advocate Press. 83 pp.

122. Cook, T.C., Jr.
     1985 "The Roles of the Church in the Community." In Gari Lesnoff-Caravoglia (ed.), *Values, Ethics, and Aging.* New York, N.Y.: Human Sciences Press. pp. 158-171.

123. Cook, Walter L.
     19-- *Send Us a Minister...Any Minister Will Do.* Rockland, Maine: Courier-Gazette. 165 pp.

124. Country Life Commission.
     1911 *The Country Church, Its Place and Power.* n.p. 12 pp.

125. Cowan, John Franklin.
     1917 *Big Jobs for Little Churches.* New York, N.Y.: Fleming H. Revell. 160 pp.

126. Crider, Donald M.
      1980   "Religion and the Rural Church" In Mary Frank (ed.),
             *Children in Contemporary Society. IYC Series: Part IV. Rural
             Children and Rural Families*. Last issue in series of four
             dedicated to the International Year of the Child. 57 pp.

127. Crooker, Joseph Henry.
      1889   "Religious Destitution of Villages." Chapter 7 in *Problems
             of American Society*. Boston, Mass.: G.H. Ellis Company.

128. Cuber, John F.
      1951   "Rural-Urban Differences in Church Participation." In
             Sociology. New York, N.Y.: Appleton-Century-Crofts, Inc.
             p. 540.

129. Cushman, James F.
      1981   *Beyond Survival: Revitalizing the Small Church*. Parsons,
             W.Va.: McClain Printing Co. 172 pp.

130. Dachauer, Alban J.
      1956   *The Rural Life Prayerbook*. Des Moines, Iowa: National
             Catholic Rural Life Conference. 410 pp.

131. Dalglish, William A.
      1982   *Models for Catechetical Ministry in the Rural Parish*.
             Washington, D.C.: National Conference of Diocesan
             Directors of Religious Education and CCD. 77 pp.

132. Dana, Malcom.
      1937   *Christ of the Countryside*. Nashville, Tenn.: Cokesbury
             Press. 128 pp.

133. Daniel, William Andrew.
      1925   *The Education of Negro Ministers: Based upon a Survey of
             Theological Schools for Negroes in the United States, Made by
             Robert L. Kelly and W.A. Daniel*. New York, N.Y.: George
             H. Doran Company. 187 pp.

134. D'Antonio, William V., James D. Davidson, Jr., and Joseph A.
      Schlangen.
      1966   *Protestants and Catholics in Two Oklahoma Communities*.
             South Bend, Ind.: University of Notre Dame, Department
             of Sociology.

135. Dascomb, Harry N.
      1900   "Men's Sunday Evening Club." Chapter 5 in Charles E.
             Hayward (ed.), *Institutional Work for the Country Church*.
             Burlington, Vt.: Free Association Press.

136. Daugherty, Mary Lee.
     1978 "Serpent Handling as Sacrament." In John D. Photiadis
     (ed.), *Religion in Appalachia: Theological, Social, and
     Psychological Dimensions and Correlates.* Morgantown,
     W.Va.: West Virginia University. pp. 103-111.

137. Daugherty, Kathleen S. and Foster R. McCurley.
     1986 *The Church and the Challenge of Rural Concerns.* n.p.:
     Lutheran Church of America.

138. Davidson, Gabriel.
     1943 *Our Jewish Farmers and the Story of the Jewish Agricultural
     Society.* New York, N.Y.: L. B. Fischer. 280 pp.

139. Davis, J.M.
     1946 *Missions and Culture Change.* Rural Life Conference Report
     No. 2. pp. 27-34.

140. Davis, Ozora S.
     1900 "Religious Instruction." Chapter 4 in Charles E. Hayward
     (ed.), *Institutional Work for the Country Church.* Burlington,
     Vt.: Free Association Press.

141. Dawber, Mark A.
     1937 *Rebuilding Rural America.* Northern Baptist
     Convention. New York, N.Y.: Friendship Press. 210 pp.

142. Dean, John P.
     1958 "Jewish Participation in the Life of Middle-Sized
     Communities." In Marshall Sklare (ed.), *The Jews: Social
     Patterns of an American Group.* New York, N.Y.: Free
     Press. pp. 304-320.

143. Debusman, Paul Marshall.
     1962 *Social Factors Affecting Selected Southern Baptist Churches in
     the Southern Appalachian Region of the United States.*
     Unpublished Ph.D. dissertation. Louisville, Ky.: Southern
     Baptist Theological Seminary. 271 pp.

144. Dennison, Doris P.
     1947 *The Church in the Small Community: A Workbook.* Nashville,
     Tenn.: Department of Christian Education of Adults,
     Board of Education, Methodist Church. 19 pp.

145. DeVisser, John.
     1976 *Pioneer Churches.* New York, N.Y.: Norton. 192 pp.

146. DeVries, Charles.
      1962 *Inside Rural America: A Lutheran View*. Chicago,
            Ill.: Division of American Missions, National Lutheran
            Council. 42 pp.

147. Dewire, Norman E.
      1975 "Where the Resources Are for Rural Development." In
            James A. Cogswell (ed.), *The Church and the Rural Poor*.
            Atlanta, Ga.: John Knox Press. pp. 95-104.

148. Donohue, George A. and Edward Gross.
      1970 "The Rural System as an Ideal Model." In Victor J.
            Klimoski and Bernard Quinn (eds.), *Church and
            Community: Nonmetropolitan America in Transition*.
            Washington, D.C.: Center for Applied Research in the
            Apostolate. pp. 23-34.

149. Douglass, Harlan Paul.
      1926 *How Shall Country Youth Be Served? A Study of the "Rural"
            Work of Certain National Character-Building Agencies*. New
            York, N.Y.: George H. Doran Company. 259 pp.

150. Douglass, Harlan Paul.
      1944 *Scranton and Lackawanna County Churches*. A Study Made
            Under the Auspices of the United Churches of Scranton
            and Lackawanna County. n.p. 41 pp.

151. Douglass, Harlan Paul.
      1946 *Some Iowa Rural Churches*. Report of a study conducted in
            1946 under the auspices of the Committee for
            Cooperative Field Research, Iowa Interchurch Council
            and Iowa Christian Rural Fellowship. New York, N.Y.:
            Committee on Cooperative Field Research of the Home
            Missions Council of North America. 70 pp.

152. Douglass, Harlan Paul.
      1949 *Rhode Island Suburban and Rural Protestant Churches, 1949*.
            A study made for the Rhode Island Council of Churches.
            n.p. 90 pp.

153. Douglass, Harlan Paul and Edmund deSchweinitz Brunner.
      1935 *The Protestant Church as a Social Institution*. New York,
            N.Y.: Harper. 368 pp. Reprinted in 1972, New York,
            N.Y.: Russell and Russell.

154. Dudley, Carl Safford.
      1977 *The Unique Dynamics of the Small Church*. Washington
            D.C.: Alban Institute. 21 pp. Reprinted 1984.

155. Dudley, Carl Safford.
     1978 *Making the Small Church Effective.* Nashville, Tenn.: Abingdon Press. 192 pp.

156. Dudley, Carl Safford.
     1979 *Where Have All Our People Gone? New Choices for Old Churches.* New York, N.Y.: Pilgrim Press. 136 pp.

157. Dudley, Carl Safford.
     1983 "The Art of Pastoring a Small Congregation." In Douglas Alan Walrath (ed.), *New Possibilities for Small Churches.* New York, N.Y.: Pilgrim Press. pp. 46-58.

158. Duel, Elva Marie (Kletzing).
     1937 *Planning to Teach in the One-Room Church.* New York, N.Y. and Cincinnati, Ohio: Methodist Book Concern. 48 pp.

159. Duncan, Dudley Otis and Albert J. Reiss, Jr.
     1956 *Social Characteristics of Urban and Rural Communities.* New York, N.Y.: John Wiley & Sons. 421 pp. Reprinted in 1976, New York, N.Y.: Russell and Russell.

160. Duncan, R.H.
     1931 *Cedar Grove Church: A Study of the Contribution of a Rural Church to Its Community.* Unpublished B.D. thesis. Atlanta, Ga.: Department of Sociology, Emory University. 31 pp.

161. Dunn, W.J.
     1956 *A Study of Secularization in the Rural Protestant Areas of Isabella County, Michigan.* Unpublished Ph.D. dissertation.

162. Earp, Edwin Lee.
     1914 *The Rural Church Movement.* New York, N.Y. and Cincinnati, Ohio: Methodist Book Concern (Association Press). 177 pp.

163. Earp, Edwin Lee.
     1918 *The Rural Church Serving the Community.* New York, N.Y.: Abingdon Press. 144 pp.

164. Earp, Edwin Lee.
     1922 *Biblical Backgrounds for the Rural Message.* New York, N.Y.: Association Press. 77 pp.

165. Eastman, Fred E. and Hermann Nelson Morse.
     1912 *A Rural Survey in Maryland: Made by the Department of
     Church and Country Life of the Board of Home Missions of
     the Presbyterian Church in the U.S.A.* New York, N.Y.:
     Redfield Brothers, Inc. 113 pp.

166. Edwards, V.A.
     1949 *The Rural Church in These Changing Times.* Nashville,
     Tenn.: Department of Christian Education, Sunday School
     Publication Board, National Baptist Convention. 39 pp.

167. Egebo, Warren I.
     1986 *"Ruth in Tears Amidst the Corn": A Case Study in Rural
     Church Conflict.* Unpublished M.A. thesis. St. Paul, Minn.:
     Luther Northwestern Theological Seminary.

168. Ekola, Giles C.
     1967 *The Christian Encounters Town and Country America.* St.
     Louis, Mo.: Concordia Publishing House. 123 pp.

169. Elliot, John Y.
     1980 *Our Pastor Has an Outside Job.* Valley Forge, Pa.: Judson
     Press. 111 pp.

170. Engstrom, Walter.
     1961 *The Rural Church and the Covenant.* Unpublished B.D.
     thesis. Chicago, Ill.: North Park Seminary.

171. Ensminger, D.
     1949 "The Rural Church and Religion." Chapter 7 in Carl C.
     Taylor, (ed.), *Rural Life in the United States.* New York,
     N.Y.: Alfred A. Knopf. pp. 116-133.

172. Erickson, Theodore A.
     1953 *The Church and 4-H Clubs.* Minneapolis, Minn.: General
     Mills, Inc. 19 pp.

173. Evangelical Covenant Church.
     1985 *Rural Evangelism, the Rural Church, and Town and Country
     Ministry.* Chicago, Ill.: Department of Church Growth and
     Evangelism, Evangelical Covenant Church.

174. Exman, Gary W.
     1987 *Get Ready--Get Set--Grow: Church Growth for Town and
     Country Congregations.* Lima, Ohio: C.S.S. Publication
     Company. 148 pp.

175. Farley, Gary.
     1982 "Typology of Churches." In Robert E. Wiley (ed.), *Change in Big Town/Small City.* Atlanta, Ga.: Home Missions Board, Southern Baptist Convention. pp. 105-128.

176. Farley, Gary.
     1986 "The 'Warm Fuzzies' of Small Churches." Atlanta, Ga.: Home Mission Board, Southern Baptist Convention. 2 pp.

177. Farley, Gary.
     1987 "Some Observations, mostly Unscientific, about Changes in Rural and Small Town Churches Affiliated with the Southern Baptist Convention." Atlanta, Ga.: Home Mission Board, Southern Baptist Convention, Atlanta. 4 pp.

178. Farm Foundation.
     1943 *The People, the Land, and the Church in the Rural West.* Chicago, Ill.: Home Missions Council, Committee on Town and Country, Farm Foundation. 172 pp.

179. Farm Foundation.
     1946 *The Land and the Rural Church in the Cumberland Plateau.* Chicago, Ill.: Committee on Town and Country, Farm Foundation. 105 pp.

180. Farmers Federation.
     1944 *The Lord's Acre Plan Succeeds in the Country Church.* Asheville, N.Car.: Farmers Federation. 40 pp.

181. Federal Council of Churches of Christ in America.
     1930 *Rural Life Sunday.* New York, N.Y.: Committee on Rural Life Sunday, Federal Council of Churches and Home Missions.

182. Federal Council of Churches of Christ in America.
     1945 *Churching the Community Cooperatively.* Church Cooperation Series No. 4. New York, N.Y.: Inter-Council Field Department, Federal Council of Churches of Christ, U.S.A.

183. Federal Council of Churches of Christ in America.
     1947 *Hymns of the Rural Spirit, with Worship Material and Rural Songs.* New York, N.Y.: Commission on Worship, Federal Council of Churches of Christ in America. 128 pp.

184. Federal Council of Churches of Christ in America.
      1948 "Social Economic Status and Outlook of Religious Groups
            in America." Study No. 10 in *Christianity and the Economic
            Order*. Bulletin No. 27 (May 15). New York, N.Y.:
            Department of Research and Educational Information
            Service, Federal Council of Churches of Christ in
            America.

185. Federal Council of Churches of Christ in America.
      1950 *Some Protestant Churches in Rural America*. Information
            Service (February). New York, N.Y.: Department of
            Research and Education, Federal Council of Churches of
            Christ in America. 4 pp.

186. Felton, Ralph Almon.
      19-- *Man's Use of God's Earth*. Nashville, Tenn.: Abingdon-
            Cokesbury.

187. Felton, Ralph Almon.
      1915 *A Rural Survey of ---- Community: The Study of a Rural
            Parish, A Method of Survey*. New York, N.Y.: Missionary
            Education Movement of the U.S. and Canada. 195 pp.

188. Felton, Ralph Almon.
      1915 *The Study of a Rural Community*. New York, N.Y.: Country
            Church Work, Board of Home Missions, Presbyterian
            Church in the U.S.A. 38 pp.

189. Felton, Ralph Almon.
      1926 *Our Templed Hills: A Study of the Church and Rural Life*.
            New York, N.Y.: Council of Women for Home Missions
            and Missionary Education Movement. 240 pp.

190. Felton, Ralph Almon.
      1930 *What's Right with the Rural Church: An Application of
            Christian Principles to the New Rural Life*. Philadelphia, Pa.:
            Presbyterian Board of Christian Education. 150 pp.

191. Felton, Ralph Almon.
      1940 *Local Church Cooperation in Rural Communities*. New York,
            N.Y.: Home Missions Council. 62 pp.

192. Felton, Ralph Almon.
      1946 *The Size of the Rural Parish*. Madison, N.J.: Department of
            the Rural Church, Drew Theological Seminary. 22 pp.

193. Felton, Ralph Almon.
      1946 *The Church Bus*. New York, N.Y.: Home Missions Council
            of North America. 21 pp.

194. Felton, Ralph Almon.
     1946 *The Church Farm*. Chicago, Ill.: McCormick Theological
     Seminary and New York, N.Y.: Committee for the
     Training of Negro Rural Pastors of the Phelps-Stokes
     Fund. 24 pp.

195. Felton, Ralph Almon.
     1946 *The Lord's Acre*. New York, N.Y.: Committee for the
     Training of Rural Pastors, Phelps-Strokes Fund. 34 pp.

196. Felton, Ralph Almon.
     1946 *The Salary of Rural Pastors*. Madison, N.J.: Department of
     the Rural Church, Drew Theological Seminary. 40 pp.

197. Felton, Ralph Almon.
     1947 *The Church and the Land*. Madison, N.J.: Department of
     the Rural Church, Drew Theological Seminary. 45 pp.

198. Felton, Ralph Almon.
     1947 *One Foot on the Land: Stories of Sixteen Successful Rural
     Churches*. Madison, N.J.: Department of the Rural Church,
     Drew Theological Seminary. 94 pp. Reprints from the
     Farm Journal and the *Progressive Farmer*.

199. Felton, Ralph Almon.
     1948 *The Art of Church Cooperation*. Madison, N.J.: Department
     of the Rural Church, Drew Theological Seminary and
     New York, N.Y.: Department of Town and Country
     Work, Division of Home Missions and Church Extension,
     Methodist Church. 63 pp.

200. Felton, Ralph Almon.
     1948 *The Home of the Rural Pastor*. Madison, N.J.: Department
     of the Rural Church, Drew Theological Seminary. 111 pp.

201. Felton, Ralph Almon.
     1949 *New Ministers*. Madison, N.J.: Department of the Rural
     Church, Drew Theological Seminary.

202. Felton, Ralph Almon.
     1950 *These My Brethren: A Study of 570 Negro Churches and
     1,542 Negro Homes in the Rural South*. Madison, N.J.:
     Department of the Rural Church, Drew Theological
     Seminary. 102 pp.

203. Felton, Ralph Almon.
      1951 *The New Gospel of the Soil: Stories of Sixteen Rural Churches
            that have Promoted Soil Conservation, Land Ownership, and
            Father-Son Partnerships, and Have Helped Young Couples Get
            Started in Farming.* Madison, N.J.: Department of the
            Rural Church, Drew Theological Seminary. 95 pp.

204. Felton, Ralph Almon.
      1952 *Go Down Moses: A Study of Twenty-One Successful Negro
            Rural Pastors.* Madison, N.J.: Department of the Rural
            Church, Drew Theological Seminary. 95 pp.

205. Felton, Ralph Almon.
      1955 *Hope Rises from the Land.* New York, N.Y.: Friendship
            Press. 136 pp.

206. Felton, Ralph Almon.
      1958 *Church Bells in Many Tongues: Stories or Account of the
            Work of 35 Rural Pastors in 19 Different Countries to Show
            the Common Elements of Successful Rural Church Work
            Around the World.* Lebanon, Penn.: Sowers Printing
            Company. 130 pp.

207. Felton, Ralph Almon.
      1960 *The Pulpit and the Plow.* New York, N.Y.: Friendship
            Press. 168 pp.

208. Felton, Ralph Almon and James McLeod Carr.
      1952 *A Survey of Town and Country Churches in the Synod of
            North Carolina Presbyterian Church in the United States: A
            Study of 238 Town and Country Churches.* Madison, N.J.:
            Department of the Rural Church, Drew Theological
            Seminary. 23 pp.

209. Fenner, Goodrich Robert.
      1935 *Episcopal Church in Town and Country.* New York, N.Y.:
            National Council, Division for Rural Work of the
            Department of Christian Social Service, Protestant
            Episcopal Church in the U.S.A. 160 pp.

210. Fetterman, John.
      1967 *Stinking Creek.* New York, N.Y.: E.P. Dutton and Co. 192
            pp. Reprinted 1970.

211. Fichter, Joseph.
      1951 *Southern Parish.* Chicago, Ill.: University of Chicago Press.
            283 pp.

212. Fiske, George Walter.
      1912 *The Challenge of the Country: A Study of Country Life
            Opportunity.* New York, N.Y.: Association Press. 283 pp.

213. Fleming, S. Bruce
      1973 *The Rural Church and the Quiet Revolution.* Unpublished
            manuscript. Minneapolis, Minn.: Bethlehem Baptist
            Church. 24 pp.

214. Foght, Harold W.
      1912 *The Country Community.* New York, N.Y.: American
            Baptist Home Mission Society and the Missionary
            Education Movement of the U.S. and Canada. 35 pp.

215. Folsom, Paul.
      1976 *Rural Ministry: A Response to Change--What Has Happened
            to the Church on Mainstreet, USA?* Unpublished pastoral
            project for D.Min. degree. Dubuque, Iowa: Aquinas
            Institute of Theology. 32 pp.

216. Ford, Thomas R.
      1967 "The Roles of the Rural Parish Minister, the Protestant
            Seminaries, and the Sciences of Social Behavior." In
            Richard D. Knudten (ed.), *The Sociology of Religion: An
            Anthology.* New York, N.Y.: Appleton-Century-Crofts.

217. Foster, Virgil E.
      1953 *Religious Education in the Small Church: A Series of Articles
            Printed in the "International Journal of Religious Education."*
            n.p.

218. Foster, Virgil E.
      1956 *How a Small Church Can Have Good Christian Education.*
            New York, N.Y.: Harper and Row. 127 pp.

219. Freeman, Harlan L.
      1914 *The Kingdom and the Farm.* New York, N.Y.: Fleming H.
            Revell Company. 121 pp.

220. Freeman, John Davis.
      1943 *Country Church: Its Problems and Their Solution.* Atlanta,
            Ga.: Home Missions Board, Southern Baptist Convention.
            127 pp.

221. Frerichs, Robert T.
      19-- *The Role of the Denominations in In-Service Training of Rural
            Clergy.* Green Lake, Wis.: Rural Church Center, American
            Baptist Home Mission Societies.

222. Freudenberger, C. Dean.
     1980 "Managing the Land and Water." In Charles P. Lutz (ed.),
           *Farming the Lord's Land: Christian Perspectives on American
           Agriculture.* Minneapolis, Minn.: Augsburg Publishing
           House, pp. 123-146.

223. Frey, Leibert Garland.
     1947 *Romance of Rural Churches.* Nashville, Tenn.: Executive
           Board, Tennessee Baptist Convention. 177 pp.

224. Fry, Charles Luther.
     1922 *The Old and New Immigrant on the Land: A Study of
           Americanization and the Rural Church.* New York, N.Y.:
           George H. Doran Company. 119 pp.

225. Fry, Charles Luther.
     1924 *Diagnosing the Rural Church: A Study in Method.* New
           York, N.Y.: George H. Doran Company. 234 pp. Also
           published as a Ph.D. thesis, New York, N.Y.: Columbia
           University, 1924.

226. Fry, Charles Luther.
     1930 *The U.S. Looks at Its Churches.* New York, N.Y.: Institute
           of Social and Religious Research. 183 pp.

227. Gallagher, Art, Jr.
     1961 "Religion in Plainville." *Plainville Fifteen Years Later.* New
           York, N.Y.: Columbia University Press. 301 pp.

228. Galpin, Charles Josiah.
     1918 *Rural Life.* New York, N.Y.: Century Company. 386 pp.
           Reprinted in 1920 and 1923.

229. Galpin, Charles Josiah.
     1925 *Empty Churches: The Rural-Urban Dilemma.* New York,
           N.Y.: Century Company. 149 pp.

230. Gardner, E. Clinton.
     1970 "The Christian Meaning of Community." In Max E. Glenn
           (ed.), *Appalachia in Transition.* St. Louis, Mo.: Bethany
           Press. pp. 43-59.

231. Gebhard, Anna Laura (Munro).
     1947 *Rural Parish! A Year from the Journal of Anna Laura
           Gebhard.* New York, N.Y.: Abingdon-Cokesbury Press. 121
           pp.

232. Gerberding, George Henry.
    1916 *The Lutheran Church in the Country: A Study, an Explanation, an Attempted Solution*. Philadelphia, Pa.: General Council Publication Board. 212 pp.

233. Gerrard, Nathan L.
    1970 "Churches of the Stationary Poor in Southern Appalachia." In John D. Photiadis and Harry K. Schwarzweller (eds.), *Change in Rural Appalachia: Implications for Actions Programs*. Philadelphia, Pa.: University of Pennsylvania Press. pp. 99-114. Reprinted in B. Ergood and B. E. Kuhre (eds.), *Appalachia: Social Context, Past and Present*, 1976. Dubuque, Iowa: Kendall/Hunt Publishing Company, pp. 274-281. Also reprinted in John D. Photiadis (ed.), *Religion in Appalachia: Theological, Social, and Psychological Dimensions and Correlates*, 1978. Morgantown, W.Va.: West Virginia University, pp. 271-284.

234. Gilbert, George B.
    1940 *Forty Years a Country Preacher*. New York, N.Y. and London, England: Harper and Brothers. 319 pp.

235. Gill, Charles Otis and Gifford Pinchot.
    1913 *The Country Church: Decline, Influence, and Remedy*. New York, N.Y.: Macmillan Company. 222 pp.

236. Gill, Charles Otis and Gifford Pinchot.
    1919 *Six-Thousand Country Churches*. New York, N.Y.: Macmillan Company. 237 pp.

237. Gillespie, J.T.
    1959 *Reaching Rural Churches*. Atlanta, Ga.: Home Mission Board, Southern Baptist Convention. 91 pp.

238. Gilmore, F.H.
    1929 *Recreational Leadership in the Rural Church*. Unpublished B.D. thesis. Atlanta, Ga.: Department of Sociology, Emory University. 41 pp.

239. Gladen, Ron.
    1985 "To Do Justice: The Rural Crisis." Fargo, N.Dak.: Red River Valley Synod of the Lutheran Church in America. 10 pp.

240. Glenn, Max E., (ed.).
    1970 *Appalachia in Transition*. St. Louis, Mo.: Bethany Press. 156 pp.

241. Glenn, Max E.
     1970 "Cooperative Mission in Appalachia." In Max E. Glenn
           (ed.), *Appalachia in Transition.* St. Louis, Mo.: Bethany
           Press. pp. 111-121.

242. Goodwin, Frederick Deane.
     1926 *Beyond City Limits: A Study of the Relation of the Church to
           Rural Life.* New York, N.Y.: National Council of the
           Protestant Episcopal Church. 230 pp.

243. Goodwin, William J.
     1978 *Approaching Rural Ministry: A City Boy Plows Through Some
           Introductory Readings on Town and Country America.*
           Atlanta, Ga.: Glenmary Research Center. 38 pp.

244. Gore, William J. and Leroy C. Hodapp, (eds.).
     1976 *Change in the Small Community: An Interdisciplinary
           Survey.* New York, N.Y.: Friendship Press. 222 pp.

245. Granger, W.A.
     19-- *The Country Church Once More.* n.p.: New York Baptist
           Missionary Convention.

246. Graybeal, David Mercer.
     1962 *Methodism in Southern Appalachia.* Philadelphia, Pa.: Board
           of Missions of the United Methodist Church. 26 pp.

247. Green, William Mercer.
     1936 *The Church and Rural Life: The 22nd Annual Hale Memorial
           Sermon Delivered October 20, 1936.* Evanston, Ill.: Seabury-
           Western Theological Seminary. 26 pp.

248. Greene, Shirley E.
     1960 *Ferment on the Fringe: Studies of Rural Churches in
           Transition.* Philadelphia, Pa.: The Christian Education
           Press. 174 pp.

249. Greene, Shirley E.
     1963 "The Church Faces Its Own Crisis in Relation to
           Community and Culture." In *The Church and Culture in
           Crisis in Town and Country.* St. Louis, Mo.: United Church
           Board for Homeland Ministries.

250. Greene, Shirley E.
     1975 "The Church's Role in Community Economic
           Development." In James A. Cogswell (ed.), *The Church
           and the Rural Poor.* Atlanta, Ga.: John Knox Press. pp. 83-
           94.

251. Greenley, Andrew M.
     1977 *No Bigger Than Necessary: An Alternative to Socialism,*
           Capitalism, and Anarchism. New York, N.Y.: New
           American Library. 181 pp.

252. Griffeth, Ross John.
     1937 *The Bible and Rural Life.* Cincinnati, Ohio: Standard
           Publishing Company. 117 pp.

253. Groves, Ernest Rutherford.
     1917 *Using the Resources of the Country Church.* New York,
           N.Y.: Association Press. 152 pp.

254. Grubbs, Bruce.
     1980 *Helping a Small Church Grow.* Nashville, Tenn.:
           Convention Press. 96 pp.

255. Guard, S.R.
     1956 *The Farmer Gives Thanks.* New York, N.Y.: Abingdon
           Press. 64 pp.

256. Gullixson, Thaddeus Frank.
     1959 *The Valley Waits.* Minneapolis, Minn.: Augsburg
           Publishing House. 100 pp.

257. Gullixson, Thaddeus Frank.
     1963 *In the Face of the West Winds.* Minneapolis, Minn.:
           Augsburg Publishing House. 104 pp.

258. Gulledge, Pat, (ed.).
     1954 *Rural Church Work at Its Best.* Atlanta, Ga.: Religious
           Education Press. 190 pp.

259. Gunther, Doyce Walter.
     1976 *Hinton Rural Life Center: A Supportive Ministry to Aid the*
           Rural Church. Unpublished S.T.D. thesis. Atlanta, Ga.:
           Emory University. 169 pp.

260. Hackenbracht, Anna.
     1980 "Direct Marketing: Is It Coming Back?" In Charles P. Lutz
           (ed.), *Farming the Lord's Land: Christian Perspectives on*
           American Agriculture. Minneapolis, Minn.: Augsburg
           Publishing House, pp. 183-199.

261. Hamner, Edward D.
     1940 *Financing the Town and Country Church.* Indianapolis, Ind.:
           United Christian Missionary Society. 56 pp.

262. Harlan, Rolvix.
      1925   *A New Day for the Country Church.* Nashville, Tenn.:
             Cokesbury Press. 166 pp.

263. Harris, Marshall Dees and Joseph Ackerman.
      1955   *Town and Country Churches and Family Farming.* New
             York, N.Y.: Land Tenure Committee,Department of Town
             and Country Church, Division of Home Missions,
             National Council of the Churches of Christ in the U.S.A.
             102 pp.

264. Hart, John.
      1984   "Land Reform and the Church." In Charles C. Geisler and
             Frank J. Popper (eds.), *Land Reform, American Style.*
             Totowa, N.J. : Rowman & Allanheld. pp. 73-87.

265. Hart, John.
      1984   *The Spirit of the Earth--A Theology of the Land.* New York,
             N.Y.: Paulist Press. 165 pp.

266. Hass, Lonnie Headley.
      1940   *Soil and the Church.* n.p. 6 pp.

267. Hassinger, Edward W.
      1978   *The Rural Component of American Society.* Danville, Ill.:
             Interstate Printers and Publishers, Inc. pp. 338-347.

268. Hassinger, Edward W. and J. Kenneth Benson.
      1978   "Interpretation of Changes in the Rural Churches of the
             Ozarks and Missouri in General." In John D. Photiadis
             (ed.), *Religion in Appalachia: Theological, Social, and
             Psychological Dimensions and Correlates.* Morgantown,
             W.Va.: West Virginia University. pp. 333-345.

269. Hassinger, Edward W., John S. Holik, and J. Kenneth Benson.
      1988   *The Rural Church: Learning from Three Decades of Change.*
             Nashville, Tenn.: Abingdon Press. 189 pp.

270. Haugen, Virgil C.
      1934   *Certain Problems of the Rural Church.* Unpublished
             thesis. St. Paul, Minn.: Luther Northwestern Seminary.

271. Haugen, Virgil C.
      1954   *The Rural Church and the Community.* Chicago, Ill.:
             Division of American Missions, National Lutheran
             Council. 27 pp.

272. Hayward, Charles E.
      1900 *Institutional Work for the Country Church*. Burlington, Vt.:
            Free Association Press. 149 pp.

273. Hendricks, Garland Alfred.
      1946 *The Contribution of Rural Churches to Moral and Civic Life*.
            n.p.: General Board of the Baptist State Convention of
            North Carolina. 9 pp.

274. Hendricks, Garland Alfred.
      1950 *Biography of a Country Church*. Nashville, Tenn.: Broadman
            Press. 137 pp.

275. Hendricks, Garland Alfred.
      1957 *How to Plan the Work of Your Church: A Study of
            Development of Churches Located in Small Communities*.
            Wake Forest, N.Car.: Extension Department, Southeastern
            Baptist Seminary. 256 pp.

276. Hendricks, Garland Alfred.
      1959 *Call to the Country*. Atlanta, Ga.: Home Mission Board,
            Southern Baptist Convention. 83 pp.

277. Hendricks, Garland Alfred.
      1965 *Appalachian Shepherd: A Story of Religion in the Southeastern
            Appalachians*. Atlanta, Ga.: Spiritual Life Publishers. 246
            pp.

278. Henry, F.E.
      1941 *The Small Church at Work for Children*. New York: N.Y.:
            Abingdon-Cokesbury Press. 121 pp.

279. Hepple, Lawrence M.
      1950 "The Church." In *Missouri: It's Resources, People, and
            Institutions*. University of Missouri Associates. pp. 543-
            558.

280. Herzel, Frank B.
      1949 *More Than Bread: An Analysis of Rural Life*. Philadelphia,
            Pa.: Muhlenberg Press. 280 pp.

281. Hester, Seth William.
      1946 *The Life and Works of Warren H. Wilson and Their
            Significance in the Beginning of the Rural Church Movement
            in America*. Unpublished thesis. Madison, N.J.: Drew
            Theological Seminary.

282. Hewitt, Arthur Wentworth.
      1926   *Steeples Among the Hills.* New York, N.Y. and Cincinnati,
             Ohio: Abingdon Press. 260 pp.

283. Hewitt, Arthur Wentworth.
      1939   *Highland Shepherds: A Book of the Rural Pastorate.* Chicago,
             Ill. and New York, N.Y.: Willett, Clark and Company.
             246 pp.

284. Hewitt, Arthur Wentworth.
      1941   *God's Back Pasture: A Book of the Rural Parish.* Chicago, Ill.
             and New York, N.Y.: Willett, Clark and Company. 144
             pp.

285. Hewitt, Arthur Wentworth.
      1943   *The Shepherdess.* Chicago, Ill.: Willett, Clark, and
             Company. 200 pp.

286. Hewitt, Arthur Wentworth.
      1966   *The Old Brick Manse.* New York, N.Y.: Harper and Row.
             246 pp.

287. Hill, Leslie G.
      1948   *The Pioneer Preachers in Missouri.* Unpublished M.A.
             thesis. Columbia, Mo.: University of Missouri.

288. Hill, Samuel S., Jr.
      1967   *Southern Churches in Crisis.* New York, N.Y.: Holt,
             Rinehart, and Winston. 234 pp. Reprinted 1968, Boston,
             Mass.: Beacon Press.

289. Hill, Samuel S., Jr., (ed.).
      1983   *On Jordan's Stormy Banks: Religion in the South, A Southern
             Exposure Profile.* Macon, Ga.: Mercer University Press. 159
             pp.

290. Hinton Rural Life Center.
      1970   *A Set of Papers Concerning the Town and Country Scene in
             the Southeast with Specific Attention to the Need for
             Administrative Renewal of the Church Parish.* Hayesville,
             N.Car.: Hinton Rural Life Center. (Various pagings.)

291. Hoge, Dean R. and David A. Roozen, (eds.).
      1979   *Understanding Church Growth and Decline: 1950-1978.* New
             York, N.Y.: Pilgrim Press. 398 pp.

292. Hoiberg, Otto G.
     1955 "The Church." Chapter 5 in *Exploring the Small Community*. Lincoln, Nebr.: University of Nebraska Press.

293. Holck, Manfred.
     1961 *Accounting Methods for the Small Church*. Minneapolis, Minn.: Augsburg Publishing House. 108 pp.

294. Hollingshead, August B.
     1961 "Religion and Religious Behavior." *Elmtown's Youth: The Impact of Social Classes on Adolescents*. (Second edition.) New York, N.Y.: Wiley.

295. Hood, Ralph W., Jr.
     1983 "Social Psychology and Religious Fundamentalism." Chapter 9 in Alan W. Childs and Gary B. Melton (eds.), *Rural Psychology*. pp. 169-198.

296. Hooker, Elizabeth Robbins.
     1931 *Hinterlands of the Church*. New York, N.Y.: Institute of Social and Religious Research. 314 pp.

297. Hooker, Elizabeth Robbins.
     1933 *Religion in the Highlands: Native Churches and Missionary Enterprises in the Southern Appalachian Area*. New York, N.Y.: Home Missions Council. 319 pp.

298. Hostetler, John Andrew.
     1953 *The Sociology of Mennonite Evangelism*. Unpublished Ph.D. thesis. State College, Pa.: Pennsylvania State College. 377 pp.

299. Houf, Walter Ralph.
     1967 *The Protestant Church in the Rural Midwestern Community, 1820-1870*. Unpublished Ph.D. thesis. Columbia, Mo.: University of Missouri. 342 pp.

300. Howard, Guy.
     1944 *Walkin' Preacher of the Ozarks*. New York, N.Y.: Harper. 273 pp.

301. Howard, Thomas E.
     1946 *Agricultural Handbook for Rural Pastors and Laymen: Religious, Economic, Social, and Cultural Implications of Rural Life*. Des Moines, Iowa and Paterson, N.J.: National Catholic Rural Life Conference. 166 pp.

302. Howes, John Baxter.
      1947   *The Rural Survey.* Nashville, Tenn.: Tidings, General Board
             of Evangelism, The Methodist Church.

303. Howes, John Baxter.
      1948   *A National Rural Policy for the Methodist Church.* New
             York, N.Y.: Department of Town and Country Church
             Work, Division of Home Missions and Church Extension,
             Methodist Church. 15 pp.

304. Howes, John Baxter.
      1952   *The Role of the Rural Church in American Protestantism.*
             Unpublished M.A. thesis. College Park, Md.: University
             of Maryland. 78 pp.

305. Hougen, Virgil Curtis.
      1954   *The Rural Church and the Community.* Chicago, Ill.:
             Division of American Missions, National Lutheran
             Council. 27 pp.

306. Hoyt, Arthur Stephen.
      1909   *The Call of the Country Church.* New York, N.Y.: Student
             Young Men's Christian Association Press. 11 pp.

307. Huff, Harold S. (chairman).
      1968   *Planning for Action: Aids for Leaders in Church Planning.*
             New York, N.Y.: Steering Committee, National
             Consultation on the Church in Community Life. 46 pp.

308. Hunter, Edwin Alfred.
      1947   *The Small Town and Country Church.* New York, N.Y. and
             Nashville, Tenn.: Abingdon-Cokesbury Press. 143 pp.

309. Hynes, Emerson.
      1951   "The Parish in the Rural Community." Chapter 5 in
             Celestine Joseph Nuesse and Thomas Joseph Harte (eds.),
             *The Sociology of the Parish: An Introductory
             Symposium.* Milwaukee, Wis.: Bruce Publishing Company.

310. Indiana Congregational Christian Conference, Rural Life
      Committee.
      1943   *Hoosier Churches: A Study of Rural Congregational Christian
             Churches of Indiana.* Muncie, Ind.: n.p. 51 pp.

311. Institute on the Church in Urban Industrial Society (ICUIS).
      1976   *Land Use Issues and the Quality of Urban and Rural Life: An
             ICUIS Working Bibliography.* ICUIS 2906 (June) n.p. 26 pp.

312. Interchurch World Movement of North America.
     1920 *Susquehanna County Survey*. New York, N.Y.: Interchurch
           Press. 52 pp.

313. Israel, Henry, (ed.).
     1913 *The Country Church and Community Cooperation*. New York,
           N.Y.: Association Press. 170 pp.

314. James, Gilbert and Robert G. Wickens.
     1968 *Town and Country Church: A Topical Bibliography*. Wilmore,
           Ky.: Department of the Church in Society, Asbury
           Theological Seminary. 137 pp.

315. Jeffreys, R.J.
     1947 *God is My Landlord*. Chicago, Ill.: Published for the
           Dynamic Kernels Foundation by Van Karupen Press. 158
           pp.

316. Jegen, Mary and Bruno Manno (eds.).
     1978 *The Earth is the Lord's: Essays on Stewardship*. New York,
           N.Y.: Paulist Press. 215 pp.

317. Jent, John William.
     1924 *The Challenge of the Country Church*. Nashville, Tenn.:
           Sunday School Board of the Southern Baptist Convention.
           206 pp.

318. Johnston, Ruby Funchess.
     1956 *The Religion of Negro Protestants: Changing Religious
           Attitudes and Practices*. New York, N.Y.: Philosophical
           Library, Inc. 224 pp.

319. Johnson, Junis William.
     1973 *The Rural Church*. Unpublished M.R.E. thesis. Kansas City,
           Mo.: Nazarene Theological Seminary. 83 pp.

320. Johnson, Merle Allison.
     1979 *How to be Happy in the Non-Electric Church*. Nashville,
           Tenn.: Abingdon Press. 112 pp.

321. Johnson, Paul C.
     1980 "Family Farming: Does It Serve the Common Good?" In
           Charles P. Lutz (ed.), *Farming the Lord's Land: Christian
           Perspectives on American Agriculture*. Minneapolis, Minn.:
           Augsburg Publishing House. pp. 41-58.

322. Jones, Ernest.
    1917 *Survey of the Rural Churches of Randolph County, Missouri.*
          Unpublished M.A. thesis. Columbia,Mo.: University of
          Missouri.

323. Jones, Loyal.
    1978 "Mountain Religion: The Outsider's View." In John D.
          Photiadis (ed.), *Religion in Appalachia.* Morgantown,
          W.Va.: West Virginia University.

324. Jones, William A., Jr.
    1970 "Communion, Communication, and Community." In Max
          E. Glenn (ed.), *Appalachia in Transition.* St. Louis, Mo.:
          Bethany Press. pp. 60-68.

325. Judy, Marvin Thornton.
    1959 *The Larger Parish and Group Ministry.* New York, N.Y.:
          Abingdon Press. 175 pp.

326. Judy, Marvin Thornton.
    1961 *The Church in Town and Country Areas.* Dallas, Tex.:
          Southern Methodist University Printing Office. 34 pp.

327. Judy, Marvin Thornton.
    1967 *The Cooperative Parish in Nonmetropolitan America.*
          Nashville, Tenn.: Abingdon Press. 208 pp.

328. Judy, Marvin Thornton.
    1968 *Frontiers in Nonmetropolitan Church Strategies.* Dallas, Tex.:
          Perkins School of Theology, Southern Methodist
          University. 15 pp.

329. Judy, Marvin Thornton.
    1973 *The Parish Development Process.* Nashville, Tenn. and New
          York, N.Y.: Abingdon Press. 207 pp. An enlargement
          and revision of *The Cooperative Parish in Nonmetropolitan
          Areas.*

330. Judy, Marvin Thornton.
    1984 *From Ivy Tower to Village Spire: A History and Contemporary
          Appraisal of the Role of the Theological Seminary in Training
          for Ministry in the Small Membership Church in Town and
          Rural Areas.* Dallas, Tex.: Perkins School of Theology,
          Southern Methodist University Printing Office. 194 pp.

331. Judy, Marvin Thornton.
    1969 *Parish Development Aids.* New York, N.Y.: Abingdon Press.
          24 pp.

Books   37

332. Julian, C.M.
      1948 *The Christian World View.* New York, N.Y.: Department of
            Town and Country Work, Division of Home Missions
            and Church Extension, Methodist Church. 16 pp.

333. Kalman, Harold.
      1976 *Pioneer Churches.* New York, N.Y.: W.W. Norton and
            Company, Inc. 192 pp.

334. Kane, Steven M.
      1976 "Holy Ghost People: The Snake Handlers of Southern
            Appalachia." In Bruce Ergood and Bruce E. Kuhre (eds.),
            Appalachia: Social Context, Past and Present. Dubuque,
            Iowa: Kendall and Hunt. pp. 288-292.

335. Kane, Steven M.
      1978 "Holiness Fire Handling in Southern Appalachia: A
            Psychophysiological Analysis." In John D. Photiadis (ed.),
            *Religion in Appalachia: Theological, Social, and Psychological
            Dimensions and Correlates.* Morgantown, W.Va.: West
            Virginia University. pp. 113-124.

336. Kaplan, Berton H.
      1971 "Religion--Traditional and Modern: A Study of Three
            Churches in the Blue Ridge Mountains." Chapter 10 in
            Blue Ridge: An Appalachian Community in Transition.
            Morgantown, W.Va.: Appalachian Center, West Virginia
            University. Reprinted in John D. Photiadis (ed.), *Religion
            in Appalachia: Theological, Social, and Psychological
            Dimensions and Correlates.* Morgantown, W.Va.: West
            Virginia University. pp. 255-270.

337. Kardoong, Terrance G.
      1985 *Prairie Church: The Diocese of Bismarck, 1910-1985.*
            Richardton, N.Dak.: Assumption Abbey Press. 258 pp.

338. Kaufman, Harold Frederick.
      1959 *Mississippi Churches: A Statistical Supplement.* Hattiesburg,
            Miss.: Social Science Research Center, Mississippi State
            University Press. 28 pp.

339. Kelley, Arleon.
      1970 "Tactics for the Church on the Offensive." In Victor J.
            Klimoski and Bernard Quinn (eds.), *Church and
            Community: Nonmetropolitan America in Transition.*
            Washington, D.C.: Center for Applied Research in the
            Apostolate. pp. 79-86.

38   Books

340.   Kephart, Horace.
       1913   *Our Southern Highlanders.* New York, N.Y.: Outing
              Publishing Company. 305 pp. Reprinted 1921, 1926,
              1941.

341.   Kerr, James M.
       1978   "A Pastor's View of Religion in Appalachia." In John D.
              Photiadis (ed.), *Religion in Appalachia: Theological, Social,
              and Psychological Dimensions and Correlates.* Morgantown,
              W.Va.: West Virginia University Press. pp. 65-78.

342.   Kim, Byong-suh.
       1968   *Religiosity as Related to Social Institutional Behavior in the
              Southern Appalachian Region.* Unpublished Ph.D. thesis.
              Atlanta, Ga.: Emory University. 243 pp.

343.   King, Horace M.
       1947   *A Rural Layman Goes to Work.* New York, N.Y. and
              Nashville, Tenn.: Abingdon-Cokesbury Press. 117 pp.

344.   Kirkpatrick, Ellis Lore.
       1942   "The Church's Part with Rural Youth." Town and
              Country Co-Operative Series No. 3. New York, N.Y.:
              Home Missions Council of North America. 8 pp.

345.   Klemme, Huber F.
       1957   *Your Church and Your Community.* Philadelphia, Pa.:
              Christian Education Press. 121 pp.

346.   Klimoski, Victor J. and Bernard Quinn, (eds.).
       1970   *Church and Community: Nonmetropolitan America in
              Transition.* Center for Applied Research in the Apostolate
              (CARA) Information Service Town and Country Report
              No. 4. Washington, D.C.: CARA. 90 pp.

347.   Klimoski, Victor J. and James F. Krile, (eds.).
       1972   *Who Needs Rural America? The Church and the Non-
              Metropolitan Community in a Changing Society.* Dubuque,
              Iowa: The Scriptory, New Melleray Abbey. 107 pp.

348.   Kraemer, Hendrik.
       1958   *A Theology of the Laity.* Philadelphia, Pa.: Westminster
              Press. 192 pp.

349.   Kreitlow, Burton W., E.W. Aiton, and Andrew P. Torrence.
       1960   "Rural Churches Working Together." Chapter 19 in
              Leadership for Action in Rural Communities. Danville, Ill.:
              Interstate Printers and Publishers.

350. Kolb, John Harrison and Edmund deSchweinitz Brunner.
      1952 "Religion and the Rural Church." In *A Study of Rural
            Society.* Cambridge, Mass.: Houghton Mifflin Co. pp. 361-
            380.

351. Kule, James and Victor J. Klimoski.
      1977 *Dimensions of Catholic Ministry: The Rural Priest.* Atlanta,
            Ga.: Glenmary Research Center. 58 pp.

352. Kuman, Alexander A.
      1962 *A Changing Church: A Study of Change in Church
            Membership and Activities Associated with Urbanization in a
            Rural County.* Unpublished Ph.D. thesis. Buffalo, N.Y.:
            University of Buffalo. 195 pp.

353. LaBare, Weston.
      1962 *They Shall Take Up Serpents: Psychology of the Southern
            Snake Handling Cults.* Minneapolis, Minn.: University of
            Minnesota Press. 208 pp.

354. Lamar, Ralph E.
      1962 *Fundamentalism and Selected Social Factors in the Southern
            Appalachian Region.* Unpublished M.S. thesis. Lexington,
            Ky.: University of Kentucky. 108 pp.

355. Lamb, Jerome D., Jerry Ruff, and William Sherman.
      1988 *Scattered Steeples: The Fargo Dioceses--A Written Celebration
            of Its Centennial.* Fargo, N.D.: Burch, Longergan, and
            Lynch, Publishers. 190 pp.

356. Landero, Gregorio.
      1980 "That Rural Peoples Might Believe and Obey." In J.
            Alexander (ed.), *Believing and Obeying Jesus Christ: The
            Urbana 79 Compendium.* Downers Grove, Ill.: Inter Varsity
            Press. pp. 191-198.

357. Landis, Benson Young.
      1922 *Rural Church Life in the Middle West, As Illustrated by Clay
            County, Iowa, and Jennings County, Indiana, With
            Comparative Data From Studies of 35 Middle Western
            Counties.* New York, N.Y.: George H. Doran Company. 88
            pp.

358. Landis, Benson Young.
      1948 "Trends in Rural Religion and the Farmers Church."
            Chapter 23 in *Rural Life in Process* (second edition). New
            York, N.Y.: McGraw-Hill Book Company.

359. Landis, Benson Young.
      1955 *National Interdenominational Rural Church Programs, 1912-
            1955: An Informal Historical Study.* New York, N.Y.

360. Langdon, David Stetson.
      1977 *The Meaning of Confirmation and Its Implications for
            Confirmation Instruction in a Rural Parish.* Unpublished
            D.Min. thesis. Madison, N.J.: Drew Theological Seminary.
            154 pp.

361. Larson, Olaf F.
      1978 "Values and Beliefs of Rural People." In Thomas R. Ford
            (ed.), *Rural USA: Persistence and Change.* Ames, Iowa:
            Iowa State University Press. pp. 91-112.

362. Lawson, John.
      1955 *Green and Pleasant Land.* Chicago, Ill.: S.C.M. Press. 126
            pp.

363. Lewis, Thomas L.
      1954 *The Function of a Pastor as a Counselor in a Rural Church
            Community.* Unpublished M.A. thesis. Louisville, Ky.:
            Southern Baptist Theological Seminary.

364. Lindgren, Alvin J.
      1965 *Foundations for Purposeful Church Administration.* New
            York, N.Y.: Abingdon Press. 302 pp.

365. Lindstrom, David Edgar.
      1939 *The Church in Rural Life.* Champaign, Ill.: Garrard Press.
            145 pp.

366. Lindstrom, David Edgar.
      1946 *Rural Life and the Church.* Champaign, Ill.: The Garrard
            Press. 205 pp. Revision of *The Church in Rural Life.* 1939.
            145 pp.

367. Lindstrom, David Edgar.
      1948 *The Methodist Church and the Rural Community.* New York,
            N.Y.: Department of Town and Country Church Work,
            Division of Home Missions and Church Extension,
            Methodist Church. 39 pp.

368. Lindstrom, David Edgar.
      1950 *America's Foundations of Religious Liberty.* Champaign, Ill.:
            Garrard Press. 107 pp.

369. Lindstrom, David Edgar.
     1948 "The Rural Church and Its Social Problem." Chapter 12
          in *American Rural Life.* New York, N.Y.: Ronald Press.
          Reprinted in 1957, Urbana, Ill.: University of Illinois
          Press.

370. Longnecker, Harold.
     1961 *The Village Church: Its Pastor and Program.* Chicago, Ill.:
          Moody Press. 192 pp.

371. Longnecker, Harold.
     1973 *Building Town and Country Churches.* Chicago, Ill.: Moody
          Press. 122 pp.

372. Loomis, Charles P. and J. Allan Beegle.
     1950 "The Character of Rural Religion." Chapter 13 in *Rural
          Social Systems.* New York, N.Y.: Prentice-Hall.

373. Loomis, Charles P. and J. Allan Beegle.
     1957 "Religious Social Systems." In *Rural Sociology: The Strategy
          of Change.* Englewood Cliffs, N.J.: Prentice-Hall.

374. Lowery, James L., Jr.
     1970 *Small Congregations and Their Clergy.* Chicago, Ill.:
          Enablement, Inc.

375. Lowery, James L., Jr.
     1974 *The Small Church Is Here to Stay and She Can Be Viable.*
          Boston, Mass.: Enablement, Inc.

376. Lutz, Charles P., (ed.).
     1980 *Farming the Lord's Land: Christian Perspectives on American
          Agriculture.* Minneapolis, Minn.: Augsburg Publishing
          House. 208 pp.

377. Lutz, Charles P.
     1980 "U.S. Farming and World Food Needs." In Charles P.
          Lutz (ed.), *Farming the Lord's Land: Christian Perspectives
          on American Agriculture.* Minneapolis, Minn.: Augsburg
          Publishing House. pp. 13-28.

378. Lutz, Charles P.
     1980 "U.S. Farmers and Our Public Food Programs." In
          Charles P. Lutz (ed.), *Farming the Lord's Land: Christian
          Perspectives on American Agriculture.* Minneapolis, Minn.:
          Augsburg Publishing House, pp. 29-40.

379. McBride, Charles Ralph.
      1940 *What I Found in Knox County.* New York, N.Y.: American
            Baptist Home Mission Society, Town and Country Work.

380. McBride, Charles Ralph.
      1949 *Rural Christians and Natural Resources.* Philadelphia, Pa.:
            Judson Press. 125 pp.

381. McBride, Charles Ralph.
      1953 *The Christian Home in a Rural Setting.* Philadelphia, Pa.:
            Judson Press. 111 pp.

382. McBride, Charles Ralph.
      1954 *An Introduction to the Rural Church Movement.* Kansas City,
            Kans.: Central Seminary Press. 130 pp.

383. McBride, Charles Ralph.
      1955 *The Rural Church: Its Message, Organization, and Program.*
            Kansas City, Kans.: Central Seminary Press. 152 pp.

384. McBride, Charles Ralph.
      1956 *The Rural Pastor: His Home and Office.* Kansas City, Kans.:
            Central Seminary Press.

385. McBride, Charles Ralph.
      1962 *Protestant Churchmanship for Rural America.* Valley Forge,
            Pa.: Judson Press. 334 pp.

386. McConnell, Charles Melvin.
      1931 *The Rural Billion.* New York, N.Y.: Friendship Press. 128
            pp.

387. McConnell, Charles Melvin.
      1956 *High Hours of Methodism in Town-Country Churches.* New
            York, N.Y.: Board of Missions of the Methodist Church.
            109 pp.

388. McLaughlin, Henry Woods.
      1926 *The New Call.* Richmond, Va.: John Knox Press. 190 pp.

389. McLaughlin, Henry Woods.
      1928 *Christ and the Country People.* Richmond, Va.: Presbyterian
            Committee of Publication. 159 pp.

390. McLaughlin, Henry Woods, (ed.).
      1930 *The Country Church and Public Affairs.* New York, N.Y.:
            Macmillan. 260 pp.

391. McLaughlin, Henry Woods.
1932 *Religious Education in the Rural Church.* New York, N.Y. and Chicago, Ill.: Fleming H. Revell Co. 220 pp.

392. MacMaster, Richard K.
1984 *Land, Piety, and Peoplehood.* Scottsdale, Pa.: Herald Press. 344 pp.

393. McNutt, Matthew Brown.
1911 *Modern Methods in the Country Church.* An address delivered before the McCormick Seminary Alumni Association, Chicago, Ill., April 28, 1910. New York, N.Y.: Missionary Education Movement and Presbyterian Board of Home Missions and New York, N.Y.: Young People's Missionary Movement of the United States and Canada. 29 pp.

394. McSwain, Harold W.
1965 *The Cooperative-Type Ministry and Renewal in Town and Country Churches.* Hayesville, N.Car.: Hinton Rural Life Center. 48 pp.

395. Madsen, Paul O.
1975 *Small Churches--Vital, Valid, Victorious.* Valley Forge, Pa.: Judson Press. 126 pp.

396. Martin, Bishop William C.
1948 *The Church in the Rural Community.* New York, N.Y.: Editorial Department, Division of Education and Cultivation, Board of Missions and Church Extension, Methodist Church. 121 pp.

397. Masters, Victor Irvine.
1916 *Country Church in the South: Arranged to Meet the Needs of Missions Study Classes, and Also of the General Reader,* Second edition. Atlanta, Ga.: Publicity Department, Home Missions Board, Southern Baptist Convention. 223 pp.

398. Mather, William G.
1948 *The Mission of the Rural Church.* New York, N.Y.: American Baptist Home Mission Society.

399. Mathews, Elmora Messer.
1965 *Neighbor and Kin: Life in a Tennessee Ridge Community.* Nashville, Tenn.: Vanderbilt University Press.

400.   Mathieson, Moira B.
       1979   *The Shepherds of the Delectable Mountains: The Story of the
              Washington County Mission Program.* Cincinnati, Ohio:
              Forward Movement Publications. 110 pp.

401.   Mattson, Alvin Daniel.
       1944   *A Study of the Mid-West Rural Churches of the Lutheran
              Augustana Synod.* Published under the Auspices of the
              Board of Home Missions, Augustana Evangelical
              Lutheran Church. Rock Island, Ill.: Augustana Book
              Concern. 35 pp.

402.   Mattson, Alvin Daniel.
       1945   *A Study of the Town and Country Churches of the Lutheran
              Augustana Synod.* Published under the Auspices of the
              Board of Home Missions, Augustana Evangelical
              Lutheran Church. Rock Island, Ill.: Augustana Book
              Concern. 61 pp.

403.   Maurer, Beryl B.
       1974   "Our Religious Heritage." In Beryl B. Maurer (ed.),
              Mountain Heritage. Morgantown, W.Va.: Morgantown
              Printing and Binding Co.

404.   Mavis, Walter Curry.
       1957   *Advancing the Smaller Local Church.* Winona Lake, Ind.:
              Light and Life Press and Grand Rapids, Mich.: Baker
              Book House. 189 pp.

405.   Mays, William E.
       1968   "The Churches of Haskell County." *Sublette Revisited:
              Stability and Change in a Rural Kansas Community after a
              Quarter Century.* New York, N.Y.: Florham Park Press.

406.   Medearis, Dale W.
       19--   *Building and Grounds for Town and Country Churches.*
              Indianapolis, Ind.: United Christian Missionary Society.

407.   Meek, Pauline Palmer.
       1975   *Ministries With Children in Small Churches.* Philadelphia,
              Pa.: Geneva Press. 30 pp.

408.   Melvin, Bruce Lee.
       1917   *Rural Church Survey of Boone County, Missouri.*
              Unpublished M.A. thesis. Columbia, Mo.: University of
              Missouri.

409. Methodist Church in the U.S.A.
194- *The Emphasis in Town and Country: Things Town and Country Churches Should Do Now.* New York, N.Y.: Board of Missions and Church Extension, Home Missions Section, Department of Town and Country Work. 11 pp.

410. Methodist Church in the U.S.A.
194- *The Changing Small Church, Town and Country.* New York, N.Y.: Board of Home Missions and Church Extension, Methodist Church. 32 pp.

411. Methodist Church in the U.S.A.
1944 *A Program and a Policy.* North Mississippi Conference, Commission on Town and Country Work. 11 pp.

412. Methodist Church.
1955 *In Town and Country: Source Book of Methodism in Town and Country.* New York, N.Y.: Department of Research and Surveys, Division of National Missions, Board of Missions, Methodist Church. 177 pp.

413. Methodist Church.
1963 *Our Church and Its Community Outreach: A Self-Study Guide Designed to Assist Methodist Churches in Gathering Data about Their Membership and Community.* Philadelphia, Pa.: Division of National Missions, Board of Missions, Methodist Church.

414. Meyer, Benjamin.
1961 *A Survey of the Town and Country Churches in Southwestern Minnesota.* Dubuque, Iowa: Presbyterian Seminary.

415. Middleton, Edwin L.
1923 *Building a Country Sunday School.* New York, N.Y.: Fleming H. Revell Company. 159 pp.

416. Miller, George Amos.
1902 *The Problems of the Town Church: A Discussion of Needs and Methods.* New York, N.Y.: Fleming H. Revell Co. 201 pp.

417. Miller, R.J.
1947 "The Papal Encyclicals and the Problems of Rural Life." In J. V. Urbain and R. J. Wilson, Jr. (eds.), *Rural America: A Catholic Sourcebook.* Cincinnati, Ohio: Catholic Students' Mission Crusade. pp. 35-40.

418. Miller, Walter W.
      1960   *The Effects of Migration on Churches in the Rural
             Fringe.* Unpublished M.S. thesis. Columbia, Ohio: Ohio
             State University.

419. Mills, Harlow Spencer.
      1914   *The Making of a Country Parish.* New York, N.Y.:
             Missionary Education Movement of the United States and
             Canada. 126 pp.

420. Miyakawa, Tetsuo Scott.
      1964   *Protestants and Pioneers.* Chicago, Ill.: University of
             Chicago Press. 306 pp.

421. Mondy, Robert William.
      1980   *Pioneers and Preachers: Stories of the Old Frontier.* Chicago,
             Ill.: Nelson Hall. 268 pp.

422. Moomaw, Ira W.
      1945   *Rural Life Objectives in the Church of the Brethren.* Elgin,
             Ill.: General Mission, Board of the Church of the
             Brethren. 19 pp.

423. Moomaw, Ira W., (ed.).
      1957   *Deep Furrows: Goals, Methods and Results of Those Who
             Work toward a Brighter Tomorrow.* New York, N.Y.:
             Agricultural Missions, Inc. and Rural Missions
             Cooperating Committee of the Division of Foreign
             Missions. 192 pp.

424. Morrison, George.
      1953   *Country Parson.* Toronto, Canada: Ryerson Press. 140 pp.

425. Morse, Hermann Nelson.
      1912   *Ohio Rural Life Survey: Church Growth and Decline in Ohio.*
             New York, N.Y.: Board of Home Missions, Department of
             Church and Country Life, Presbyterian Church in the
             U.S.A. 32 pp.

426. Morse, Hermann Nelson.
      1922   *The Country Church in Industrial Zones: The Effects of
             Industrialization upon the Church Life of Adjacent Rural Areas
             as Illustrated Typical Counties.* New York, N.Y.: George H.
             Doran. 120 pp.

427. Morse, Hermann Nelson and Edmund deSchweinitz Brunner.
     1923 *The Town and Country Church in the United States: As Illustrated by Data From 179 Counties and by Intensive Studies of 29.* New York, N.Y.: George H. Doran Company. 179 pp. Reprinted 1925.

428. Mosher, Arthur T.
     1945 *Christian Mission among Rural People.* New York, N.Y.: John Riesner. 334 pp.

429. Mosher, Arthur T.
     1945 *Sourcebook of Rural Missions: Volume I. Selected Readings.* New York, N.Y.: Agricultural Missions, Inc. 235 pp.

430. Mueller, Elwin William, (ed.).
     19-- *The Lutheran Church in Town and Country.* Minneapolis, Minn.: Augsburg Publishing House.

431. Mueller, Elwin William.
     1954 *A Profile of the Lutheran Church.* Chicago, Ill.: Division of American Missions, National Lutheran Council. 210 pp.

432. Mueller, Elwin William.
     1957 *The Church and the Stewardship of the Land.* Chicago, Ill.: Division of American Missions, National Lutheran Council.

433. Mueller, Elwin William.
     1958 *Serving Churches in Town and Country.* Chicago, Ill.: Division of American Missions, National Lutheran Council. 29 pp.

434. Mueller, Elwin William.
     1960 *The Look Ahead.* Chicago, Ill.: Division of American Missions, National Lutheran Council. 14 pp.

435. Mueller, Elwin William.
     1963 *Stewardship in the Countryside.* Chicago, Ill.: National Lutheran Council.

436. Mueller, Elwin William.
     1970 "Is the Church on the Offensive?" In Victor J. Klimoski and Bernard Quinn (eds.), *Church and Community: Nonmetropolitan America in Transition.* Washington, D.C.: Center for Applied Research in the Apostolate. pp. 67-78.

437. Mueller, Elwin William and Giles C. Ekola, (eds.).
      1963 *The Silent Struggle for Mid-America: The Church in Town
            and Country Today.* Minneapolis, Minn.: Augsburg
            Publishing House. 167 pp.

438. Mueller, Elwin William and Giles C. Ekola, (eds.).
      1966 *Mission in the American Outdoors: Concerns of the Church in
            Leisure-Recreation.* St. Louis, Mo.: Concordia Publishing
            House. 165 pp.

439. Mueller, Elwin William and Betty Westrom Skold.
      1957 *First the Blade.* Chicago, Ill.: Division of American
            Missions, National Lutheran Council. 16 pp.

440. Mueller, Elwin William and Betty Westrom Skold.
      1957 *Planting the Cross on the Contour.* Chicago, Ill.: Division of
            American Missions, National Lutheran Council. 16 pp.

441. Mueller, Elwin William and Betty Westrom Skold.
      1960 *Pastor, How Can You Expect....* Chicago, Ill.: Division of
            American Missions, National Lutheran Council. 20 pp.

442. Myers, Alexander John William and Edwin Einer Sundt.
      1930 *The Country Church As It Is: A Case Study of Rural
            Churches and Leaders.* Chicago, Ill.: Fleming H. Revell
            Company. 189 pp.

443. National Catholic Rural Life Conference.
      19-- *Developing Rural Industry.* Des Moines, Iowa: National
            Catholic Rural Life Conference.

444. National Catholic Rural Life Conference.
      1939 *Manifesto on Rural Life.* Bishop Aloisius P. Muench,
            Imprimatur. Milwaukee, Wis.: Bruce Publishing Co. 222
            pp.

445. National Catholic Rural Life Conference.
      194- *Christ to the Country--the Country to Christ.* Des Moines,
            Iowa: National Catholic Rural Life Conference.

446. National Catholic Rural Life Conference.
      1948 *A Survey of Catholic Weakness.* With an introduction and a
            plan by Monsignor Ligutti. Des Moines, Iowa: National
            Catholic Rural Life Conference. 61 pp.

447. National Catholic Rural Life Conference.
      1958 *National Catholic Rural Life Conference in Review, 1957:
            Serving Rural America 35 Years.* Des Moines, Iowa:
            National Catholic Rural Life Conference. 18 pp.

448. National Catholic Rural Life Conference.
    1962 *Developing Rural Resources: An Appraisal of Rural Areas Development Program.* Des Moines, Iowa: National Catholic Rural Life Conference.

449. National Council of Churches of Christ in the U.S.A.
    1955 *Christian Stewardship of the Land.* New York, N.Y.: Division of Home Missions, National Council of Churches of Christ in the U.S.A. 48 pp.

450. National Council of Churches of Christ in the U.S.A.
    1955 *Be a Rural Pastor.* New York, N.Y.: Department of the Ministry, National Council of Churches of Christ in the U.S.A.

451. National Council of Churches of Christ in the U.S.A.
    1957 *Rural Missions Perspective for the Years Ahead.* New York, N.Y.: Rural Missions Cooperating Committee, National Council of Churches of Christ in the U.S.A. 15 pp.

452. National Council of Churches of Christ in the U.S.A.
    1959 *Church and the Rural Development Program.* New York, N.Y.: Department of Town and Country Church, Division of Home Missions, National Council of Churches of Christ in the U.S.A.

453. National Council of Churches of Christ in the U.S.A.
    1960 *Church and the Rural Community: A Proposal and a Guide for One-Day Institutes Dealing With Farm Family Problems.* New York, N.Y.: Department of the Town and Country Church, Division of Home Missions, National Council of Churches of Christ in the U.S.A.

454. National Council of Churches of Christ in the U.S.A.
    1961 *The Church and Rural Reconstruction: A Report on Program and Policy for the Years Ahead.* New York, N.Y.: Rural Missions Cooperating Committee and Agricultural Missions, Inc. 30 pp.

455. National Council of Churches of Christ in the U.S.A.
    1970 *Ethical Issues in Commercial Agriculture.* New York, N.Y.: Working Group on Agriculture and Rural Life Issues, National Council of Churches of Christ in the U.S.A. 18 pp.

456.   National Council of Churches of Christ in the U.S.A.
       1970   *The Ethical Challenge of Rural Poverty.* New York, N.Y.:
              Working Group on Agriculture and Rural Life Issues,
              National Council of Churches of Christ in the U.S.A. 19
              pp.

457.   National Lutheran Council of American Missions.
       19--   *Lutheran Higher Education in Service to Rural People.*
              Chicago, Ill.: Division of American Missions.

458.   National Lutheran Council.
       1962   *The Church's Concern for Town and Country Communities in
              Mid-America.* New York, N.Y.: National Lutheran Council.

459.   National Lutheran Council.
       1964   *The Nature and Mission of the Church in Town and Country.*
              National Lutheran Council: New York, N.Y.

460.   Neff, Lois.
       1913   *Ohio Rural Life Survey: Country Churches of Distinction.*
              New York, N.Y.: Board of Home Missions, Department of
              Church and Country Life, Presbyterian Church in the
              U.S.A. 48 pp.

461.   Neigh, Kenneth G.
       1961   *Crisis in Town and Country: A Call to the Church.* New
              York, N.Y.: Department of Town and Country Church
              and Indian Work, Board of National Missions, United
              Presbyterian Church in the U.S.A. 28 pp.

462.   Nelsen, Hart M.
       1978   "Consequences of Church-Sect Heterogeneity for Local
              Church Dissension: An Assessment of Causes of Church
              Bickering." In John D. Photiadis (ed.), *Religion in
              Appalachia: Theological, Social, and Psychological Dimensions
              and Correlates.* Morgantown, W.Va.: West Virginia
              University. pp. 347-358.

463.   Nelsen, Hart M. and Raymond H. Potvin.
       1974   *Appalachian Religion Transplanted.* Columbus, Ohio:
              Academy of Contemporary Problems.

464.   Nelson, Glenn I.
       1965   *Social Change, Reference Groups and the Self Concept: A
              Study of Change in Rural Churches.* Unpublished Ph.D.
              thesis.

465. Nelson, Lowry.
     1946 *Red Wing Churches During the War*. Minneapolis, Minn.: University of Minnesota Press. 21 pp.

466. Nelson, Lowry.
     1952 "The Church as a Social Institution." Chapter in *Rural Sociology*. New York, N.Y.: American Book Company.

467. Nelson, Lowry.
     1954 "Rural Church." Chapter in *American Farm Life*. Cambridge, Mass.: Harvard University Press.

468. Nelson, Lowry.
     1955 "Religion in the Rural Church." Chapter 17 in *Rural Sociology*. New York, N.Y.: American Book Company.

469. Nelson, Richard Henry.
     1906 "The Training of Men for Rural Missions Work." New York, N.Y.: n.p. 9 pp.

470. Nesius, Ernest J.
     1967 *A New Town and Country Community*. Valley Forge, Pa.: Home Mission Societies.

471. Nida, Eugene Albert.
     1960 *Message and Mission: The Communication of the Christian Faith*. New York, Harper and Row. 253 pp. Reprinted in 1975, South Pasadena, Cal.: William Cary Library.

472. Niederfrank, E.J.
     1956 *Town and Country Churches and Family Farming: A Study Guide*. New York, N.Y.: Department of Town and Country Church, Division of Home Missions, National Council of Churches of Christ in the U.S.A. 15 pp.

473. Nielsen, Charles Emmet.
     1963 *Adjustment of the Church and the Community to Population Change in a Rural South Dakota Community*. Unpublished M. A. thesis. Brookings, S.Dak.: South Dakota State University. 116 pp.

474. Nuckols, Elizabeth H.
     1927 *Working With Children in Rural and Village Sunday Schools*. Nashville, Tenn.: Sunday School Board of the Southern Baptist Convention. 172 pp.

475. Nuesse, Celestine Joseph and Thomas Joseph Harte (eds.)
     1951 *The Sociology of the Parish: An Introductory Symposium*. Milwaukee, Wis.: Bruce Publishing Company. 354 pp.

476. Obenhaus, Victor.
     1963 *The Church and Faith in Mid-America.* Philadelphia, Pa.:
          Westminster Press. 174 pp.

477. O'Hara, Edwin V.
     1927 *The Church and the Country Community.* New York, N.Y.:
          Macmillan Company. 115 pp. Reprinted in 1978, New
          York, N.Y.: Arno Press.

478. O'Hara, Edwin V., W.H. Bishop, and J.V. Urbain.
     1947 "Why the Catholic Church is Interested in the Rural
          Life." In Urbain, J.V. and R.J. Wilson, Jr. (eds.), *Rural
          America: A Catholic Sourcebook.* Cincinnati, Ohio: Catholic
          Students' Mission Crusade. pp. 1-6.

479. Olson, Merlyn J.
     1974 *Prophetic and Priestly Aspects of Caring for the Community.*
          Unpublished thesis. St. Paul, Minn.: Luther Northwestern
          Seminary.

480. Olson, Merlyn J.
     1977 *Forgotten Challenge: Town and Country Ministry.*
          Worthington, Minn.: n.p.

481. Ormond, Jesse Marvin.
     1931 *The Country Church in North Carolina: A Study of the
          Country Churches of North Carolina in Relation to the
          Material Progress of the State.* Durham, N.Car.: Duke
          University Press. 369 pp.

482. Ormond, Jesse Marvin.
     1936 *By the Waters of Bethesda.* Nashville, Tenn.: Department of
          Education and Promotion, Board of Missions, Methodist
          Episcopal Church, South. 153 pp.

483. Palmer, James M.
     1977 "The Vital Ministry of the Rural and Small Church."
          Atlanta, Ga.: Home Mission Board, Southern Baptist
          Convention. 7 pp.

484. Papus, Tony.
     1988 *Entering the World of the Small Church.* Washington, D.C.:
          Albin Institute.

485. Partick, June W.
     1950 *The Development of an Adequate Vacation School Program for
          the Rural Church.* Unpublished M.R.E. thesis. Wilmore,
          Ky.: Asbury Theological Seminary. 66 pp.

486. Patten, Marjorie.
     1922 *The Country Church in Colonial Counties: As Illustrated by
     Addison County, Vt., Tompkins County, N.Y. and Warren
     County, N.Y.* New York, N.Y.: George H. Doran
     Company. 106 pp.

487. Pearsall, Marion.
     1959 "Supernatural Sanctions." *Little Smoky Ridge: The Natural
     History of a Southern Appalachian Neighborhood.* Tuscaloosa,
     Ala.: University of Alabama Press. 205 pp.

488. Pepper, Clayton A.
     1962 *A Manual for Yoked Church Fields.* Valley Forge, Pa.:
     American Baptist Home Mission Societies, Division of
     Church Missions, American Baptist Convention.

489. Pepper, Clayton A.
     1962 *Work Together as One--Federated Churches.* Valley Forge,
     Pa.: American Baptist Home Mission Societies, Division
     of Church Missions, American Baptist Convention.

490. Pepper, Clayton A.
     1973 *Streams of Influence: An Historical Evaluation of the Town
     and County Movement within the American Baptist
     Convention.* Valley Forge, Pa.: Judson Press. 160 pp.

491. Perrin, Noel.
     1980 *Second Person Rural: More Essays on a Sometimes Farmer.*
     Boston, Mass.: D. R. Godine. 152 pp. Reprinted in 1981,
     New York, N.Y.: Penguin Books and Boston, Mass.: G.K.
     Hall.

492. Peterkin, George William.
     1912 *The Country Minister and His Work.* Reinecke Lecture
     delivered at the Virginia Seminary during the sessions
     1911-1912. 40 pp.

493. Photiadis, John D.
     1966 "The Changing Rural Church." In *Science Serves Your Farm
     and Home.* Morgantown, W.Va.: West Virginia University.

494. Photiadis, John D., (ed.).
     1978 *Religion in Appalachia: Theological, Social, and Psychological
     Dimensions.* Morgantown, W.Va.: West Virginia
     University. 422 pp.

495. Photiadis, John D.
      1978 "A Theoretical Supplement." In John D. Photiadis (ed.),
            *Religion in Appalachia: Theological, Social, and Psychological
            Dimensions.* Morgantown, W.Va.: West Virginia
            University. pp. 7-27.

496. Photiadis, John D.
      1978 "Change and Stability of the Religious Institution in Rural
            Appalachia: Why American Religion is Most Successful."
            In John D. Photiadis (ed.), *Religion in Appalachia:
            Theological, Social, and Psychological Dimensions.*
            Morgantown, W.Va.: West Virginia University. pp. 285-
            322.

497. Pielstick, Don F.
      194- *A Study of Protestant Churches in Douglas, Hancock, and
            Whiteside Counties, Illinois, 1947.* New York, N.Y.:
            Committee on Cooperative Field Research of the Home
            Missions Council of North America.

498. Piper, David Roy, (compiler).
      1922 *A Handbook of the Community Church Movement in the
            United States.* Excelsior Springs, Mo.: The Community
            Churchman Company. 83 pp.

499. Piper, David Roy.
      1928 *Community Churches: The Community Church Movement.*
            Chicago, Ill.: Willett, Clark & Colby Company. 158 pp.

500. Plunkett, Sir Horace Curzon.
      1910 *The Rural Life Problem in the United States: Notes of an Irish
            Observer.* New York, N.Y.: Macmillan. 174 pp. Reprinted
            in 1911, 1912, 1913, and 1919.

501. Poage, Bennett D.
      1975 "The Cooperative Movement Among the Southern Rural
            Poor." In James A. Cogswell (ed.), *The Church and the
            Rural Poor.* Atlanta, Ga.: John Knox Press. pp. 27-46.

502. Pope, Liston.
      1942 *Millhands and Preachers: A Study of Gastonia.* New Haven,
            Conn.: Yale University Press. 369 pp. Reprinted in 1946,
            1958, 1965, 1973, and 1976.

503. Presbyterian Church in the U.S.A.
      1912 "Church Growth and Decline in Ohio." In *Ohio Rural Life
            Survey.* New York, N.Y.: Board of Home Missions,
            Department of Church and Country Life, Presbyterian
            Church in the U.S.A. 32 pp.

504. Presbyterian Church in the U.S.A.
     1926 *What Presbyterians Are Doing for Country People.* New
     York, N.Y.: Board of National Missions, Presbyterian
     Church in the U.S.A. 16 pp.

505. Presbyterian Church in the U.S.A.
     1953 *The Achievement Goals for Town and Country Churches.* New
     York, N.Y.: Department of Town and Country Churches,
     Presbyterian Church in the U.S.A.

506. Presbyterian Church in the U.S.A.
     1961 *Crisis in Town and Country: A Call to the Church.* New
     York, N.Y.: Board of National Missions, The Presbyterian
     Church in the U.S.A. 28 pp.

507. Presbyterian Church in the U.S.A.
     1975 *Learning in the Small Church.* Atlanta, Ga.: John Knox
     Press; General Assembly Mission Board, Presbyterian
     Church of the U.S.A. Six booklets. 137 pp.

508. Price, Clay.
     1975 *The Rural-Urban Church on the Metro Fringe.* (Inter-Agency
     Council Project CC-CPC-29). Atlanta, Ga.: Inter-agency
     Council, Office of Survey and Special Studies, Home
     Missions Board, Southern Baptist Convention. 63 pp.

509. Princeton Religious Research Center.
     1978 *The Unchurched American.* Princeton, N.J.: Princeton
     Religious Research Center. 64 pp.

510. Quillian, William F.
     1951 *Improving and Beautifying Rural Church Grounds.* Atlanta,
     Ga.: Rural Work Department, Southeastern Jurisdictional
     Council, The Methodist Church.

511. Quinn, Bernard.
     1967 *The Protestants' Approach to the Town and Country: A Study
     Guide for Catholics.* Washington, D.C.: Center for Applied
     Research in the Apostolate. 31 pp.

512. Quinn, Bernard.
     1967 *Understanding the Small Community: Some Informed
     Resources for the Town and Country Apostolate.* Washington,
     D.C.: Center for Applied Research in the Apostolate. 58
     pp.

513.   Quinn, Bernard.
       1968   *Mission, Missions and the Creative Planing Process.* Atlanta,
              Ga.: The Glenmary Research Center. 50 pp. Reprinted in
              Resonance (Winter), 1968.

514.   Quinn, Bernard.
       1970   *The Changing Context of Town and Country
              Ministry.* Washington, D.C.: Center for Applied Research
              in the Apostolate. 42 pp.

515.   Quinn, Bernard.
       1980   *The Small Rural Parish.* Washington, D.C.: The Glenmary
              Research Center and New York, N.Y.: National
              Conference of Catholic Bishops. 118 pp.

516.   Quinn, Bernard, and Douglas Johnson, (eds.).
       1970   *Atlas of the Church in Appalachia: Administrative Units and
              Boundaries.* Knoxville, Tenn.: Commission on Religion in
              Appalachia. (Variously paged.)

517.   Randolph, Henry S.
       1949   "The Church's Stake in the Family Farm." In Marshall
              Dees Harris and Joseph Ackerman (eds.), *Agrarian Reform
              and Moral Responsibility.* New York, N.Y.: Agricultural
              Missions. pp. 17-25.

518.   Randolph, Henry S.
       1960   *The Golden Harvest: The Presbyterian Town and Country
              Church Movement.* Boone, Iowa: Sunstrom-Miller Press.
              285 pp.

519.   Randolph, Henry S. and Alice Maloney.
       1945   *A Manual for Town and Country Churches.* New York, N.Y.:
              Department of the Rural Church of National Mission,
              Board of National Missions, Presbyterian Church, U.S.A.
              215 pp. Reprinted 1950, 172 pp.

520.   Randolph, Henry S. and Betty Jean Patton.
       1961   *Orientation to the Town and Country Church: A Discussion of
              United Presbyterian Philosophy, Organization, and
              Methods.* New York, N.Y.: Board of National Missions,
              United Presbyterian Church in the U.S.A. and
              Philadelphia, Pa.: Board of National Missions, United
              Presbyterian Church in U.S.A. 228 pp.

521. Rapking, Aaron Henry, (ed.).
     1943 *The Town and Country Pulpit: Suggestions for Worship by and for Town and Country Pastors.* New York, N.Y.: Board of Missions and Church Extension, The Methodist Church. 206 pp.

522. Rapking, Aaron Henry.
     1951 *The Group Ministry Plan.* Department of Town and Country Work, Board of Missions and Church Extension, The Methodist Church, New York, N.Y.

523. Rapking, Aaron Henry.
     1967 *Stick to It Farmer Boy: An Autobiography.* Nashville, Tenn.: Parthenon Press. 188 pp.

524. Rapking, Aaron Henry.
     1938 *Building the Kingdom of God in the Countryside.* Nashville, Tenn.: Abingdon-Cokesbury Press and New York, N.Y. and Cincinnati, Ohio: Methodist Book Concern. 60 pp

525. Raper, A.F.
     1948 *Land Policy and Church Stability.* New York, N.Y.: Department of Town and Country Work, Division of Home Missions and Church Extension, Methodist Church. 35 pp.

526. Ray, David R.
     1982 *Small Churches Are the Right Size.* New York, N.Y.: Pilgrim Press. 224 pp.

527. Reeves, Don.
     1980 "How Can the Smaller Farm Be Saved?" In Charles P. Lutz (ed.), *Farming the Lord's Land: Christian Perspectives on American Agriculture.* Minneapolis, Minn.: Augsburg Publishing House, pp. 59-78.

528. Rich, Mark.
     1940 *The Rural Minister's Problems.* New York, N.Y.: American Baptist Home Mission Society.

529. Rich, Mark.
     1937 *The Larger Parishes of Tompkins County, New York.* Ithaca, N.Y.: Cornell University Press.

530. Rich, Mark (compiler).
     1941 *Rural Life Prayers for Rural Life Sunday, Harvest Home Services, and Other Occasions.* New York, N.Y.: Commission on Worship, Federal Council of the Churches of Christ in America. 52 pp.

531. Rich, Mark.
     1942 "The Rural Pastor's Message to His People." New York,
           N.Y.: Town and Country Department, Church Extension
           Division, Board of Home Missions, Congregational and
           Christian Churches. 7 pp.

532. Rich, Mark.
     1950 *Rural Prospect.* New York, N.Y.: Friendship Press. 183 pp.

533. Rich, Mark.
     1957 *The Rural Church Movement.* Columbia, Mo.: Juniper Knoll
           Press. 251 pp.

534. Rich, Mark, Mossie Allman Wyker, and Mary Heald Williamson.
     1940 *Youth Work in the Rural Church.* St. Louis, Mo.: The
           Bethany Press. 112 pp.

535. Richardson, Harry van Buren.
     1947 *Dark Glory: A Picture of the Church among Negroes in the
           Rural South.* New York, N.Y.: Published for the Home
           Missions Council of North America and Phelps-Stokes
           Fund by Friendship Press. 209 pp.

536. Richerson, William Robert.
     1940 *Criteria for the Total Program of the Rural Church.*
           Unpublished B.D. thesis. Atlanta, Ga.: Department of
           Sociology, Emory University. 183 pp.

537. Riedel, Robert and Jon Wefald.
     1980 "Strengthening Rural Communities." In Charles P. Lutz
           (ed.), *Farming the Lord's Land: Christian Perspectives on
           American Agriculture.* Minneapolis, Minn.: Augsburg
           Publishing House, pp. 107-122.

538. Riley, Royce W.
     1987 *The Group Parish and Extended Ministry: The Lifeline of the
           Small Rural United Methodist Church.* Unpublished D.Min.
           thesis. Madison, N.J.: Drew Theological Seminary. 220 pp.

539. Roads, Charles.
     1909 *Rural Christendom and the Problems of Christianizing Country
           Communities.* Philadelphia, Pa.: American Sunday School
           Union. 322 pp.

540. Robinson, Ruth B.
     1958 *A Guide to the Literature of Rural Life.* New York, N.Y.:
           Department of Town and Country, National Council of
           the Churches of Christ in the U.S.A. 16 pp.

541. Rogers, Everett M. and Rabel J. Burdge.
     1972 "The Rural Church in a Changing Society." Chapter 8 in
     Social Change in Rural Societies. New York, N.Y.:
     Appleton-Century-Crofts. pp. 205-226.

542. Rogerson, Phillip E.
     198- *Planbook for Town and Country Churches.* Missions
     Department, Division of Ministries, Virginia Baptist
     General Board. 16 pp.

543. Romer, James and Bernard Quinn, (eds.).
     1972 *Town and Country Idea Book: Twenty Creative Ministries.*
     Washington, D.C.: Center for Applied Research in the
     Apostolate. 39 pp.

544. Rother, Kathleen and Carol A. Gosse.
     1976 *National Catholic Rural Life Conference Idea Book for Small
     Town Churches.* Atlanta, Ga.: The Glenmary Research
     Center. 120 pp.

545. Rubin, Morton.
     1962 "The Church and the Belief System." *Plantation County.*
     (Revised edition). Chapel Hill, N.Car.: University of
     North Carolina Press.

546. Rupp, William J.
     1944 *Recommended Reading.* New York, N.Y.: Committee on
     Town and Country. 12 pp.

547. Rural Church Institute.
     19-- *The Rural Church Institute for Religious Workers.* Ithaca,
     N.Y.: Rural Church Institute.

548. Rural Missions Cooperating Committee.
     1945 *Christian Mission among Rural People, Volume III in Studies
     in the World Mission of Christianity.* New York, N.Y.: Rural
     Missions Cooperating Committee of the Foreign Missions
     Conference of North America. 334 pp.

549. Rural Missions Cooperating Committee.
     1963 *Rural Welfare in a Revolutionary World: A Guide to Christian
     Participation.* New York, N.Y.: Rural Missions Cooperating
     Committee. 16 pp.

550. Sanders, William E.
     1970 "A New Commitment to Mission." In Max E. Glenn (ed.),
     Appalachia in Transition. St. Louis, Mo.: Bethany Press. pp.
     147-156.

551. Sandt, Eleanor E., (ed.).
      1964 *Education in the Small Church: An Anthology of Materials
      from the Small Church School Bulletin.* New York, N.Y.:
      Seabury Press. 128 pp.

552. Sanchagrin, Kenneth M.
      1986 *Ministry in Rural Contexts.* New Orleans, La.: Institute for
      Ministry, Loyola University. 68 pp.

553. Sandridge, Sidney E.
      1959 *A Study of the Relationship Between Ecclesiastical Effectiveness
      and Community Outreach in Town and Country Methodist
      Churches in the United States, 1957.* Unpublished Ph.D.
      thesis. Evanston, Ill.: Northwestern University.

554. Schaller, Lyle E.
      1967 *The Churches' War on Poverty.* Nashville, Tenn.: Abingdon
      Press. 160 pp.

555. Schaller, Lyle E.
      1977 *Survival Tactics in the Parish.* Nashville, Tenn.: Abingdon
      Press. 208 pp.

556. Schaller, Lyle E.
      1982 *The Small Church is Different!* Nashville, Tenn.: Abingdon
      Press. 192 pp.

557. Schaller, Lyle E.
      1985 *The Middle-Sized Church: Problems and
      Prescription.* Nashville, Tenn.: Abingdon Press. 160 pp.

558. Schirer, Marshall and Mary Ann Forehand.
      1984 *Cooperative Ministry: Hope for Small Churches.* Valley Forge,
      Pa.: Judson Press. 94 pp.

559. Schisler, J.Q.
      1946 *The Educational Work of the Small Church.* Nashville, Tenn.:
      Methodist Publishing House. 150 pp.

560. Schlingman, Edward L.
      1947 *Good Times In the Rural Church.* Philadelphia, Pa. and St.
      Louis, Mo.: Christian Education Press. 79 pp.

561. Schmidt, Karla, (ed.).
      1987 *Renew the Spirit of My People: A Handbook for Ministry in
      Times of Rural Crisis.* Des Moines, Iowa: Prairiefire Rural
      Action, Inc. 99 pp.

562. Schmiedeler, Edgar.
    1938 *A Better Rural Life.* New York, N.Y.: Joseph F. Wagner,
          Inc. 304 pp.

563. Schnucker, Calvin T., (ed.).
    1943 *The Job of the Rural Church in this Day.* Dubuque, Iowa:
          Dubuque Presbyterian Press. 31 pp.

564. Schnucker, Calvin T.
    1954 *How to Plan the Rural Church Program.* Philadelphia, Pa.:
          Westminster Press. 158 pp.

565. Schroeder, William Widwick.
    1960 *Religion in Midwestern County: An Empirical Investigation of
          Ecclesiastical, Theological, Sociological, and Psychological
          Factors.* Unpublished thesis. Chicago, Ill.: University of
          Chicago. 156 pp.

566. Schroeder, William Widwick and Victor Obenhaus.
    1964 *Religion in American Culture: Unity and Diversity in a
          Midwestern County.* New York, N.Y.: Free Press. 254 pp.

567. Schwarzweller, Harry K., James S. Brown, and J.J. Mangalam.
    1971 *Mountain Families in Transition: A Case Study of
          Appalachian Transition.* University Park, Pa.: Pennsylvania
          State University Press. 300 pp.

568. Seifert, Harvey.
    1952 *The Church in Community Action.* New York, N.Y.:
          Abingdon-Cokesbury Press. 240 pp.

569. Sengel, William R.
    1970 "Ecumenical Trends in Appalachia." In Max E. Glenn
          (ed.), *Appalachia in Transition.* St. Louis, Mo.: Bethany
          Press. pp. 140-146.

570. Sheaff, Robert L.
    1900 "The Church Paper." Chapter 6 in Charles E. Hayward
          (ed.), *Institutional Work for the Country Church.* Burlington,
          Vt.: Free Association Press.

571. Sherrill, Lewis Joseph.
    1932 *Religious Education in the Small Church.* Philadelphia, Pa.:
          Westminster Press. 208 pp.

572. Shriver, Donald W., Jr.
      1975   "Bread for Life: the Churches and Rural Economic
             Development." In James A. Cogswell (ed.), *The Church
             and the Rural Poor*. Atlanta, Ga.: John Knox Press. pp.
             49-66.

573. Sills, Horace S., (ed.).
      1967   *Grassroots Ecumenicity: Case Studies in Local Church
             Consolidation*. Philadelphia, Pa.: United Church Press. 140
             pp.

574. Sills, Horace S., (ed.)
      1967   *The Small Church Situation in the United Church of Christ*.
             New York, N.Y.: Department of the Church in Town and
             Country, Division of Church Extension, United Church
             Board for Homeland Ministries.

575. Simmons, David S.
      1983   *A Marriage Enrichment Program for Rural Parish Ministry*.
             D.Min. thesis. Madison, N.J.: Drew Theological Seminary.
             144 pp.

576. Simpkins, O. Norman.
      1972   "Culture." No. 7 in *Mountain Heritage Series*. Appalachia
             Center, West Virginia University.

577. Skolas, Argyle.
      1980   "Chemical Dependency: Can We Break the Addiction?" In
             Charles P. Lutz (ed.), *Farming the Lord's Land: Christian
             Perspectives on American Agriculture*. Minneapolis, Minn.:
             Augsburg Publishing House. pp. 165-182.

578. Skrabanek, Robert L.
      1958   "The Rural Church: Characteristics and Problems." In
             Alvin L. Bertrand (ed.), *Rural Sociology: An Analysis of
             Contemporary Life*. New York, N.Y.: McGraw-Hill.

579. Slocum, Walter L.
      1962   "Rural Religious Systems." Chapter in *Agricultural
             Sociology: A Study of Sociological Aspects of American Farm
             Life*. New York, N.Y.: Harper.

580. Smathers, Eugene.
      1944   *A Primer for Friends of the Soil*. Black Mountain, N.Car.:
             Fellowship of Southern Churchmen. 28 pp.

581. Smathers, Eugene.
     1946 "Rural Pastor." In John Oliver Nelson (ed.), *We Have This Ministry: Church Vocations for Men and Women*. New York, N.Y.: Association Press. pp. 11-19.

582. Smathers, Michael.
     1970 "Suspicion and Community in Appalachia." In Max E. Glenn (ed.), *Appalachia in Transition*. St. Louis, Mo.: Bethany Press. pp. 69-81.

583. Smith, Page.
     1966 "Religion in the Town." Chapter in *As a City Upon a Hill: The Town in American History*. New York, N.Y.: Knopf. Reprinted in 1973, Cambridge, Mass.: M.I.T. Press.

584. Smith, Timothy Lawrence.
     1980 *Revivalism and Social Reform In Mid-Nineteenth Century America*. Baltimore, Md.: Johns Hopkins University Press. 269 pp.

585. Smith, Rockwell Carter.
     1945 *The Church in Our Town: A Study of the Relationship between the Church and the Rural Community*. New York, N.Y. and Nashville, Tenn.: Abingdon-Cokesbury Press. 190 pp. Republished in 1950 and 1955, 220 pp.

586. Smith, Rockwell Carter.
     1953 *Rural Church Administration*. Nashville,Tenn.: Abingdon-Cokesbury Press. 176 pp.

587. Smith, Rockwell Carter.
     1959 *People, Land, and Churches*. New York, N.Y.: Friendship Press. 164 pp.

588. Smith, Rockwell Carter.
     1971 *Rural Ministry and the Changing Community*. Nashville, Tenn. and New York, N.Y.: Abingdon Press. 206 pp.

589. Smith, Rockwell C., Clifford M. Black, Stephen G. Cobb, S. Burkett Milner, and Judith L. Betler.
     1969 *The Role of Rural Social Science in Theological Education: With Particular Application to the Town and Country Ministry in the Methodist Church*. Evanston, Ill.: Bureau of Social and Religious Research, Garrett Theological Seminary. 88 pp.

590. Smith, T. Lynn and Paul E. Zopf.
     1970 "Religion and the Rural Church." *Principles in Inductive Rural Sociology*. Philadelphia, Pa.: Davis.

591. Smucker, O.C.
      1953   "Adult Education in the Rural Church." In *Study of Adult
             Education in Rural Areas. Rural Social Systems and Adult
             Education.* Michigan State College Press. pp. 196-229.

592. Somerndike, John Mason.
      1924   *The Sunday School in Town and Country.* Philadelphia, Pa.:
             Westminster Press. 151 pp.

593. Sorokin, Pitrim and Clarke C. Zimmerman.
      1929   "Rural-Urban Religious Culture, Belief, and Convictions."
             Chapter 18 in *Principles of Rural-Urban Sociology.* New
             York, N.Y.: Holt and Company.

594. Sorokin, Pitrim, Clarke C. Zimmerman, and Charles Galpin,
      (eds.).
      1965   "Rural Religious Organizations." Chapter 14 in *A
             Systematic Sourcebook of Rural Sociology*, Volume II. New
             York, N.Y.: Russell and Russell.

595. Soule, William E.
      1958   *Music in the Town and Country Church.* New York, N.Y.:
             Division of Town and Country Work, National Council
             of the Episcopal Church. 48 pp.

596. Southern Baptist Convention.
      19--   *Studies of the Church in the Rural-Urban Fringe.* Atlanta,
             Ga.: Urban-Rural Missions Department, Home Missions
             Board, Southern Baptist Convention.

597. Southern Baptist Convention.
      1955   *Long-Range Rural Church Program of Southern Baptists.*
             Atlanta, Ga.: Home Missions Board, Southern Baptist
             Convention.

598. Stacy, William H. and John L. Tait.
      1968   *Adult Education Programs with Church Leaders.* Ames, Iowa:
             Iowa State University.

599. Strong, Josiah.
      1893   "The Problem of the Country." Chapter 8 in *The New Era.*
             New York, N.Y.: Baker and Taylor Company. pp. 164-
             177.

600. Strout, Joseph Woodbury.
      19--   *The Rural Problem and the Country Minister.* Social Service
             Bulletin No. 26. Boston, Mass.: Department of Social and
             Public Service, American Unitarian Association. 17 pp.

601. Stroup, N.W.
     19-- *The Country Church, the Country's Hope.* Cleveland, Ohio:
           The Methodist Union. 14 pp.

602. Stubbs, Charles William.
     1887 *The Church in the Villages: Principles and Ideal--An Address
           to the Church Council and Wardens of the United Parishes of
           Stokenham, Chivelstone, and Sherford.* Hanover, N.H.:
           Dartmouth College, Cranford's Library. 48 pp.

603. Sturm, Roy Albert.
     1949 *Research and Survey in the Town and Country Churches of
           Methodism.* New York, N.Y.: Department of Town and
           Country Work, Division of Home Missions and Church
           Extension, Methodist Church. 28 pp.

604. Sturm, Roy Albert.
     1959 "Some Aspects of Iowa Methodism." New York, N.Y.:
           Department of Research and Surveys, Division of
           National Missions, Board of Missions, Methodist Church.
           6 pp.

605. Sturm, Roy Albert.
     1959 *West Virginia Methodism.* New York, N.Y.: Department of
           Research and Surveys, Division of National Missions,
           Board of Missions, Methodist Church.

606. Sundt, Edwin Einer.
     1932 *The Country Church and Our Generation.* New York, N.Y.
           and Chicago, Ill.: Fleming H. Revell. 160 pp.

607. Surface, William "Bill".
     1971 *The Hollow.* New York, N.Y.: Coward-McCann. 190 pp.

608. Surrey, Peter J.
     1981 *The Small Town Church.* Creative Leadership Series.
           Nashville, Tenn.: Abingdon Press. 128 pp.

609. Swagerty, June Mignon.
     1939 *A Study of the Status and Trends in Rural Vacation Church
           Schools.* Unpublished B.D. thesis. Atlanta, Ga.: Religious
           Education Department, Emory University.

610. Taylor, Lee and Arthur R. Jones, Jr.
     1964 "Church Organization from National Parks to Suburbia."
           In *Rural Life and Urbanized Society.* New York, N.Y.:
           Oxford University Press.

611. Teague, Margaret W.
     19-- *Forward Into Rural America.* New York, N.Y.: National
           Council, Protestant Episcopal Church.

612. Thomas, Evan.
     1900 "Library and Reading Room." Chapter 9 in Charles E.
           Hayward (ed.), *Institutional Work for the Country Church.*
           Burlington, Vt.: Free Association Press.

613. Thompson, Edgar T.
     1972 "God and the Southern Plantation System." In Samuel S.
           Hill (ed.), *Religion and the Solid South.* Nashville, Tenn.:
           Abingdon Press. pp. 57-91.

614. Thompson, Richard.
     1970 *Rural Church in Transition.* St. Paul, Minn.: Bethel
           Theological Seminary.

615. Thornton, Martin.
     1948 *Rural Synthesis: The Religious Basis of Rural Culture.* New
           York, N.Y. and London, England: Steffington. 124 pp.

616. Tipple, Ezra Squier.
     1911 *Some Famous Country Parishes.* New York, N.Y. and
           Cincinnati, Ohio: Abingdon Press. 244 pp. Reprinted
           1914.

617. Tjaden, George K.
     1970 "Protestant and Ecumenical Response to the Church's
           Town and Country Mission." In Victor J. Klimoski and
           Bernard Quinn (eds.), *Church and Community:
           Nonmetropolitan America in Transition.* Washington, D.C.:
           Center for Applied Research in the Apostolate. pp. 60-66.

618. Trexler, Edgar R.
     1969 "Eight Rural Churches Think Big." In Edgar R. Trexler
           (ed.), *Ways to Wake Up Your Church.* Philadelphia, Pa.:
           Fortress Press. 152 pp.

619. Tripp, Thomas Alfred.
     1939 *Factors Affecting the Future of Rural Churches in North
           Dakota.* Preliminary report prepared by the Commission
           on the Study of the Rural Churches of the
           Congregational Conference of North Dakota. New York,
           N.Y.: Town and Country Department, Church Extension
           Division, Board of Home Missions, Congregational and
           Christian Churches. 26 pp.

620. Tripp, Thomas Alfred.
    1939 *Rural People and the Church.* New York, N.Y.: Council for Social Action, Congregational and Christian Churches.

621. Tripp, Thomas Alfred.
    1941 *The Farmer's Search for Economic Democracy.* New York, N.Y.: Council for Social Action, Congregational Christian Churches. 38 pp. Also in *Social Action* 7(April 15, 1941).

622. Tripp, Thomas Alfred.
    1945 *Rural Americans on the Move.* New York, N.Y.: Friendship Press. 24 pp.

623. Tripp, Thomas Alfred.
    1953 *Successful Rural Church Methods.* Prepared for the Committee on the Marginal Church, Town and Country Department, Board of Home Missions. 61 pp.

624. Tyree, Vernon C.
    1930 *The Church of the Open Country.* Unpublished Th.D. thesis. Denver, Colo.: Iliff School of Theology. 102 pp.

625. Tyson, William Ainsworth.
    1944 *White Harvest Fields: A Survey of Thirty-Nine Counties in North Mississippi.* Tupelo, Miss.: Office Supply Company. 144 pp.

626. United Christian Missionary Society.
    19-- *Clarifying Terms for Rural Leaders.* Indianapolis, Ind.: Department of Church Development and Evangelism, United Christian Missionary Society.

627. United Christian Youth Movement.
    1946 *Christian Youth and the Rural Task: A Guide to Action for Christian Young People and Their Leaders in the United Christian Youth Movement.* Chicago, Ill.: United Christian Youth Movement and the International Council of Religious Education. 28 pp.

628. United Church of Christ.
    1961 *The Church in Town and Country: Self-Studies in Community Context.* St. Louis, Mo.: Department of Town and Country, United Church of Christ.

629. United Church of Christ.
    1976 *Good to Be Together: Suggestions for Effective Church Meetings.* St. Louis, Mo.: Office for Church Life and Leadership, United Church of Christ. 11 pp.

630. United Methodist Church.
      19-- *Arrangement and Equipment for Small Churches.* Nashville,
            Tenn.: United Methodist Church.

631. United Methodist Church.
      1973 *Ways of Learning in Small Churches.* Nashville, Tenn.:
            Discipleship Resources.

632. United Presbyterian Church in the U.S.A.
      1961 *A Survey of the United Presbyterian Church in the U.S.A. in
            Town and Country.* A Report Prepared by the Committee
            on Study of the Town and Country Church. New York,
            N.Y.: Board of National Missions, United Presbyterian
            Church in the U.S.A.

633. United Presbyterian Church U.S.A. and the Presbyterian Church
      U.S.
      1969 *Strategy for Change: Presbyterians, Churches and Education in
            Appalachia.* Philadelphia, Pa. and Richmond, Va.: Boards
            of Christian Education, United Presbyterian Church
            U.S.A. and the Presbyterian Church U.S.

634. Upjohn, Richard.
      1852 *Upjohn's Rural Architecture: Designs, Working Drawings, and
            Specifications for Wooden Churches and Other Rural
            Structures.* New York, N.Y.: Da Capo Press. 13 pp.
            Reprinted 1975.

635. Urbain, J.V.
      1947 "Problems and Opportunities of the Church in Rural
            America." In Urbain, J. V. and R. J. Wilson, Jr. (eds.),
            Rural America: A Catholic Sourcebook. Cincinnati, Ohio:
            Catholic Students' Mission Crusade. pp. 65-71.

636. Urbain, J.V. and R.J. Wilson, Jr., (eds.).
      1947 *Rural America: A Catholic Sourcebook.* Cincinnati, Ohio:
            Catholic Students' Mission Crusade. 106 pp.

637. Van Saun, Arthur Carlos.
      1932 *Replanning the Rural Church.* Quincy, Pa.: Quincy
            Orphanage Press. 178 pp.

638. Vance, Rupert.
      1945 *All These People.* Chapel Hill, N.Car.: North Carolina
            University Press. 504 pp.

639. Vidich, Arthur and Joseph Bensman.
    1968 "Religion and the Affirmation of the Present." Chapter in *Small Town in Mass Society: Class, Power, and Religion in a Rural Community.* (Revised edition.) Princeton, N.J.: Princeton University Press.

640. Vier, Lester B.
    1979 *The Pastor's Role in Creating a Task Force to Examine Its Future.* Unpublished D.Min. Madison, N.J.: Drew Theological Seminary. 140 pp.

641. Virginia Council of Churches.
    1950 *Watchers of the Springs: A Collection of Rural Life Sermons and Addresses.* Richmond, Va.: Virginia Council of Churches. 132 pp.

642. Voelker, Stanley Walter.
    1962 *Economic and Sociological Trends Affecting Town and Country Churches in North Dakota.* Fargo, N.Dak.: North Dakota Council of Churches. 37 pp.

643. Vogt, Paul Leroy.
    1921 *Church Cooperation in Community Life.* New York, N.Y. and Cincinnati, Ohio: The Abingdon Press. 171 pp.

644. Wagner, James Elvin.
    1920 *Rural Evangelism.* New York, N.Y.: Methodist Book Concern. 176 pp.

645. Walker, J. Marshall.
    1946 *The Rural Minister Looks at His Work.* General Board of the Baptist State Convention of North Carolina. 9 pp.

646. Walrath, Douglas Alan, (ed.).
    1983 *New Possibilities for Small Congregations.* New York, N.Y.: Pilgrim Press. 101 pp.

647. Waltner, Sherman K.
    1969 *The Changing Rural Church in Missouri 1952-1967: An Analysis of Organizational Complexity.* Unpublished M.A. thesis. Columbia, Mo.: University of Missouri. 172 pp.

648. Warehime, Hal M.
    1975 "Theology for the Wretched of the Earth." In James A. Cogswell (ed.), *The Church and the Rural Poor.* Atlanta, Ga.: John Knox Press. pp. 67-80.

649. Warner, R. Stephen.
     1988 *New Wine in Old Wineskins: Evangelicals and Liberals in a*
           Small-Town Church. Berkeley, Calif.: University of
           California Press. 387 pp.

650. Weatherford, W.D. and Earl D.C. Brewer.
     1962 *Life and Religion in Southern Appalachia: An Interpretation of*
           Selected Data from the Southern Appalachian Studies. New
           York, N.Y.: Friendship Press. 165 pp.

651. Webber, Frederick Roth.
     1939 *The Small Church: How to Build and Furnish It With Some*
           Account of the Improvement of Existing Buildings. Cleveland,
           Ohio: J.H. Jansen. 324 pp.

652. Weller, Jack E.
     1965 "The Mountaineer and the Church." Chapter 7 in Jack E.
           Weller (ed.), *Yesterday's People: Life in Contemporary*
           Appalachia. Lexington, Ky.: University of Kentucky Press.
           pp. 121-133.

653. Weller, Jack E.
     1970 "How Religion Mirrors and Meets Appalachian Culture."
           In Max E. Glenn (ed.), *Appalachia in Transition.* St. Louis,
           Mo.: Bethany Press. pp. 122-139.

654. Weller, Jack E.
     1969 "Salvation is Not Enough." In John D. Photiadis (ed.),
           Religion in Appalachia: Theological, Social, and Theological
           Dimensions and Correlates. Morgantown, W.Va.: West
           Virginia University. pp. 395-399. Also in *Mountain Life &*
           Work. (45, March).

655. Wells, George Frederick.
     1908 "The Country Church." *The Cyclopedia of American*
           Agriculture, Volume IV. New York, N.Y.: Macmillan
           Company.

656. West, James.
     1945 "Religion." In *Plainville, USA.* New York, N.Y.: Columbia
           University Press.

657. White, Reuel Clyde.
     1928 *Denominationalism in Certain Rural Communities in Texas.*
           Indianapolis, Ind.: Training Course for Social Work in
           Indiana University. 116 pp.

658. Whitley, Oliver Read.
    1961 *The Rural Church: Its Response to the Changing Society.*
    Denver, Colo.: Iliff School of Theology. 12 pp. Reprint
    from *The Iliff Review* (Fall 1961).

659. Whitman, Lauris Burchard.
    1953 *An Ecological Study of the Rural Churches in Four
    Pennsylvania Counties.* State College, Pa.: Department of
    Sociology, Pennsylvania State University.

660. Whitman, Lauris Burchard and Anne O. Liveley.
    1958 *A Study of Low-Income Farm Families in Two Southern Rural
    Communities.* Chicago, Ill.: Bureau of Research and Survey
    for the Department of Town and Country Church,
    National Council of the Churches of Christ in the U.S.A.
    65 pp.

661. Whitman, Lauris Burchard and Glen W. Trimble.
    1963 *The United States and Its Churches: Some Facts and Trends.*
    New York, N.Y.: National Council of the Churches of
    Christ in the U.S.A. 21 pp.

662. Widner, Ralph R.
    1970 "Building an Appalachian Alliance for Growth." In Max
    E. Glenn (ed.), *Appalachia in Transition.* St. Louis, Mo.:
    Bethany Press. pp. 15-24.

663. Wiley, Robert E., (ed.).
    1982 *Change in Big Town/Small City.* (313-15P). Atlanta, Ga.:
    Home Mission Board, Southern Baptist Convention. 136
    pp.

664. Wiley, Robert E.
    1982 "Implications for Churches in Big Towns/Small Cities." In
    Robert E. Wiley (ed.), *Change in Big Town/Small City.*
    Atlanta, Ga.: Home Missions Board, Southern Baptist
    Convention. pp. 133-135.

665. Wiley, Robert E.
    1982 *Our Church On Mission* (313-10P). Atlanta, Ga.: Home
    Mission Board, Southern Baptist Convention. 24 pp.

666. Wilkinson, Loren, (ed.).
    1980 *Earthkeeping: Christian Stewardship of Natural Resources.*
    Grand Rapids, Mich.: Eerdmans. 317 pp.

667. Wilkinson, Theodore S.
      1970 *Churches at the Testing Point: A Study in Rural Michigan.*
      World Council of Churches Studies in Mission Series.
      New York, N.Y.: Friendship Press. 200 pp.

668. Williams, Colin W.
      1964 "Dialogue on Issues and Trends." In Henry A. McCanna
      (ed.), *The Church Meeting Human Needs.* New York:
      National Council of Churches of Christ in the U.S.A.

669. Williamson, Mary Heald.
      1940 *The Countrywoman and Her Church.* New York, N.Y. and
      Nashville, Tenn.: Abingdon-Cokesbury Press. 80 pp.

670. Williamson, Ralph L.
      1951 *Factors of Success and Failure in Federated Churches.*
      Madison, N.J. n.p.

671. Williamson, Ralph L.
      1951 *Federated Churches: A Study of Success and Failure.* Ithaca,
      N.Y.: Rural Church Institute, Cornell University. 40 pp.

672. Willimon, William H. and Robert L. Wilson.
      1980 *Preaching and Worship in the Small Church.* Nashville,
      Tenn.: Abingdon Press. 126 pp.

673. Wilson, Charles Earnest, Jr.
      1961 *The Changing Role of the Town and Country Church in
      Vermont.* Unpublished Th.D. thesis. Boston, Mass.: School
      of Theology, Boston University. 313 pp.

674. Wilson, Warren Hugh.
      19-- "The Church and Country Life Work of the Board of
      Home Missions." New York, N.Y.: Board of Home
      Missions, Presbyterian Church in the U.S.A. (leaflet).

675. Wilson, Warren Hugh.
      19-- *The Church and the Country Life Movement.* Department of
      Town and Country Church and Indian Work, Board of
      National Missions, United Presbyterian Church in the
      U.S.A. (manuscript).

676. Wilson, Warren Hugh.
      19-- *The Community Pastor in the Country.* New York, N.Y.:
      Church and Country Life Work, Board of Home
      Missions, Presbyterian Church in the U.S.A. 18 pp.

677. Wilson, Warren Hugh.
    19-- "The Country Church Program." New York, N.Y.: Board of Home Missions, Presbyterian Church in the U.S.A. (leaflet).

678. Wilson, Warren Hugh.
    19-- *The Problem of the Department and What It Has Accomplished for the Survival and Efficiency of the Country Church.* Department of Town and Country Church and Indian Work, Board of National Missions, United Presbyterian Church in the U.S.A. (manuscript).

679. Wilson, Warren Hugh.
    19-- *Realignment of Religious and Moral Forces for Country Life.* Department of Town and Country Church and Indian Work, Board of National Missions, United Presbyterian Church in the U.S.A. (manuscript).

680. Wilson, Warren Hugh.
    19-- *The Rural Church and Rural Morale.* Department of Town and Country Church and Indian Work, Board of National Missions, United Presbyterian Church in the U.S.A. (manuscript).

681. Wilson, Warren Hugh.
    19-- *The Services of the Church to the Community and the Support of the Church by the Community.* Department of Town and Country Church and Indian Work, Board of National Missions, United Presbyterian Church in the U.S.A. (manuscript).

682. Wilson, Warren Hugh.
    19-- *The Struggle of the Country Church.* Department of Town and Country Church and Indian Work, Board of National Missions, United Presbyterian Church in the U.S.A. (manuscript).

683. Wilson, Warren Hugh.
    19-- *Training of the Country Minister.* Department of Town and Country Church and Indian Work, Board of National Missions, United Presbyterian Church in the U.S.A. (manuscript).

684. Wilson, Warren Hugh.
    1911 *The Church of the Open Country: A Study of the Church for the Working Farmer.* Cincinnati, Ohio: Jennings and Graham and New York, N.Y.: Missionary Education Movement of the United States and Canada. 238 pp.

685. Wilson, Warren Hugh.
      1912 *The Evolution of the Country Community.* Boston, Mass. and
            New York, N.Y.: Pilgrim Press. 221 pp.

686. Wilson, Warren Hugh.
      1914 *The Church at the Center.* New York, N.Y.: Missionary
            Education Movement of the United States and Canada.
            98 pp.

687. Wilson, Warren Hugh.
      1915 *The Second Missionary Adventure.* New York, N.Y.: Fleming
            H. Revell Company. 32 pp.

688. Wilson, Warren Hugh.
      1924 *The Efficient Country Pastor.* New York, N.Y.: Board of
            National Missions, Presbyterian Church in the U.S.A. 30
            pp.

689. Wilson, Warren Hugh.
      1925 *The Farmers' Church.* New York, N.Y.: Century Company.
            264 pp.

690. Wilson, Warren Hugh.
      1927 *Rural Religion and the Country Church.* New York, N.Y.:
            Fleming H. Revell Company. 141 pp.

691. Wilson, Warren Hugh, Frank A. Starrett, Edmund deSchweinitz
      Brunner, and Ward Platt.
      1915 *The Rural Church.* New York, N.Y.: Board of Home
            Missions, Presbyterian Church in the U.S.A. 31 pp.

692. Wintermeyer, Herbert H.
      1947 *Rural Worship.* Philadelphia, Pa. and St. Louis, Mo.:
            Christian Education Press. 99 pp.

693. Wolking, M. L.
      1947 "Cooperatives and Catholic Rural Life." In J.V. Urbain
            and R.J. Wilson, Jr. (eds.), *Rural America: A Catholic
            Sourcebook.* Cincinnati, Ohio: Catholic Students' Mission
            Crusade. pp. 49-55.

694. Wood, Richard R.
      1973 *The Church and Community Organization.* Unpublished
            D.Min. thesis. Wesley Theological Seminary. 193 pp.

695. Woodall, Thomas E. and Beryl B. Maurer.
     1970 "A Case Study in Community: Cooperative Creativity by
          Community, University, and Church." In Max E. Glenn
          ed.), *Appalachia in Transition*. St. Louis, Mo.: Bethany
          Press. pp. 93-110.

696. Wright, William D.
     1982 *The Rite of Christian Initiation of Adults (RICA) in the Rural
          Setting: Some Important Considerations.* Atlanta, Ga.:
          Glenmary Research Center.

697. Wuthnow, Robert and Kevin Christiano.
     1979 "The Effects of Residential Migration on Church
          Attendance in the United States." In Robert Wuthnow
          (ed.), *The Religious Dimension: New Directions in
          Quantitative Research.* New York, N.Y.: Academic Press,
          Inc. pp. 257-276.

698. Wyker, James D.
     1949 "Redemption in the Rural Community." Chicago, Ill.:
          International Council of Religious Education. 6 pp.

699. Wyker, James D.
     1952 *Program of the Rural Church: A Manual for Developing the
          Rural Church Community.* Columbia, Mo.: Rural Seminary,
          Bible College at the University of Missouri. 72 pp.

700. Yoder, Robert A.
     1983 *Seeking First the Kingdom: Called to Faithful Stewardship.*
          Scottsdale, Pa.: Herald Press. 99 pp.

701. Ziegler, Edward Krusen.
     1942 *Country Alters: Worship in the Church.* New York, N.Y.:
          Commission on Worship, Federal Council of Churches of
          Christ in America. 47 pp.

702. Ziegler, Edward Krusen.
     1943 *Rural People at Worship.* New York, N.Y.: Agricultural
          Missions, Inc. 118 pp.

703. Ziegler, Edward Krusen.
     1948 *A Bibliography on Worship for the Rural Church.* Worship in
          the Church Series, Bulletin No. 1. (Spring). New York,
          N.Y.: Agricultural Missions, Inc. 10 pp.

704. Ziegler, Edward Krusen.
     1954 *Rural Preaching.* Westwood, N.J.: Fleming H. Revell
          Company. 176 pp.

705. Ziegler, Edward Krusen.
      1959   *The Village Pastor: His Work and Training for Tomorrow's World.* New York, N.Y.: Agricultural Missions, Inc. 110 pp.

706. Zunkel, C. Wayne.
      1982   *Growing the Small Church.* Elgin, Ill.: David C. Cook. 109 pp.

Academic
Journal
Articles

Academic Journal Articles

707. Anderson, W.A.
     1944 "Social Participation and Religious Affiliation in Rural Areas." *Rural Sociology* 9(September): 242-250.

708. Anderson, W.A. and Ralph Williamson.
     1942 "The Community Church as a Sociological Form in New York." *Rural Sociology* 7(December): 415-423.

709. Arrington, Leonard J.
     1951 "Property Among the Mormons." *Rural Sociology* 16 (December): 339-352.

710. Arrington, Leonard J.
     1954 "The Mormon Tithing House: A Frontier Business Institution." *Business History Review* 28(March): 24-58.

711. Bahr, H.M. and B.A. Chadwick.
     1985 "Religion and Family in Middletown, USA." *Journal of Marriage and the Family* 47(May): 407-414.

712. Bardis, Panos D.
     1959 "A Comparative Study of Familism." *Rural Sociology* 24(December): 362-371.

713. Barnett, Henlee H.
     1954 "Problems of the Rural Preacher." *Review and Expositor* 51(July): 358-363.

714. Beekman, Darold H.
     1986 "Ministry Among the People of the Land in the '80s." *Word and World: Theology for Christian Ministry* 6(1): 5-17.

715.   Beers, Howard W.
       1958   "Social Components of Community Development." *Rural
              Sociology* 23(March): 13-24.

716.   Bennett, G. Willis.
       1959   "Social Environment and Its Influence on Counseling
              Procedure in the Rural Church." *Pastoral Psychology* 10(5):
              31-36.

717.   Binkley, Olin T.
       1959   "Task of the Church in Rural America." *Pastoral
              Psychology* 10(September): 9-13.

718.   Blizzard, Samuel W.
       1967   "The Roles of the Rural Parish Minister, the Protestant
              Seminaries, and the Sciences of Social Behavior." *Religious
              Education* 7(November-December, 1955): 382-392. (Also in
              Richard D. Knudten (ed.), *The Sociology of Religion: An
              Anthology.* New York, N.Y.: Appleton-Century-Crofts.)

719.   Boisen, A.T.
       1916   "Factors Which Have to do with the Decline of the
              Country Church." *American Journal of Sociology*
              22(September): 177-192.

720.   Boos, Merle W.
       1985   "The New Face of Town and Country America and Its
              Challenge for the Church." *Word and World: Theology for
              Christian Ministry* 5(Winter): 43-48.

721.   Boycott, W.S.
       1951   "Christ and the Land: The Role of Agriculture in
              Christian Life." *Church Quarterly Review* 151(January-
              March): 213-235.

722.   Brinkerhoff, Merlin B. and Jeffrey C. Jacob.
       1987   "Quasi-Religious Meaning Systems, Official Religion, and
              Quality of Life in an Alternative Lifestyle: Survey, Back-
              to-the-Land Movement." *Journal for the Scientific Study of
              Religion* 26(March): 63-80.

723.   Brown, James Stephen.
       1951   "Social Class, Intermarriage, and Church Membership in a
              Kentucky Community." *American Journal of Sociology* 57(3):
              232-242.

724. Buie, T.S.
1944 "The Land and the Church." *Rural Sociology* 9(September): 251-257. (Also published by Washington, D.C.: Soil Conservation Service, U.S. Department of Agriculture. 12 pp.)

725. Bultena, Louis.
1944 "Rural Churches and Community Integration." *Rural Sociology* 9(September): 257-264.

726. Burchard, Waldo W.
1963 "A Comparison of Urban and Rural Churches." *Rural Sociology* 28(September): 271-278.

727. Burchinal, Lee G.
1961 "Farm-Nonfarm Differences in Religious Beliefs and Practices." *Rural Sociology* 26(4): 414-418.

728. Cantrell, Randolph, James F. Krile, and George A. Donohue.
1980 "The External Adaptation of Religious Organizations." *Sociological Analysis* 41(4): 351-364.

729. Cantrell, Randolph, James F. Krile, and George A. Donohue.
1982 "Community Involvement of Yoked Parishes." *Rural Sociology* 47(Spring): 81-90.

730. Cantrell, Randolph, James F. Krile, and George A. Donohue.
1983 "Parish Autonomy: Measuring Denominational Differences." *Journal for the Scientific Study of Religion* 22(3): 276-287.

731. Carter, Michael Vaughn.
1982 "Local Congregations as Actors in Appalachian Development." *Richard Montgomery Foundation* (Summer): 24-25.

732. Carter, Michael Vaughn.
1984 "Religion in Appalachian Culture: A Brief Look." *New England Sociologist* (Special Edition: Religion--the Cutting Edge) 5(1): 134-142.

733. Carter, Michael Vaughn.
1988 "Local Churches Improving Life in Appalachia: A Collective Action Commentary." *The Rural Sociologist* 8(August): 354-359.

734. Carter, Michael Vaughn.
      1988 "The Rural Church: Can It Be an Arena for Change? An
            Example from Appalachia." *Human Services in the Rural
            Environment* 11(Winter): 31-33.

735. Christensen, John R., John W. Payne, and Kenneth J. Brown.
      1963 "Church Participation and College Desires of Rural Youth
            in Utah." *Rural Sociology* 28(June): 176-185.

736. Cisin, Ira H.
      1955 "Comment on an Application of Scale Analysis to the
            Study of Religious Groups by Coughenour." *Rural
            Sociology* 20(September/December): 208-211.

737. Clark, Carl A.
      1955 "Specialized Seminary Training for the Rural Minister."
            Review and Expositor 52(July): 336-342.

738. Clawson, M.
      1966 "Factors and Forces Affecting the Optimum Future Rural
            Settlement." *Economic Geography* 42(October): 283-293.

739. Cleland, Charles.
      1988 "The Church in Rural Tennessee." *The Rural Sociologist*
            8(August): 360-366.

740. Comfort, Richard O.
      1948 "Survey of Activities and Training of Selected Rural
            Ministers in the United States." *Rural Sociology*
            12(December): 375-387.

741. Comfort, Richard O.
      1959 "Education for the Rural Ministry." *Pastoral Psychology*
            10(October): 37-43.

742. Coughenour, C. Milton.
      1955 "An Application of Scale Analysis to the Study of
            Religious Groups." *Rural Sociology* 20
            (September/December): 197-207. Comment by Ira H.
            Cisin on pp. 208-211. Rejoinder by C. Coughenour on p.
            211.

743. Cummings, Scott, Richard Briggs, and James Mercy.
      1977 "Preachers Versus Teachers: Local-Cosmopolitan Conflict
            Over Textbook Censorship in an Appalachian
            Community." *Rural Sociology* 42(Spring):7-21.

744. Davis, Kenneth S.
     1955   "Challenge to the Country Churches." *New York Times*
            (May 22): 26-27.

745. Davis, J. Merle.
     1949   "Missionary Strategy and the Rural Church." *International
            Review of Mission* 38(October): 401-411.

746. DeJong, Gordon F. and Thomas R. Ford.
     1965   "Religious Fundamentalism and Denominational
            Preference in the Southern Appalachian Region." *Journal
            for the Scientific Study of Religion* 5(1): 24-33.

747. Dillingham, H.C.
     1965   "Protestant, Religion, and Social Status." *American Journal
            of Sociology* 72(January): 416-422.

748. Dyer, William G.
     1956   "Development of a Mormon Line Community." *Rural
            Sociology* 21(June): 181-182.

749. Dynes, Russell R.
     1956   "Rurality, Migration, and Sectarianism." *Rural Sociology*
            21(March): 25-28.

750. Ericksen, Eugene P., Julia A. Ericksen, and John A. Hostetler.
     1980   "The Cultivation of the Soil as a Moral Directive:
            Population Growth, Family Ties, and the Maintenance of
            Community among the Old Order Amish." *Rural Sociology*
            45(Spring): 49-68.

751. Feuer, Lewis S. and Mervyn S. Perrine.
     1965   "Religion in a Northwestern Vermont Town: A Cross-
            Century Comparative Study." *Journal for the Scientific
            Study of Religion* 5(4): 367.

752. Fisher, Elliot L.
     1942   "A Church-Centered Community." *Rural Sociology*
            7(December): 445-446.

753. Ford, Thomas R.
     1960   "Status, Residence, and Fundamentalist Religious Beliefs
            in the Southern Appalachians." *Social Forces* 39(October):
            41-49.

754.   Ford, Thomas R.
       1961   "Religious Thought and Beliefs in the Southern
              Appalachians as Revealed by an Attitude Survey." *Review
              of Religious Research* 3(Summer). (Also in Richard D.
              Knudten (ed.), (1967) *The Sociology of Religion: An
              Anthology.* New York, N.Y.: Appleton-Century-Crofts.)

755.   Foster, Thomas W.
       1984   "Separation and Survival of Amish Society." *Sociological
              Focus* 17(1): 1-15.

756.   Foster, Virgil E.
       1952   "Religious Education in the Small Church." *International
              Journal of Religious Education.* (July-August): 3,8-9,12-13.

757.   Freudenberger, C. Dean.
       1986   "Food and Politics: Business as Usual Has Run Its
              Course--What Are the Options?" *Word and World: Theology
              for Christian Ministry* 6(Winter): 40-53.

758.   Gentilcore, R. Louis.
       1961   "Missions and Mission Lands of Alta, California." *Annals
              of the Association of American Geographers* 51(March): 46-72.

759.   Gibbons, Cecil W.
       1949   "The Church and the Land." *International Review of
              Missions* 38(January): 95-99.

760.   Goatley, W.H.
       1973   "Black Church in Rural America." *Review and Expositor*
              70(Summer): 357-363.

761.   Goldschmidt, W.R.
       1944   "Class Denominationalism in Rural California Churches."
              American Journal of Sociology 49(January): 348-355.

762.   Griffin, Kenyon N., John C. Martin, and Oliver Walter.
       1976   "Religious Roots and Rural Americans' Support for Israel
              during the October War." *Journal of Palestine Studies* 6(1):
              104-114.

763.   Hadaway, Christopher Kirk.
       1980   "The Demographic Environment and Church Membership
              Change." *Journal for the Scientific Study of Religion* 20(1):
              77-89.

764. Hassinger, Edward Wesley, J. Kenneth Benson, and John S. Holik.
     1972 "Changes in Program and Suborganization of Rural Churches in Missouri in a 15-Year Period." *Rural Sociology* 37(September): 428-435.

765. Hassinger, Edward Wesley and John S. Holik.
     1970 "Changes in the Number of Rural Churches in Missouri: 1952-1967." *Rural Sociology* 35(September): 354-366.

766. Hendricks, Garland A.
     1959 "Guiding a Rural Church in a World of Change." *Pastoral Psychology* 10(5): 25-30.

767. Herron, Roy Brasfield.
     1965 "The Land, the Law, and the Poor." *Word and World: Theology for Christian Ministry* 6(Winter): 76-84.

768. Holik, John S.
     1957 "An Index of Religious Group Action." *Rural Sociology* 22(September): 268-270.

769. Holland, J.B. and C.P. Loomis.
     1948 "Goals of Life of Rural Ministers." *Sociometry* 11(August): 217-229.

770. Hollingshead, August B.
     1937 "The Life Cycle of Nebraska Rural Churches." *Rural Sociology* 2(June): 180-191.

771. Holt, Arthur.
     1927 "The Ecological Approach to the Church." *American Journal of Sociology* 33(July); 72-79.

772. Hostetler, John A.
     1954 "Religious Mobility in a Sect Group: The Mennonite Church." *Rural Sociology* 19(September): 244-255.

773. Hostetler, John A.
     1955 "Old World Extinction and New World Survival of the Amish: A Study of Group Maintenance and Dissolution." *Rural Sociology* 20 (September/December): 212-219.

774. Hultgren, Arland J., (ed.)
     1986 "Land Values and Ministry." *Word and World: Theology for Christian Ministry* 6(1): 3-4.

775. Hunt, Giles.
      1980   "The Church: Two Points of View." *Theology* 83(July): 257-
             262.

776. Jackson, Allen K.
      1961   "Religious Beliefs and Expressions of the Southern
             Highlander." *Review of Religious Research* (Summer): 21-39.

777. Jackson, M.J.
      1963   "Rural Church and the Sociology of Religion." *Church
             Quarterly Review* 164(January-March): 94-102.

778. Jones, Loyal.
      1976   "Mountain Religion: The Outsider's View." *Mountain
             Review* 2(3). (Reprinted in John D. Photiadis (ed.),
             *Religion in Appalachia: Theological, Social, and Psychological
             Dimensions and Correlates*, 1978. Morgantown, W.Va.: West
             Virginia University Press, pp. 401-407.)

779. Kan, Stephen H. and Yun Kim.
      1981   "Religious Affiliation and Migration Intentions in
             Nonmetropolitan Utah." *Rural Sociology* 46(Winter): 669-
             687.

780. Kane, Steven M.
      1974   "Holy Ghost People: The Snake Handlers of Southern
             Appalachia." *Appalachian Journal* 1(4): 255-262.

781. Kane, Steven M.
      1974   "Ritual Possession in a Southern Appalachian Religious
             Sect." *Journal of American Folklore* 87(October-December):
             293-302.

782. Kanten, Anne.
      1986   "The Erosion of Soil and Culture." *Word and World:
             Theology for Christian Ministry* 6(Winter): 35-39.

783. Kaplan, B.H.
      1965   "Structure of Adaptive Sentiments in a Lower Class
             Religious Group in Appalachia." *Journal of Social Issues*
             21(January): 126-141.

784. Klietsch, Ronald G.
      1963   "Social Change, Ethnicity, and the Religious System in a
             Rural Community." *American Catholic Sociological Review*
             24(Fall): 222-230.

785. Kluegel, James R.
1980 "Denominational Mobility: Current Patterns and Recent Trends." *Journal for the Scientific Study of Religion* 19(1): 26-39.

786. Kollmorgen, W.L.
1943 "The Agricultural Stability of the Old Order Amish and Old Order Mennonites of Lancaster County, Pennsylvania." *American Journal of Sociology* 49(November): 233-241.

787. Landis, Edward Bryant.
1909 "Rural Church in Its Educational and Social Opportunities." *Religious Education* 15(5).

788. Lee, J.O.
1950 "The Religious Life and Needs of Negro Youth." *Journal of Negro Education* 19(Summer): 298-309.

789. McIntosh, W. Alex, S.D. Fitch, J.B. Wilson, and K.L. Nyberg.
1981 "The Effect of Mainstream Religious Social Controls on Adolescent Drug Use in Rural Areas." *Review of Religious Research* 23(September): 54-75.

790. McKinney, William and Dean R. Hoge.
1983 "Community and Congregational Factors in the Growth and Decline of Protestant Churches." *Journal for the Scientific Study of Religion* 22(1): 51-66.

791. Madison, James H.
1986 "Reformers and the Rural Church, 1900-1950." *Journal of American History* 73(December): 645-668.

792. March, John L. and Karl E. Nordberg.
1980 "The Country Church: A Study in 19th Century Taste and 20th Century Commitment." *Presbyterian History* 58(Spring): 3-16.

793. Marshall, Douglas G.
1950 "The Decline in Farm Family Fertility and its Relationship to Nationality and Religious Background." *Rural Sociology* 15(March): 42-49.

794. Martin, R.R.
1941 "The Church and Changing Ecological Dominance." *Sociology and Social Research* 25(January-February): 246-257.

795.   Mitchell, John B., Eldon C. Schriner, and E.D. Lafontaine.
       1970   "Influentials and the Church in Small Communities."
              Review of Religious Research 11(Spring): 192-196.

796.   Moomaw, Ira W.
       1953   "Our Christian Mission and the Rural World."
              International Review of Mission : 249-256.

797.   More, Jamieson.
       1926   "Rural Churches Dying in America." *Current History*
              25(1926-1927): 343-347.

798.   Nelsen, Hart M.
       1970   "Attitudes Toward Religious Education in Appalachia."
              Religious Education 65(January/February): 50-55.
              (Reprinted in John D. Photiadis (ed.), *Religion in
              Appalachia: Theological, Social, and Psychological Dimensions
              and Correlates*, 1978. Morgantown, W.Va.: West Virginia
              University. pp. 323-332.)

799.   Nelsen, Hart M. and Eleanor Frost.
       1971   "Residence, Anomie, and Receptivity to Education Among
              Southern Appalachian Presbyterians." *Rural Sociology*
              36(4): 521-532.

800.   Nelsen, Hart M. and Raymond H. Potvin.
       1977   "The Rural Church and Rural Religion: Analysis of Data
              from Children and Youth." *Annals of the Academy of
              Political and Social Science.* 429(January): 103-114.

801.   Nelsen, Hart M. and William E. Snizek.
       1976   "Musical Pews: Rural and Urban Models of Occupational
              and Religious Mobility." *Sociology and Social Research*
              60(April): 279-289.

802.   Nelsen, Hart M. and Raytha L. Yokley.
       1970   "Civil Rights Attitudes of Rural and Urban
              Presbyterians." *Rural Sociology* 35(June): 161-174.

803.   Nelsen, Hart M., Raytha L. Yokley, and Thomas W. Madron.
       1971   "Rural-Urban Differences in Religiosity." *Rural Sociology*
              36(September): 389-396.

804.   Nelson, Lowry.
       1952   "Education and the Changing Size of Mormon Families."
              Rural Sociology 17(December): 335-342.

805. Nelson, Lowry.
1954 "Comment on: The Effects of Geographical Position on Belief and Behavior in a Rural Mormon Village by O'Dea." *Rural Sociology* 19(December): 364.

806. Nesmith, G.T.
1903 "The Problem of the Rural Community with Special Reference to the Rural Church." *American Journal of Sociology* 8(May).

807. Nuesse, C.J.
1948 "The Relation of Financial Assessment to Status in a Rural Parish." *American Catholic Sociological Review* 9: 26-38.

808. Nuesse, C.J.
1957 "Membership Trends in a Rural Catholic Parish." *Rural Sociology* 22(June): 123-130.

809. Nuesse, C.J.
1963 "Recent Catholic Fertility in Rural Wisconsin." *Rural Sociology* 28(December): 379-393.

810. Oates, Wayne E.
1959 "The Rural Pastor as Counselor." *Pastoral Psychology* 10(5): 14-24.

811. Obenhaus, Victor and W. Widick Schroeder.
1963 "Church Affiliation and Attitudes Toward Selected Public Questions in a Typical Midwest County." *Rural Sociology* 28(March): 35-47.

812. Obenhaus, Victor, W. Widick Schroeder, and Charles D. England.
1958 "Church Participation Related to Social Class and Type of Center." *Rural Sociology* 23(September): 298-308.

813. O'Dea, Thomas F.
1954 "The Effects of Geographical Position on Belief and Behavior in a Rural Mormon Village." *Rural Sociology* 19(December): 358-364. Comment by Lowry Nelson, p. 364.

814. Olson, Dennis T.
1986 "Biblical Perspectives on the Land." *Word and World: Theology for Christian Ministry* 6(Winter): 18-27.

815. Olson, Lynette J., Walter R. Schumm, Stephan R. Bollman, and Anthony P. Jurich.
1985 "Religion and Anomia in the Midwest." *Journal of Social Psychology* 125(February): 131-132.

816. Ostendorf, David L.
1986 "Toward Wholeness and Community: Strategies for Pastoral and Political Response to the American Rural Crisis." *Word and World: Theology for Christian Ministry* 6(Winter):55-65.

817. Peter, Karl and Ian Whitaker.
1983 "The Hutterite Economy: Recent Changes and Their Social Correlates." *Anthropos* 78(3-4): 535-546.

818. Photiadis, John D. and John Schnobel.
1977 "Religion: A Persistent Institution in a Changing Appalachia." *Review of Religious Research* 19(1): 32-42.

819. Ploch, Louis A.
1986 "Religion and the Rural Community--A New Beginning?" *The Rural Sociologist* 6(September): 376-384.

820. Rathge, Richard W. and Gary A. Goreham.
1989 "The Influence of Economic and Demographic Factors on Rural Church Viability." *Journal for the Scientific Study of Religion* 28(1): 59-74.

821. Rhoades, J. Benton.
1975 "Agricultural Missions Today and Yesterday." *International Review of Mission* 64(October): 346-353.

822. Ricken, William
1987 "Salvation Army Programs in Rural Areas." *Human Services in the Rural Environment* 10(Winter): 32-33.

823. Roberts, Harry W.
1947 "The Rural Negro Minister: His Work and Salary." *Rural Sociology* 12(September): 284-297.

824. Roberts, Harry W.
1948 "The Rural Negro Minister: His Educational Status." *Journal of Negro Education* 17(Fall): 478-487.

825. Roberts, Harry W.
     1949 "The Rural Negro Minister: His Personal and Social
           Characteristics." *Social Forces* 27(March): 291-300.

826. Rodehaver, Myles W.
     1948 "Ministers on the Move: A Study of Mobility in Church
           Leadership." *Rural Sociology* 13(December): 400-410.

827. Rowles, Graham D.
     1985 "The Rural Elderly and the Church." *Journal of Religion
           and Aging* 2(1-2): 79-98.

828. "Rural Ministry."
     1962 *Pastoral Psychology* 13(October): 48-56.

829. Salamon, Sonya.
     1985 "Ethnic Communities and the Structure of Agriculture."
           Rural Sociology 50(September): 323-340.

830. Scanzoni, J.
     1965 "Innovation and Constancy in Church." *American Journal
           of Sociology* 71(November): 320-327.

831. Schaffer, Albert.
     1959 "The Rural Church in a Metropolitan Area." *Rural
           Sociology* 24(September):236-245.

832. Schoenfeld, Eugen.
     1970 "Small-Town Jews Integration into Their Communities."
           Rural Sociology 35(June): 175-190.

833. Schwarz, Berthold E.
     1960 "Ordeal by Serpents, Fire, and Strychnine: A Study of
           Some Provocative Psychosomatic Phenomena." *Psychiatric
           Quarterly* 34: 405-429.

834. Seaver, LaRoy E.
     1959 "Counseling Needs in the Rural Church." *Pastoral
           Psychology* 10(5): 43-49.

835. Shissler, Henry.
     1957 "An Experiment in Attitudinal Outcomes Resulting From
           Seminary Courses in 'The Church and Community.'"
           Rural Sociology 22(September): 250-257.

836. Shortridge, James R.
1976 "Patterns of Religion in the United States." *Geographical Review* 66(October):420-434.

837. Smith, Elmer Lewis.
1958 "Personality Differences Between Amish and Non-Amish Children." *Rural Sociology* 23(December): 371-376.

838. Smith, Wilford E.
1959 "The Urban Threat to Mormon Norms." *Rural Sociology* 24(December): 355-361.

839. Sorenson, James A.
1986 "Living on the Land: Imaging Our Ways." *Word and World: Theology for Christian Ministry* 6(Winter): 29-34.

840. Southard, Samuel.
1965 "The Personal Life of the Frontier Minister." *Journal for the Scientific Study of Religion* 5(4): 213.

841. Sparks, James A.
1975 "The Land-Grant University: A Major Resource for Clergy Continuing Education." *Journal of the Academy of Parish Clergy* 5(March): 30-33.

842. Stoddard, Robert H.
1970 "Changing Patterns of Some Rural Churches." *Rocky Mountain Social Science Journal* 17(1): 61-68.

843. Swanson, Merwin.
1977 "The 'Country Life Movement' and the American Churches." *Church History* 46(3): 358-373.

844. Tansey, B.R.
1967 "Plea for Help in Town and Country Church." *Pastoral Psychology* 19(November): 50-52.

845. Tellis-Nayak, V.
1982 "The Transcendent Standard: The Religious Ethos of the Rural Elderly." *Gerontologist* 22(August): 359-363.

846. Theobald, Robin.
1985 "From Rural Population to Practical Christianity: The Seventh Day Adventists Movement." *Archives de Sciences Sociales des Religions* 60(1): 109-130.

847. Tinker, George E.
1986 "Native Americans and the Land: 'The End of the Living, and the Beginning of Survival.'" *Word and World: Theology for Christian Ministry* 6(Winter): 66-74.

848. Tripp, Thomas Alfred.
1942 "Rural Churches and the War." *Rural Sociology* 7 (June): 210-211.

849. Tuberville, Gus.
1949 "Religious Schism in the Methodist Church: A Sociological Analysis of the Pine Grove Case." *Rural Sociology* 14(March): 29-39.

850. Turner, Eldon R.
1983 "Peasants and Parsons: Readers and the Intellectual Location of John Wise's 'Churches Quarrel Espoused.'" *Early American Literature* 18(20): 146-170.

851. Vangerud, Richard D.
1969 "The Dynamics of Depression in Contemporary Town and Country: Pastoral Assessment and Response." *Journal of Pastoral Care* 23(3): 129-141.

852. Wasserman, Ira M.
1978 "Religious Affiliation and Homicide: Historical Results from the Rural South." *Journal for the Scientific Study of Religion* 17(December): 415-418.

853. Wells, George Frederick.
1907 "An Answer to the New England Country Church Question." *Bibliotheca Sacra* (April):314-330.

854. Wilson, John, Ida Harper Simpson, and David K. Jackson.
1987 "Church Activism among Farm Couples: Measuring the Impact of the Conjugal Unit. *Journal of Marriage and the Family* 49(November): 875-882.

855. Wilson, Warren Hugh.
1911 "The Church and the Rural Community." *American Journal of Sociology* 16(March):668-693. Discussion of article by various authors on pp. 693-702.

856. Wolters, Gilbert.
1956 "The Human Crop of a Rural Catholic Parish." *Rural Sociology* 21(September-December): 297-298.

857.   Woolridge, Nancy Bullock.
       1945   "The Slave Preacher--Portrait of a Leader." *Journal of
              Negro Education* 14(1): 28-37.

858.   Wright, George Frederick.
       1890   "The Country Church." *Bibliotheca Sacra* (April): 267-284.

859.   Zimmer, B.G. and A.H. Hawley.
       1959   "Suburbanization and Church Participation." *Social Forces*
              37(May): 348-354.

U.S. Government and Land-Grant University Publications

U.S. Government and
Land-Grant University Publications

860. Arvold, Alfred Gilmeiden.
   1940 "Neighborhood Activities in Country Communities."
   North Dakota Extension Service Circular No. 171. Fargo,
   N.Dak.: Extension Service, North Dakota Agricultural
   College. 79 pp.

861. Aylesworth, Phillip F.
   1961 "Church Leaders: Channel for Telling the Agriculture
   Story." *Extension Service Review* (May): 95,104.

862. Aylesworth, Phillip F. and E.J. Niederfrank.
   1958 "In-Service Training for Rural Clergy." Washington, D.C.:
   U.S. Department of Agriculture. 4 pp.

863. Baker, Oliver Edwin.
   1938 "The New Significance of the Rural People to America
   and the Christian Church." New Brunswick, N.J.:
   Extension Service.

864. Becker, W.J.
   1947 "The Rural Church." *Kansas State Board of Agriculture
   Report* 76: 24-30.

865. Beecher, A.A.
   1954 "Landscaping the Church Grounds." Agricultural
   Extension Bulletin No. 220. (September). Blacksburg, Va.:
   Extension Service, Virginia Polytechnic Institute and State
   University. 12 pp.

866. Belew, M. Wendell, Henry A. McCanna, Elwin William Mueller,
   and Edward W. O'Rourke.
   1962 "The Church and Agricultural Progress." (May)
   Washington, D.C.: U.S. Department of Agriculture,
   Centennial Committee. 8 pp.

867. Bielfeld, Wolfgang, Randolph Cantrell, and George A. Donohue.
      1987 "Long Pastor Tenure Means Fewer Linkages:
            Organizational Linkages of Local Churches." *Sociology of
            Rural Life* 9(3): 5-6. St. Paul, Minn.: University of
            Minnesota.

868. Bielfeld, Wolfgang, Randolph Cantrell, and George A. Donohue.
      1988 "Economic Activism of Minnesota Churches in Two
            Regions." *Sociology of Rural Life* 10(Summer/Fall): 5-6, 8.
            St. Paul, Minn.: University of Minnesota.

869. Blizzard, Samuel W.
      1953 "The Rural Church and Its Community Relations."
            Lexington, Ky.: Cooperative Extension Work In
            Agriculture and Home Economics, College of Agriculture
            and Home Economics, University of Kentucky.

870. Blizzard, Samuel W., Beryl B. Maurer, and G.A. Lee.
      1956 "Rural Ministers--Work Long Day." *Science for the Farmer*
            3(4): 14. University Park, Penn.: Agricultural Experiment
            Station, Pennsylvania State University.

871. Blume, George T. and Lawrence M. Hepple.
      1960 "The Church in Rural Missouri: Part VI, Spatial and
            Social Relationships." Missouri Agricultural Experiment
            Station Bulletin 633F (September). Columbia, Mo.:
            Missouri Agricultural Experiment Station, University of
            Missouri, Columbia. pp. 313-344.

872. Boyd, V.A.
      1953 "Open-Country Churches in Anderson County, South
            Carolina." Bulletin No. 107 (February). Clemson, S.Car.:
            Department of Agricultural Economics and Rural
            Sociology, Clemson University. 13 pp.

873. Boyd, F., M. Oyler, and W.D. Nicholls.
      1936 "Factors in the Success of Rural Organizations."
            Agricultural Experiment Station Bulletin No. 364
            (September). Lexington, Ky.: Agricultural Experiment
            Station, University of Kentucky. pp. 83-105.

874. Brooks, J.B.
      1944 "The Rural Church." In *Looking Toward the Post-War World*.
            Clemson, S.Car.: Clemson Agricultural College of South
            Carolina, Clemson University. 46 pp.

875. Buie, T.S.
1943 "Saving the Rural Church through Soil Conservation."
Spartanburg, S.Car. 8 pp.

876. Bureau of the Census, U.S. Department of Commerce.
1911 "Religious Bodies, 1906. Volume I: Summary and Detailed
Tables." Washington, D.C.: Government Printing Office.

877. Bureau of the Census, U.S. Department of Commerce.
1921 "Religious Bodies, 1916. Volume I: Summary and Detailed
Tables." Washington, D.C.: Government Printing Office.

878. Bureau of the Census, U.S. Department of Commerce.
1931 "Religious Bodies, 1926. Volume I: Summary and Detailed
Tables." Washington, D.C.: Government Printing Office.

879. Bureau of the Census, U.S. Department of Commerce.
1941 "Religious Bodies, 1936. Volume I: Summary and Detailed
Tables." Washington, D.C.: Government Printing Office.

880. Bureau of the Census, U.S. Department of Commerce.
1958 "Religion Reported by the Civilian Population of the
United States: March 1957." Current Population Reports,
Population Characteristics, Series P-20, No. 79.
Washington, D.C.: Government Printing Office.

881. Burtt, Edwin A.
1958 "The Impact of Religion on Cultural Change."
Comparative Extension Publication No. 6 (October):
Ithaca, N.Y.: Cooperative Extension Service, New York
State College of Agriculture, Cornell University. 10 pp.

882. Cantrell, Randolph L., James F. Krile, and George A. Donohue.
1980 "Church Activity and the Yoked Parish: A Structural
Adaptation to Scarcity." *Sociology of Rural Life* 3(Winter):
1-2,8. St. Paul, Minn.: University of Minnesota.

883. Carter, Michael V. and J.G. Pankhurst.
1981 "Local Congregations and Their Provision of Collective
Goods in the Appalachian Region." ESO Paper #781.
Columbus, Ohio: Department of Agricultural Economics
and Rural Sociology, Ohio State University.

884. Cleland, Courntney B.
      1957 "The Little Church Back Home." North Dakota
            Agricultural Experiment Station Project RR-507. *North
            Dakota Farm Research Bimonthly Bulletin*
            19(January/February): 80-84. Fargo, N.Dak.: North Dakota
            State University.

885. Coons, I.M.
      1945 "Christian Living, Rural Communities, Recreation,
            Returning Veterans, World Peace: A List of References on
            the Subjects Considered at the Short Course for Pastors
            in Farm Communities, July 9-14, 1945." Fort Collins,
            Colo.: Colorado Agricultural College Library. 4 pp.

886. Cottom, H.R.
      1942 "Trends in Religious Bodies in Pennsylvania, 1906-1936."
            Pennsylvania Agricultural Experiment Station Journal.
            University Park, Pa.: Agricultural Experiment Station,
            Pennsylvania State University. 9 pp.

887. Coughenour, Milton and Lawrence M. Hepple.
      1957 "The Church in Rural Missouri, Midway in the 20th
            Century, Part II: Religious Groups in Rural Missouri."
            Missouri Agricultural Experiment Station Research
            Bulletin No. 633B (September). Columbia, Mo.:
            Agricultural Experiment Station, University of Missouri-
            Columbia. pp. 41-156.

888. Dawson, Marshall.
      1922 "The Rural Church." Extension Bulletin No. 54. Storrs,
            Conn.: Connecticut Agricultural College.

889. Dyer, Delwyn A.
      1969 "Community Understanding and Action, Unit 9: Religion
            and Churches (Preliminary Draft)." Washington, D.C.:
            Federal Extension Service, U.S. Department of
            Agriculture. 12 pp.

890. Ensminger, Douglas.
      1945 "If I Were a Rural Pastor." Washington, D.C.: Cooperative
            Extension Service, U.S. Department of Agriculture. 3 pp.

891. Eshleman, R.F. and David Edgar Lindstrom.
1945 "The Church of the Brethren in the Rural Community: A Study of 34 Churches in the Two Illinois Districts of the Church of the Brethren." Illinois Agricultural Experiment Station RSM16. Urbana, Ill.: Agricultural Experiment Station, University of Illinois. 12 pp.

892. Farrell, F.D.
1949 "Kansas Rural Institutions: V. Three Effective Rural Churches." Kansas Agricultural Experiment Station Circular No. 256 (June). Manhattan, Kans.: Agricultural Experiment Station, Kansas State University. 35 pp.

893. Farrell, F.D.
1950 "Three Effective Rural Churches." Manhattan, Kans.: Agricultural Experiment Station, Kansas State University.

894. Farrell, F.D.
1956 "Rural Churches Are Important." *Kansas Board of Agriculture Biennial Report* 39: 78-79.

895. Fluharty, M.
1985 "Churches Work Together in Vinton County." 15(July): 8-9. Washington, D.C.: U.S. Department of Agriculture.

896. Fonda, Morris E.
1951 "The Lord's Land." U.S. Soil Conservation Service. Chicago, Ill.: Sears-Roebuck Foundation.

897. Francis, R.G., C.E. Ramsey, and J.A. Toews.
1955 "The Church in the Rural Fringe." *Minnesota Farm and Home Science* 12(February): 8,13.

898. Freuhling, R. and E.J. Niederfrank.
1953 "Three Churches Put on a Community 4-H Fair." *Extension Service Review* (June): 115.

899. Galpin, Charles Josiah
1917 "The Country Church: An Economic and Social Force." University of Wisconsin. Agricultural Experiment Station Bulletin No. 278. Madison, Wis.: Agricultural Experiment Station, University of Wisconsin. 48 pp.

900. Garnett, William Edward.
      1957 "The Virginia Rural Church and Related Influences: 1900-
            1950." Virginia Agricultural Experiment Station Bulletin
            No. 479. (May). Blacksburg, Va.: Virginia Agricultural
            Experiment Station, Virginia Polytechnic Institute. 88 pp.

901. Garnett, William Edward and P.B. Gaston.
      1955 "Virginia Rural Church Trends." *Virginia University
            Newsletter* (November 1): 1.

902. Gessaman, Paul Hayden.
      1979 *Your Community: Parts and Functions.* Lincoln, Neb.: 4-H
            Youth and Development, University of Nebraska-Lincoln.

903. Gessner, Amy A.
      1940 "Selective Factors in Migration From a New York Rural
            Community." New York Agricultural Experiment Station
            Bulletin No. 736. Ithaca, N.Y.: Cornell University.

904. Gilmer, M. and David Edgar Lindstrom.
      1948 "A Study of the Lutheran Church in Rural Illinois, 1946."
            Urbana, Ill.: Cooperative Extension Service, College of
            Agriculture, Illinois University. 20 pp.

905. Gluck, J.C.
      1961 "Our Early Churches and Their Leaders." West Virginia
            Agricultural College Cooperative Extension Service *Good
            Living Series* 28. Morgantown, W.Wa.: West Virginia
            University. 8 pp.

906. Greene, Shirley E.
      1963 "Theology of Rural Life: A Protestant Perspective." In
            Conference on Goals and Values in Agricultural Policy
            (ed.) *Farm Goals in Conflict: Family Farm, Income, Freedom,
            Security.* Ames, Iowa: Iowa State University Center for
            Agricultural and Economic Development, Iowa State
            University Press. pp. 15-32.

907. Grimsley, C.J.
      1953 "Faith is a Family Affair." North Carolina State
            Agricultural College Extension Miscellaneous Pamphlet
            No. 144 (April). Raleigh, N.Car.: North Carolina State
            University. 12 pp.

908. Hamilton, Charles Horace and William Edward Garnett.
    1929 "The Role of the Church in Rural Community Life in
        Virginia." Virginia Agricultural Experiment Station
        Bulletin No. 267 (June). Blacksburg, Va.: Virginia
        Agricultural Experiment Station, Virginia Polytechnic
        Institute. 191 pp.

909. Harris, J.
    1950 "Landscaping Church Grounds." Extension Circular No.
        357 (November). Raleigh, N.Car.: North Carolina
        Agricultural College. 8 pp.

910. Hassinger, Edward Wesley, J. Kenneth Benson, James H. Dorsett,
    and John S. Holik.
    1971 "The Rural Church in Missouri, 1967." Agricultural
        Experiment Station Research Bulletin No. 984 (December).
        Columbia, Mo.: Missouri Agricultural Experiment Station,
        University of Missouri, Columbia. 28 pp.

911. Hassinger, Edward Wesley, J. Kenneth Benson, James H. Dorsett,
    and John S. Holik.
    1973 "A Comparison of Rural Churches and Ministers in
        Missouri over a 15 Year Period." Agricultural Experiment
        Station Research Bulletin No. 999 (November). Columbia,
        Mo.: Agricultural Experiment Station, University of
        Missouri, Columbia. 26 pp.

912. Hassinger, Edward Wesley, J. Kenneth Benson, James H. Dorsett,
    and John S. Holik.
    1973 "Ministers in Rural Churches of Missouri." Agricultural
        Experiment Station Research Bulletin No. 995 (February).
        Columbia, Mo.: Agricultural Experiment Station,
        University of Missouri, Columbia. 44 pp. Also printed in
        John D. Photiadis (ed.) (1978) *Religion in Appalachia:
        Theological, Social, and Psychological Dimensions and
        Correlates*. Morgantown, W.Va.: West Virginia University.

913. Hassinger, Edward Wesley, J. Kenneth Benson, James H. Dorsett,
    and John S. Holik.
    1974 "A Comparison of Rural and Urban Churches and
        Ministers of Missouri." Agricultural Experiment Station
        Research Bulletin No. 1004 (May). Columbia, Mo.:
        Agricultural Experiment Station, University of Missouri,
        Columbia. 28 pp.

914. Hepple, Lawrence M.
1957 "The Church in Rural Missouri, Midway in the 20th Century: Part I, Introduction." Agricultural Experiment Station Bulletin No. 633A. (September). Columbia, Mo.: Agricultural Experiment Station, University of Missouri, Columbia. pp. 1-39.

915. Hepple, Lawrence M.
1958 "The Church in Rural Missouri, Midway in the 20th Century: Part III, Clergymen in Rural Missouri." Agricultural Experiment Station Bulletin No. 633C (December). Columbia, Mo.: Agricultural Experiment Station, University of Missouri, Columbia. pp. 157-244.

916. Hepple, Lawrence M.
1959 "The Church in Rural Missouri, Midway in the 20th Century: Part IV, Rural-Urban Churches Compared." Agricultural Experiment Station Bulletin No. 633E (July). Columbia, Mo.: Agricultural Experiment Station, University of Missouri, Columbia. pp. 281-313.

917. Hepple, Lawrence M. and Milton Coughenour.
1961 "The Church in Rural Missouri: Part VII, What Rural People Think of Church." Agricultural Experiment Station Bulletin No. 633G (September). Columbia, Mo.: Agricultural Experiment Station, University of Missouri, Columbia. pp. 344-385.

918. Hochbaum, Hans Weller.
1929 "The Rural Church and Cooperative Extension Work: An Outline of What Extension Work Is and How It May Aid the Rural Church in Community Improvement." U.S. Department of Agriculture Circular No. 57 (January). Washington, D.C.: U.S. Department of Agriculture. 25 pp.

919. Holik, John S. and Lawrence M. Hepple.
1959 "The Church in Rural Missouri, Midway in the 20th Century, Part IV: Index of Religious Group Action." Agricultural Experiment Station Bulletin No. 633D (January). Columbia, Mo.: Agricultural Experiment Station, University of Missouri, Columbia. pp. 247-279.

920. Hostetler, John A. and William G. Mather.
     1952 "Participation in the Rural Church: A Summary of
     Research in the Field." Pennsylvania Agricultural
     Experiment Station Paper No. 1762 (October). State
     College, Pa.: Agricultural Experiment Station, Department
     of Agricultural Economics and Rural Sociology,
     Pennsylvania State College. 64 pp.

921. Illinois University.
     1943 "Memorandum for Bishops of the Methodist Church,
     Session of Council at Princeton, N.J., December 14, 1943,
     'American Agriculture and the Country Church.'" Home
     Economics Bulletin No. 2138. Urbana, Ill: Department of
     Home Economics, Illinois Agriculture College. 8 pp.

922. Johnston, A.P. and Wiles, David K.
     1982 "Christian Schools and Public Schools In Small Rural
     Communities of the Northeast." Research report for
     Spencer Foundation, Chicago, Ill. Burlington, Vt.:
     Vermont University. College of Education and Social
     Services. 58 pp.

923. Kaufman, Harold Frederick.
     1948 "Religious Organization in Kentucky." Agriculture
     Experiment Station Bulletin No. 524 (August). Lexington,
     Ky.: Agricultural Experiment Station, University of
     Kentucky. 44 pp.

924. Kaufman, Harold Frederick.
     1949 "Rural Churches in Kentucky, 1947." Agriculture
     Experiment Station Bulletin No. 530 (April). Lexington,
     Ky.: Agricultural Experiment Station, University of
     Kentucky. 48 pp.

925. Kaufman, Harold Frederick.
     1959 *Mississippi Churches: A Half Century of Change.*
     Hattiesburg, Miss.: Social Science Research Center,
     Mississippi State University Press. 31 pp. Reprinted from
     Mississippi Quarterly 12(3), 1959.

926. Kolb, John Harrison and C.J. Bornman.
     1924 "Rural Religious Organizations: A Study of the Origin
     and Development of Religious Groups." Agricultural
     Experiment Station Bulletin No. 60. Madison, Wis.:
     Agricultural Experiment Station, University of Wisconsin.
     63 pp.

927.   Korbobo, R.P., R.B. Farnham, and C.H. Connors.
        1946   "Improving the Church Grounds." Agricultural College
                Extension Bulletin No. 243. New Brunswick, N.J.: New
                Jersey State College of Agriculture and Mechanical Arts,
                Cooperative Extension Service, Rutgers University. 12 pp.

928.   Krile, James F., Randolph L. Cantrell, and George A. Donohue.
        1981   "The Power Structure and Social Activism of Rural
                Churches." Sociology of Rural Life 4(Spring): 3-4,8. St.
                Paul, Minn.: Agricultural Extension Service, University of
                Minnesota.

929.   Krile, James F., Randolph L. Cantrell, and George A. Donohue.
        1985   "Effects of Centralized Control on Local Church
                Activities." Sociology of Rural Life. 7(Summer): 1-2,7. St.
                Paul, Minn.: Agricultural Extension Service, University of
                Minnesota.

930.   Krile, James F., G. C. Sponaugle, Randolph L. Cantrell, and
        George A. Donohue.
        1985   "Who Participates in Church and Community?"
                Sociology of Rural Life 7(Spring): 3-4,8. St. Paul, Minn.:
                Agricultural Extension Service, University of Minnesota.

931.   Kumlien, Wendell F.
        1935   "The Social Problem of the Church in South Dakota."
                Agricultural Experiment Station Bulletin No. 294 (May).
                Brookings, S.Dak.: Agricultural Experiment Station,
                Department of Rural Sociology, South Dakota State
                College of Agriculture and Mechanical Arts. 46 pp.

932.   Kumlien, Wendell F.
        1942   "The Problem of Over-Churched and Under-Churched
                Areas in Aurora County." Rural Sociology Pamphlet No.
                107 (August). Brookings, S.Dak.: South Dakota
                Agricultural Experiment Station, South Dakota State
                College of Agriculture and Mechanical Arts. 8 pp.

933.   Kumlien, Wendell F.
        1942   "The Problem of Over-Churched and Under-Churched
                Areas in Marshall County." Rural Sociology Pamphlet No.
                108 (August). Brookings, S.Dak.: South Dakota
                Agricultural Experiment Station, South Dakota State
                College of Agriculture and Mechanical Arts. 8 pp.

934. Lancaster, J.J.
1966 "Non-Extension Organization." Chapter 26 in H. C. Sanders (ed.) *The Cooperative Extension Service.* Englewood Cliffs, N.J.: Prentice-Hall, Inc. pp. 276-283.

935. Losey, James Edwin.
1957 "The Rural Church Situation in Indiana." Agricultural Experiment Station Research Bulletin No. 153 and Cooperative Extension Service Bulletin No. EC-15. Lafayette, Ind.: Purdue University. 9 pp.

936. McCanna, Henry A.
1963 "Goals and Values in American Agriculture: The Protestant Program." In Conference on Goals and Values in Agricultural Policy (ed.) *Farm Goals in Conflict: Family Farm, Income, Freedom, and Security.* Ames, Iowa: Iowa State University Center for Agricultural and Economic Development, Iowa State University Press. pp. 112-128.

937. McNair, H.A. and David Edgar Lindstrom.
1947 "Contributions of Presbyterian Churches to Rural Life in Illinois." Agricultural Experiment Station No. RSM-17. Urbana, Ill.: Agricultural Experiment Station, University of Illinois. 19 pp.

938. Mather, William G., Jr.
1934 "The Rural Churches of Allegheny County, New York." Agricultural Experiment Station Bulletin No. 587 (March). Ithaca, N.Y.: Agricultural Experiment Station, Cornell University. 31 pp.

939. Maurer, Beryl B.
1982 "Continuing Education for Church Leaders at West Virginia University." Morgantown, W.Va.: Center for Extension and Continuing Education, West Virginia University. 9 pp. First published in 1979, 8 pp.

940. Minnesota Agricultural Extension Service.
1968 "Working with Church and Community." Extension Program Report No. 10 (March). St. Paul, Minn.: Agricultural Extension Service, University of Minnesota.

941.   Minor, W.A.
       1951   "The Church and Agriculture." An address at the
              Religion in Life Week, Raleigh, N.Car., November 6,
              1951. Washington, D.C.: U.S. Department of Agriculture.
              7 pp.

942.   Mitchell, John B.
       1963   "The Church in Town and Country." *U.S.D.A. Yearbook of
              Agriculture.* Washington, D.C.: Government Printing
              Office. pp. 198-200.

943.   Mitchell, John B., Eldon C. Shriner, and E.D. Lafountain.
       1968   "In Small Communities, Are Churches Still Important
              Influences?" *Ohio Research and Development*
              53(November/December): 85-87.

944.   Morse, T.D.
       1955   "New Opportunities for Church Leadership: Notes Used
              in an Address before the National Convocation on the
              Church in Town and Country, Sringfield, Mass., October
              18, 1955." Washington, D.C.: U.S. Department of
              Agriculture. 4 pp.

945.   National Association of Soil Conservation Districts.
       1956   "Selected Sermons on Soil Stewardship from 1956."
              League City, Tex.: National Association of Soil
              Conservation Districts Press.

946.   Niederfrank, E.J.
       1950   "Challenges of the Changing Community and Town-
              Country Churches." Washington, D.C.: Extension Service,
              U.S. Department of Agriculture.

947.   Niederfrank, E.J.
       1960   "Cooperation for Community Development and Town-
              Country Churches." AEP-29(3-60) (February). Washington,
              D.C.: Federal Extension Service, U. S. Department of
              Agriculture. 16 pp.

948.   Nelsen, Hart M.
       1968   "The Appalachian Presbyterian: Some Rural-Urban
              Differences." Research Bulletin No. 5. (February). Bowling
              Green, Ky.: Western Kentucky University, College of
              Commerce Office of Research and Services. 59 pp.

949. Nelsen, Hart M. and Anne K. Nelsen.
1967 "Bibliography on Appalachia: A Guide to Studies Dealing with Appalachia in General and Including Rural and Urban Working Class Attitudes Toward Religion, Education, and Social Change." Bulletin No. 4. (April). Bowling Green, Ky.: Western Kentucky University, College of Commerce, Office of Research and Services. 73 pp.

950. Nelson, Glenn I.
1965 "Social Change and Religious Organizations of Meeker County." University of Minnesota Agriculture Experiment Station Bulletin No. 477 (May). St. Paul, Minn.: University of Minnesota, St. Paul. 55 pp.

951. Nelson, Lowry.
1948 "Rural Churches in Minnesota." *Minnesota Farm and Home Science* (March 15): 1-2. St. Paul, Minn.: Minnesota Agricultural Experiment Station, University of Minnesota.

952. Nelson, William R. and Joe A. Porter.
1966 "Planning for a Better Church Landscape." Cooperative Extension Service Circular No. 938. Urbana, Ill.: College of Agriculture, Cooperative Extension Service, University of Illinois. 18 p.

953. Nesius, Ernest J.
1966 "Rural Society in Transition: An Historical Examination of the Rural Society with Emphasis on Ways to Assist our Rural Society to Maximize Its Economic and Social Position during the Present Period of Rapid Transition to an Urban-Industrial Culture." Public Affairs Series No. 3 (April). Morgantown, W.Va.: Office of Research and Development, West Virginia Center for Appalachian Studies and Development, West Virginia University. 66 pp.

954. Obst, Jennifer.
1985 "Look at How Rural Communities Work." *Minnesota Science* 40(3): 14-15. St. Paul, Minn.: Agricultural Experiment Station, University of Minnesota.

955. O'Rourke, Edward W.
      1963 "Goals and Values Underlying Programs of the Catholic
            Church in Rural U.S.A." In Conference on Goals and
            Values in Agricultural Policy (ed.) *Farm Goals in Conflict:
            Family Farm, Income, Freedom, Security.* Ames, Iowa: Iowa
            State University Center for Agricultural and Economic
            Development, Iowa State University Press. pp. 129-134.

956. Oyler, M.
      1936 "Community and Neighborhood Groupings in Knott
            County." Agricultural Experiment Station Bulletin No.
            366 (October). Lexington, Ky.: Agricultural Experiment
            Station, University of Kentucky. pp. 123-156.

957. Page, James Franklin and I.R. LaCamp.
      1930 "The Oklahoma Rural Church." Agricultural Experiment
            Station Bulletin. Stillwater, Okla.: Agricultural
            Experiment Station, Oklahoma State University.

958. Patten, J.
      1967 "The Aberdeen Area Ministry." Agricultural Experiment
            Station Economics Pamphlet No. 127 (September).
            Brookings, S.Dak.: Agricultural Experiment Station, South
            Dakota State University. pp. 49-50.

959. Pennsylvania State University.
      1960 "Observing Rural Life Sunday." Extension Special Circular
            No. 50 (April). State College, Pa.: Cooperative Extension
            Service, Schools of Agriculture and Home Economics,
            Pennsylvania State University. 8 pp.

960. Photiadis, John D.
      1970 "Social and Socialpsychological Characteristics of West
            Virginians in Their Own State and in Cleveland, Ohio:
            Summary and Conclusions of a Comparative Social
            Study." Information Report No. 3. Morgantown, W.Va.:
            Appalachian Center, West Virginia University. Revised
            1975.

961. Photiadis, John D. and Beryl B. Maurer.
1974 "Religion in an Appalachian State." Research Report No.
6. Morgantown, W. Va.: Division of Personal and Family
Development, West Virginia University. Reprinted in
John D. Photiadis (ed.) (1978) *Religion in Appalachia:
Theological, Social, and Psychological Dimensions and
Correlates*. Morgantown, W.Va.: West Virginia University.
pp. 171-228.

962. Reuss, C.F.
1944 "Trends in Virginia Church Membership and Finance,
1926-1936." *Virginia University Newsletter* 20(April 1): 1.

963. Rich, Mark.
1939 "The Larger Parish, An Effective Organization for Rural
Churches." Extension Bulletin No. 408 (May). Ithaca, N.Y.:
New York State College of Agriculture, Cornell
University.

964. Samson, A'Delbert.
1958 "Church Groups in Four Agricultural Settings in
Montana." Agricultural Experiment Station Bulletin No.
538 (March). Bozeman, Mont.: Agricultural Experiment
Station, Montana State College. 43 pp.

965. Samson, A'Delbert.
1958 "Church Pastors in Four Agricultural Settings in
Montana." Agricultural Experiment Station Bulletin No.
539 (April). Bozeman, Mont.: Agricultural Experiment
Station, Montana State College. 27 pp.

966. Scheifele, Theodore C. and William G. Mather.
1949 "Closed Rural Pennsylvania Churches." Agricultural
Experiment Station Bulletin No. 512 (May). University
Park, Pa.: Agricultural Experiment Station, State College
of Pennsylvania. 17 pp.

967. Sneed, Melvin W. and Douglas Ensminger.
1935 "The Rural Church in Missouri." Agricultural Experiment
Station Bulletin No. 225 (June). Columbia, Mo.:
Agricultural Experiment Station, University of Missouri,
Columbia. 75 pp.

968. Soil Conservation Service.
     19--   "Influence of Soils on the Effectiveness of the Country
            Church: A Study of the Economics of Christianity in 222
            South Carolina Rural Churches." Washington, D.C.: U.S.
            Department of Agriculture. 1 p.

969. South Dakota State College of Agriculture and Mechanical Arts.
     1961   "Rural Life Sunday Bulletin." Brookings, S.Dak.:
            Cooperative Extension Service, South Dakota State
            College of Agriculture and Mechanical Arts. 13 pp.

970. Speltz, G.H.
     1963   "Theology of Rural Life: A Catholic Perspective." In
            Conference on Goals and Values in Agricultural Policy
            (ed.) *Farm Goals in Conflict: Family Farm, Income, Freedom,
            Security.* Ames, Iowa: Iowa State University Center for
            Agricultural and Economic Development, Iowa State
            University Press. pp. 33-49.

971. Sponaugle, G.C., James F. Krile, Randy Cantrell, and George A.
     Donohue.
     1984   "Family, Church and Community Involvement in Rural
            Minnesota." *Sociology of Rural Life* 6(3):1-2,5. St. Paul,
            Minn.: Agricultural Extension Service, University of
            Minnesota.

972. Stacy, W.H.
     1946   "Iowa Christian Rural Fellowship." *Iowa Yearbook of
            Agriculture, 1945.* pp. 451-456.

973. Taves, M.J.
     1953   "Factors Influencing Personal Religion of Adults."
            Washington Agricultural Experiment Station Bulletin No.
            544 (November). Pullman, Wash.: Agricultural Experiment
            Station, Washington State University. 30 pp.

974. Thompson, T.
     1963   "Evaluation of an Ethical Basis." In Conference on Goals
            and Values in Agricultural Policy (ed.) *Farm Goals in
            Conflict: Family Farm, Income, Freedom, Security.* Ames,
            Iowa: Iowa State University Center for Agricultural and
            Economic Development, Iowa State University Press. pp.
            145-155.

975. Ulrey, O.
     1946 "The Churches and Agriculture." Washington, D.C.:
          Bureau of Agricultural Economics, U.S. Department of
          Agriculture. 8 pp.

976. United States Department of Agriculture.
     1949 "The Rural Clergyman as a Parish Leader." Washington,
          D.C.: U.S. Extension Service, U.S. Department of
          Agriculture. 5 pp.

977. United States Department of Agriculture.
     1962 "Rural Areas Development and the Churches." U.S.
          Department of Agriculture Pamphlet No. PA-508.
          Washington, D.C.: Government Printing Office. 8 pp.

978. University of Virginia, Extension Division.
     1947 "The Schools Can Help: A Rural Church Institute Trains
          Local Leadership." Extension Division Pamphlet, New
          Dominion Series No. 85. Charlottesville, Va.: University
          of Virginia. 7 pp.

979. Vezina, Jacqueline Pauli
     1980 "Transference among Rural Women." Research Report.
          Chadron, Neb.: Chadron State College. 84 pp.

980. Wakeley, Ray E.
     1946 "It's Sunday in Exira: Survey Shows Youth Chief Source
          of Church Strength; Problem is to Maintain Interest." *Iowa
          Farm Science* 1(November): 15-16. Ames, Iowa: Iowa State
          College.

981. Warren, Gertrude L.
     1950 "Observance of Rural Life Sunday by 4-H Clubs, 1950
          Theme: Better Living for a Better World." Washington,
          D.C.: Extension Service, U.S. Department of Agriculture.
          28 pp.

982. Webb, Charles G.
     1941 "Churches Prosper as Conservation Comes to the Land."
          Washington, D.C.: Soil Conservation Service, U.S.
          Department of Agriculture. Reprint from *Soil Conservation*
          6(7).

983.   Whitman, Lauris B. and William G. Mather.
        1952   "The Rural Churches of Four Pennsylvania Counties."
                Progress Report No. 76 (June). State College, Pa.: School
                of Agriculture, Agricultural Experiment Station,
                Pennsylvania State College. 48 pp.

984.   Wileden, A.F.
        19--   "Rethinking Roles in In-Service Training for Rural
                Clergy." Madison, Wis.: Rural Sociology Department,
                University of Wisconsin.

985.   Wilson, L.G.
        1922   "The Church and the Landless Men." University of North
                Carolina Extension Bulletin (March 1). Chapel Hill,
                N.Car.: University Extension Division, University of
                North Carolina. 26 pp.

Proceedings
and Presented
Papers

Proceedings and Presented Papers

986. A & M College of Texas Agricultural Extension Service and
      Agricultural Experiment Station and Texas Town and Country
      Church Conference.
      1962 *The Dignity of Man in Town and Country Living.*
            Seventeenth Annual Town and Country Church
            Conference, College Station, Tex., October 17-19, 1962.
            College Station, Tex.: A & M College of Texas.

987. A & M College of Texas Agricultural Extension Service and
      Agricultural Experiment Station and Texas Town and Country
      Church Conference.
      1963 *The Town and Country Church Meeting Our Spiritual,
            Mental, Social, and Physical Needs.* Eighteenth Annual
            Town and Country Church Conference, College Station,
            Tex., October 16-18, 1963. College Station, Tex.: A & M
            College of Texas.

988. A & M College of Texas Agricultural Extension Service and
      Agricultural Experiment Station and Texas Town and Country
      Church Conference.
      1964 *Building a Climate of Love in Town and Country Areas.*
            Nineteenth Annual Town and Country Church
            Conference, College Station, Tex., October 14-16, 1963.
            College Station, Tex.: A & M College of Texas.

989. All New England Conference on the Rural Church.
      1938 *The Church and Rural Life in New England.* Proceedings of
            the All New England Conference on the Rural Church,
            Keene, N.H., May 10-13, 1938.

990. Alleger, D.E.
      1963 "Contributions of Southern Social, Political, and Religious
            Institutions to Economic Growth and Development." In
            *Association of Southern Agricultural Workers, Agricultural
            Economics and Rural Sociology Section Proceedings, 60th
            Annual Convention*, Volume 2: 353-364.

991. Beeman, Hulbert G.
      1912 "The Problem of the Rural Church." In *Proceedings of the
            Baptist Congress* 7: 130-141.

992. Belcher, John C.
      1979 "Religious Membership and Rural Retirement Lifestyles."
            Paper presented at the annual meeting of the Southern
            Sociological Society, 1979.

993. Boisen, Anton.
      1943 "Economic Distress and the Rise of the Holiness Sects." In
            *The People, the Land, and the Church in the Rural West: A
            Study Prepared as a Result of a Series of Conferences.*
            Chicago, Ill.: Farm Foundation. pp. 101-116.

994. Brewer, Earl D.C.
      1960 "Methodism in the Space Age." Address for the Town
            and Country Program of the 1960 Session of the W.N.C.
            Conference, Lake Junalaska, N.Car.

995. Brewer, Earl D.C. and Theodore H. Runyon.
      1966 *A Chart Book of Urban Parish and Rural Parish: Materials
            Drawn from a Case Study of Urban Parish and Rural Parish
            for Use in the Fourth Quadrennial Methodist Convocation on
            Urban Life in America, 1966.* Atlanta, Ga.: Religious
            Research Center, Candler School of Theology, Emory
            University. 53 pp.

996. Butterfield, Kenyon Leech.
      1925 "A Challenge to the Christian Farmer." In *Proceedings of
            the Seventh National Country Life Conference, American
            Country Life Association.* Chicago, Ill.: University of
            Chicago Press.

997. Callahan, Kennon L. (chairman).
      1978 *Religion and Rural Life Festival.* Indianapolis, Ind., July 31-
            August 3, 1978. Decatur, Ga.: Committee on Religion and
            Rural Life. 7 pp.

998. Cantrell, Randolph, James F. Krile, and George A. Donohue.
1980 "External Adaptation of Religious Organizations." Paper presented at the annual meeting of the Rural Sociological Society, 1980.

999. Carter, Michael Vaughn.
1981 "Religious Language and Collective Action: A Study of Voluntarism in a Rural Appalachian Church." Chapter 5 in Wilson Somerville (ed.), *Appalachia/America: Proceedings of the 1980 Appalachian Studies Conference*. Johnson City, Tenn.: Appalachian Consortium Press, East Tennessee State University. pp. 218-229.

1000. Cleland, Charles L.
1988 "Requirements for Rural Social Action: The Church." Paper presented at the annual meeting of the Rural Sociological Society, Athens, Ga., August 19-23, 1988.

1001. Colliver, McGuire C. and Paul D. Warner.
1979 "Appalachian Values: A Longitudinal Analysis." Paper presented at the annual meeting of the Rural Sociological Society, Burlington, Vt., August 26, 1979. 23 pp.

1002. Commission on Religion in Appalachia.
1966 *A United Approach to Fulfilling the Church's Mission in Appalachia*. Proceedings, 1966. Knoxville, Tenn.: Commission on Religion in Appalachia. 100 pp.

1003. Committee on Continuing Education for Clergy at Land-Grant and State Universities.
1976 *Continuing Education--Now More than Ever*. 1975 Clergy and Land-Grant University Conference, Madison, Wis., September 15-17, 1975. Chicago, Ill.: Lutheran Council in the U.S.A.

1004. Committee on Town and Country.
1944 *What Emphasis for the Church in Town and Country?* A report of the National Convocation on the Church in Town and Country, Columbus, Ohio, September 6-8, 1943. New York, N.Y.: Committee on Town and Country, Home Missions Council, Federal Council of the Churches of Christ in America. 103 pp.

1005. Congregational Churches of Massachusetts.
1908 "Report on the Committee on the Federation of Churches." In *Minutes of the 1908 Meeting of the Congregational Churches of Massachusetts.*

1006. Considine, John H., (ed.).
1960 *Fordham Rural Life Socio-Economic Conference, Maryknoll, N.Y., 1958.* Westminster, Md.: Newman Press. 330 pp.

1007. Copp, James H.
1962 "The People In Stable and Declining Town-Country Communities." Paper presented at the Northeast Conference on the Rural Non-Farm Population, June 27-29, 1961, Gettysburg College, Gettysburg, Pa. Chicago, Ill: Church in Town and Country, National Lutheran Council.

1008. Dawber, Mark A.
1943 *The Meaning of Christianity for Rural Life and of Rural Life for Christianity.* Report of the National Convocation on the Church in Town and Country.

1009. Dawson, H.A.
1952 "Does Modern Youth Feel a Responsibility to Church, Home, School, and Community?" In *American Country Life Association Proceedings* 31:68-71.

1010. Emory University.
1953 "Report of the Ninth Annual Town and Country School, July 14-29, 1953." Atlanta, Ga.: School for Town and Country Ministers, Emory University. 33 pp.

1011. Fairbanks, Henry.
1886 "The Problem of the Evangelization of Vermont." In *Ninety-First Meeting of the Congregational Ministers in Churches in Vermont: Supplement to the Minutes.* Congregational Conference in Vermont.

1012. Farley, Gary.
19-- "The Response of the Christian Denominations to the Farm Crisis." Paper presented at the annual meeting of the Southern Rural Sociological Society, Atlanta, Ga., May 18-20.

1013. Farley, Gary.
    1987 "Observations and Explanations of Data on Rural and Small Town Congregations Affiliated with the Southern Baptist Convention." Paper presented at annual meeting of the Rural Sociological Society, Madison, Wis., August 13, 1987.

1014. Farley, Gary, Ray Dalton, and Greg Hoover.
    1988 "The Farm Crisis and the Response of the Rural Church." Paper presented at the annual meeting of the Rural Sociological Society, Athens, Ga., August 19-23, 1988.

1015. Farm Foundation.
    1945 *The Land and the Rural Church in the Cumberland Plateau.* Proceedings of a Conference on Church and Community, Crossville, Tenn. Chicago, Ill.: Farm Foundation. 105 pp.

1016. Farm Foundation.
    1960 *Planning In-Service Training for Rural Clergy by Land-Grant Colleges*: National Conference, University of Wisconsin, Madison, Wis., May 24-26, 1960. Chicago, Ill.: Farm Foundation. 17 pp.

1017. Fry, John R., (ed.).
    1965 *The Church and Community Organization.* A Report of the Consultation on Community Development and Community Organization, Sponsored by the Division of Home Missions, National Council of the Churches of Christ in the U.S.A., Philadelphia, Penn., December 7-10, 1964. New York, N.Y.: Division of Christian Life and Mission, Department of Publication Services, National Council of Churches of Christ in the U.S.A. 179 pp.

1018. Gibbons, W.J.
    1948 "The Church and the Land." In *Association of Southern Agricultural Workers Proceedings* 45: 163-164.

1019. Goldschmidt, Walter R.
    1943 "Class Denominationalism in Rural California Churches." In *The People, the Land, and the Church in the Rural West: A Study Prepared as a Result of a Series of Conferences.* Chicago, Ill.: Farm Foundation. pp. 117-129.

1020. Goreham, Gary A. and Richard W. Rathge.
      1987 "Impact and Response of Rural Transition on Rural North
            Dakota Churches: An Exploratory Study." Paper
            presented at annual meeting of the Great Plains
            Sociological Association, Brookings, S.Dak., November,
            1987.

1021. Harris, Marshall.
      1949 "Rural Church and Farm Land Tenure; Analytical
            Summary." In Marshall Harris and Joseph Ackerman
            (eds.), *Agrarian Reform and Moral Responsibility: Report of
            an International Conference on the Rural Church and Farm
            Land Tenure.* New York, N.Y.: Agricultural Missions, Inc.
            pp. 1-16.

1022. Hart, John.
      1979 *Rural Ministry in the Eighties: Reflections from Colloquium
            '79.* Des Moines, Iowa: Rural Ministries Institute. 43 pp.

1023. Hays, B.
      1958 "The Role of the Churches and Religions Organizations in
            Rural Development. (condensed version)" In *Conference
            on Rural Development Program Proceedings* pp. 37-41.

1024. Hessel, Dieter T., (ed.).
      1980 *The Agricultural Mission of Churches and Land-Grant
            Universities: A Report of an Informal Consultation.* Informal
            Consultation on the Response of Land-Grant Universities
            to World Hunger. John T. Conner, convener and Dieter
            T. Hessel, editor. Ames, Iowa: Iowa State University
            Press. 146 pp.

1025. Holdredge, Gene R.
      1962 "Two Points of View of the Rural Church." Address
            made at the Group Ministry Conference, W.N.C.
            Commission on Town and Country Work, Hinton
            Memorial Rural Life Center, Hayesville, N.Car.

1026. Holik, John S. and James S. Dorsett.
      1965 "The Rural Church in a Changing Society." Paper
            presented at the Rural Sociology Session of the annual
            meeting of the American Sociological Association,
            Chicago, Ill., 1965.

1027. Holik, John S., Edward W. Hassinger, and Bernadette A. Kulas.
      1983 "Changes in Rural Churches Over a 30 Year
            Period." Paper presented at the annual meeting of the
            Rural Sociological Society, Lexington, Ky., August 17-20,
            1983.

1028. Holik, John S., Edward W. Hassinger, and Bernadette A. Kulas.
      1984 "The Demographic and Social Context of Changes in
            Missouri Rural Church Membership: 1952-1982." Paper
            presented at the annual meeting of the Rural Sociological
            Society, 1984.

1029. Home Missions Council.
      1936 *The Church and the Agricultural Situation.* Report of the
            National Conference on the Rural Church, Ames, Iowa,
            November 23-25, 1936. New York, N.Y.: Home Missions
            Council. 85 pp.

1030. Home Missions Council.
      1944 *Urgent Tasks of the Church in Town and Country.* Report of
            the National Convocation of the Church in Town and
            Country, Elgin, Ill., November 14-16, 1944. New York,
            N.Y.: Committee on Town and Country, Home Missions
            Council of North America, The Federal Council of the
            Churches of Christ in American and the International
            Council of Religious Education. 88 pp.

1031. Home Missions Council.
      1947 *Report of the Third National Convocation of the Church in
            Town and Country.* New York, N.Y.: Committee on Town
            and Country, Home Missions Council of North America,
            The Federal Council of the Churches of Christ in
            America and the International Council of Religious
            Education. 108 pp.

1032. Home Missions Council.
      1947 *The Rural Church in these Moving Times.* Report on the
            National Convocation on the Church in Town and
            Country. Des Moines, Iowa, November 12-14, 1946. New
            York, N.Y.: Committee on Town and Country, Home
            Missions Council of North America, The Federal Council
            of the Churches of Christ in America and the
            International Council of Religious Education. 119 pp.

1033. Home Missions Council.
        1953   *The Redemption of Rural Life.* Report to the National
                Convocation on the Church in Town and Country, St.
                Paul, Minn., October 27-29, 1953. New York, N.Y.:
                Committee on Town and Country, Home Missions
                Council of North America and the Federal Council of
                Churches of Christ in America. 64 pp.

1034. Home Missions Council.
        1954   *A United Christian Witness for Rural America.* Report to the
                National Convocation on the Church in Town and
                Country, Salina Kansas, October 26-28, 1954. New York,
                N.Y.: Committee on Town and Country, Home Missions
                Council of North America and the Federal Council of
                Churches of Christ in America. 79 pp.

1035. Home Mission Council and Council of Women for Home
        Missions.
        1936   *The Rural Church Today and Tomorrow.* Report of the
                National Conference on the Rural Church, Washington,
                D.C., January,1936. New York, N.Y.: The Home Missions
                Council and the Council of Women for Home Missions.
                90 pp.

1036. Hooker, G.E.
        1893   *The Problem of Interdenominational Comity among Country
                Churches in Home Missionary Territory; Christianity
                Practically Applied.* Report of the Chicago Conference of
                the Evangelical Alliance, 1893.

1037. Howard, Robert West, G. Ross Freeman, and James W. Sells.
        1959   *The Bench Mark.* A serendipity about, of, and for the
                American South, developed during the 15th annual
                Church and Community Workshop, Emory University,
                Atlanta, Ga., July 1959. Atlanta, Ga.: Church and
                Community Press. 138 pp.

1038. Humon, S. (chairman).
        1964   "Panel Discussion: Contributions of the Rural Church to
                Purposeful Recreation." In *American Country Life
                Association Proceedings.* 43rd Conference. pp. 25-33.

1039. Hussell, Oscar J.
      1962 *United Presbyterian Mountain Churches--Culture and Christian Education: A Working Paper.* A Report for the Boards of National Missions and Christian Education. New York, N.Y. and Philadelphia, Pa.: United Presbyterian Church, U.S.A.

1040. Hyde, William DeWitt.
      1901 *The Social Mission of the Country Church.* Minutes of the National Council of the Congregational Churches of the United States, Portland, Oreg., October, 1901.

1041. Israel, Henry, (ed.).
      1913 *The Country Church and Community Cooperation.* Third conference in a series by the International Committee of the Young Men's Christian Associations. New York, N.Y.: Association Press. 170 pp.

1042. Israel, Henry, (ed.).
      1919 *The Young Men's Christian Association in Town and Country: The Gist of a National Conference, in which Various Types and Interests of Association and Other Allied Agencies Cooperated.* Held at the Edgewater Beach Hotel, Chicago, Ill., October 18-20, 1928. New York, N.Y.: Association Press. 116 pp.

1043. Johansen, John P.
      1946 *Orientation of the Churches Toward Life in the Great Plains.* Address given at the mid-winter convocation of the Lutheran Theological Seminary, St. Paul, Minn., January 31, 1946. St. Paul, Minn.: Luther Theological Seminary.

1044. Judy, Marvin T., (ed.).
      1961 *Institute on the Church in Town and Country.* Dallas, Tex.: Southern Methodist University Printing Office.

1045. Larson, Robert W., Elwin William Mueller, and Emil F. Wendt.
      1960 *Social Change and Christian Responsibility in Town and Country.* Report of two workshops on social trends in rural America resulting from different land use, Palos Park, Ill., January 16-17, 1957 and February 12-13, 1958. Chicago, Ill.: Division of American Missions, Church in Town and Country, National Lutheran Council. 44 pp.

1046. Long, James S.
       1986   "Growing Responsive Organizations: The Experience of
              Rural Ministry Resources, Inc." Paper presented at the
              American Association for Adult and Continuing
              Education, Hollywood, Fl., October 24, 1986.

1047. Kaufman, Harold F. and Mary B. Whitmarsh, (eds.).
       1957   *The Ministry of Community Improvement.* Proceedings of
              the Ninth Annual Institute for Town and Country
              Leaders. State College, Miss.: Division of Sociology and
              Rural Life. 74 pp.

1048. Martin, A.W.
       1943   "A Philosophy of Rural Work." In *The Methodist Church in
              Town and Country: Proceedings of the National Methodist
              Rural Pastors Conference, Columbus, Ohio, 1943.* New York,
              N.Y.: Department of Town and Country, Methodist
              Church. pp. 18-24.

1049. Medearis, Dale W. (chairman).
       1955   *Christian Stewardship of the Land.* Proceedings of the
              Conference on the Christian Stewardship of the Land
              Held at the Louisville Presbyterian Seminary, Louisville,
              Ky., June 2-4, 1955. New York, N.Y.: Department of
              Town and Country Church, Division of Home Missions,
              National Council of the Churches of Christ in the U.S.A.
              48 pp.

1050. Methodist Church.
       1943   *The Methodist Church in Town and Country. Proceedings of
              the National Methodist Rural Pastors Conference, Columbus,
              Ohio, 1943.* New York, N.Y.: Department of Town and
              Country, Methodist Church. 84 pp.

1051. Methodist Church.
       1946   *Opportunities for Action in the Rural Church: A Study Guide.*
              Committee on Program and Arrangements for the
              National Methodist Rural Life Conference. 48 pp.

1052. Methodist Church.
       1947   *National Methodist Rural Life Conference: Condensed Report.*
              Atlanta, Ga.

1053. Methodist Church.
1951 *Methodists in Town and Country.* Report of the National
Methodist Town and Country Conference, Sioux City,
Iowa, July 21-24, 1951. Mount Vernon, Iowa: The Cornell
College Press. 139 pp.

1054. Methodist Church.
1959 *Emerging Patterns in Town and Country Methodism
Regarding Beliefs, Organization, Leadership, and Outreach.*
Prepared for the National Methodist Town and Country
Conference, Wichita, Kansas, July 21-24, 1959.
Philadelphia, Pa.: Department of Town and Country,
Department of Research and Survey, Division of National
Missions, Board of Missions, Methodist Church. (various
pagings).

1055. Methodist Episcopal Church.
1923 *Rural Leaders' Problems.* Papers presented at the Fourth
Annual Rural Leadership Council, Garrett Biblical
Institute, March 26-31, 1923. Philadelphia, Pa.:
Department of Rural Work, Board of Home Missions and
Church Extension, Methodist Episcopal Church. 141 pp.

1056. Men and Religion Forward Movement.
1912 *The Rural Church.* Revised Reports of the Commissions
Presented at the Congress of the Men and Religion
Forward Movement, April, 1912. New York, N.Y. and
London, England: Funk and Wagnalls. 267 pp.

1057. Mississippi Christian Community Fellowship and the Mississippi
State Univeristy Cooperative Extension Service Cooperating.
1965 *The Less Fortunate in Our Midst.* Seventeenth Annual
Church Leadership Institute, Mississippi State University,
State College, Miss., January 11-13, 1965. State College,
Miss.: Mississippi Christian Community Fellowship and
the Cooperative Extension Service, Mississippi State
University. 62 pp.

1058. Mississippi Christian Community Fellowship and the Mississippi
State Univeristy Cooperative Extension Service Cooperating.
    1966   *Responsible Family Life.* Eighteenth Annual Church
Leadership Institute, Mississippi State University, State
College, Miss., January 24-26, 1966. State College, Miss.:
Mississippi Christian Community Fellowship and the
Cooperative Extension Service, Mississippi State
University. 50 pp.

1059. Mississippi Christian Community Fellowship and the Mississippi
State University Cooperative Extension Service Cooperating.
    1967   *The Church and Poverty.* Nineteenth Annual Church
Leadership Institute, Mississippi State University, State
College, Miss., January 23-25, 1967. State College, Miss.:
Mississippi Christian Community Fellowship and the
Cooperative Extension Service, Mississippi State
University. 47 pp.

1060. Mueller, Elwin William.
    1963   "The Church." In *American Country Life Association
Proceedings.* 42nd Conference. pp. 48-51.

1061. Mueller, Elwin William.
    1970   *New Landmarks: A Series of Papers Dealing with Some of the
Economic, Social, and Spiritual Interests of the American
Farmer.* St. Paul, Minn.: National Catholic Rural Life
Conference. 4 Volumes.

1062. National Catholic Rural Life Conference.
    1935   *Catholic Rural Life Objectives.* Conference held Rochester,
N.Y., October 27, 1935. Des Moines, Iowa: National
Catholic Rural Life Conference.

1063. National Conference on Prevention and Control of Juvenile
Delinquency.
    1947   *Church Responsibilities.* Report No. 14. Conference held in
Washington, D.C. in 1946. Washington, D.C.: Government
Printing Office.

1064. National Council of Churches in Christ in the U.S.A.
    1955 *The Christian Mission in the Rural-Social Process.* Report of the National Convocation on the Church in Town and Country, Springfield, Mass., October 18-20, 1955. New York, N.Y.: Department of the Town and Country Church, Division of Home Missions, National Council of Churches of Christ in the U.S.A. 90 pp.

1065. National Council of Churches in Christ in the U.S.A.
    1956 *New Horizons for Town and Country Churches.* A Report of the National Convocation on the Church in Town and Country, St. Louis, Missouri, October 16-18, 1956. New York, N.Y.: Department of Town and Country Work, National Council of Churches of Christ in the U.S.A. 116 pp.

1066. National Council of Churches of Christ in the U.S.A.
    1960 *In-Service Training Study. Summary of a Conference held in Rye, N.Y., 1958.* New York, N.Y.: Division of Home Missions, Department of Town and Country Church, National Council of Churches of Christ in the U.S.A.

1067. National Council of Churches in Christ in the U.S.A.
    1962 *The Challenge of Change for the Church in Town and Country.* Report to the National Convocation on the Church in Town and Country, Iowa State University, Ames, Iowa, October 16-18, 1962. New York, N.Y.: Committee on Town and Country, Division of Home Missions, National Council of Churches of Christ in the U.S.A. 89 pp.

1068. National Country Life Conference.
    1925 *Religion in Country Life.* Proceedings from the Seventh National Country Life Conference, Columbus, Ohio, 1924. Chicago, Ill.: University of Chicago Press. 216 pp.

1069. National Lutheran Council.
    1965 *Thoughts Before Action.* Glenburn Area Workshop, Glenburn, N.Dak., October 11-13, 1965. Chicago, Ill.: National Lutheran Council. 23 pp.

1070. National Lutheran Council.
    1943 *Papers Presented at the Lutheran Home Missions Conference on Christ for Town and Country, Decorah, Iowa, October 27-28, 1943.* Chicago, Ill.: Division of American Missions, National Lutheran Council.

1071. National Lutheran Council.
    1953   *The Rural Congregation and Community Health.* Report of a
           rural health workshop, Wartburg Theological Seminary,
           Dubuque, Iowa, June 24-26, 1952. Chicago, Ill.: R. C.
           Thune. 58 pp.

1072. National Lutheran Council.
    1954   *Lutheran Church in the Upper Great Plains.* Conference in
           Hettinger, N.Dak., February 24-26, 1954. Chicago, Ill.:
           National Lutheran Council. 80 pp.

1073. National Lutheran Council.
    1955   *Lutheran Home Missions Conference, Decorah, Iowa, 1954.*
           Chicago, Ill.: Division of American Missions, National
           Lutheran Council.

1074. National Lutheran Council.
    1955   *Christ for Town and Country.* Report on the National
           Lutheran Council Home Missions Conference, Iowa.
           Chicago, Ill.: Division of American Missions, National
           Lutheran Council. 92 pp.

1075. National Lutheran Council.
    1957   *Local Workshop Report for Seven Northeastern Nebraska
           Counties.* Chicago, Ill.: Division of American Missions,
           National Lutheran Council. 20 pp.

1076. National Lutheran Council.
    1957   *The Lutheran Church in the Timberland Area: Minnesota,
           Wisconsin, and the Upper Peninsula of Michigan*: Conference
           at Grand Rapids, Mich., February 7-8, 1957 and at
           Phillips, Wis., February 11-12, 1957. Chicago, Ill.: Division
           of American Missions, National Lutheran Council. 130
           pp.

1077. National Lutheran Council.
    1958   *The Lutheran Church in Brenham Conference, Texas.* Chicago,
           Ill.: Division of American Missions, National Lutheran
           Council. 63 pp.

1078. National Lutheran Council.
    1958   *Town and Country Workshop*: Randolph, Nebr., November
           11, 1957. Chicago, Ill.: National Lutheran Council.

1079. National Lutheran Council.
1959 *Sunrise on the Flatlands of Northern Minnesota.* Chicago, Ill.:
Division of American Missions, National Lutheran
Council. 56 pp.

1080. National Lutheran Council.
1959 *The Lutheran Church in the Eastern Pennsylvanian
Countryside.* Chicago, Ill.: Division of American Missions,
National Lutheran Council. 68 pp.

1081. National Lutheran Council.
1959 *Town and Country Workshop.* Round Top, Tex., September
29-30, 1958. Chicago, Ill.: National Lutheran Council.

1082. National Lutheran Council.
1959 *Town and Country Workshop, Western Conference, Ohio.*
Chicago, Ill.: Division of American Missions, National
Lutheran Council. 80 pp.

1083. National Lutheran Council.
1960 *The Lutheran Church in Southern Iowa.* Chicago, Ill.:
Division of American Missions, National Lutheran
Council. 110 pp.

1084. National Lutheran Council.
1961 *Mid-Nebraska Town and Country Workshop.* Chicago, Ill.:
Division of American Missions, National Lutheran
Council. 57 pp.

1085. National Lutheran Council.
1961 *Northeastern Montana Town and Country Workshop.*
Conference at Sidney, Mont., March 20-21, 1961. Chicago,
Ill.: Division of American Missions, National Lutheran
Council. 52 pp.

1086. National Lutheran Council.
1962 *New Thousands in Town and Country: The Church's Concern
for Communities with a Rural Nonfarm Population in the
Northeast U.S.A.* A report of a workshop held at
Gettysburg College, Gettysburg, Pa., June 27-29, 1961.
Chicago, Ill.: Church in Town and Country, National
Lutheran Council. 127 pp.

1087. National Lutheran Council.
    1962 *The Northeast Sandhills Area Workshop.* North Platte,
          Nebr., October 11-12, 1962. American Lutheran Church,
          Lutheran Church in America, and Lutheran Church-
          Missouri Synod--Sponsors in cooperation with the Church
          in Town and Country, National Lutheran Council.
          Chicago, Ill.: National Lutheran Council.

1088. National Lutheran Council.
    1963 *West of the Cascades Workshop.* Conference at Corbett,
          Oreg., February 18-19, 1963. Chicago, Ill.: National
          Lutheran Council.

1089. National Lutheran Council.
    1965 *Your Church and Community in a Changing Illinois.*
          Conference at Pontiac, Ill., February 14-15, 1965. Chicago,
          Ill.: National Lutheran Council.

1090. National Lutheran Council.
    1966 *Church and Community Development in Southern Indiana.*
          Town and Country Area Workshop, Cortland, Ind.,
          September 19-20, 1966. Chicago, Ill.: National Lutheran
          Council.

1091. National Lutheran Council.
    1966 *Studying Our Mission in the Mountains.* Town and
          Country Area Workshop, Franklin, W.Va., September 11-
          12, 1966. Chicago, Ill.: National Lutheran Council.

1092. National Methodist Rural Life Conference.
    1947 *Committee Reports of the Eight Study Groups from the
          National Methodist Rural Life Conference, Lincoln, Nebraska,
          July 29-31, 1947.* n.p.: Methodist Church.

1093. Nesius, Ernest J.
    1966 "The Role of the Church in Appalachia." In *Proceedings--
          Commission on Religion in Appalachia, 1966.* October 18,
          1966. Knoxville, Tenn.: Commission on Religion in
          Appalachia, Inc.

1094. Norris, Merlin K., (ed.).
    1964 *The Dubuque Conference in Perspective.* Chicago, Ill.:
          National Lutheran Council.

1095. North Carolina State University.
 1969 *Religion and Social Change: A Series of Seminars.* Raleigh,
 N.Car.: Agricultural Policy Institute, School of Agriculture
 and Life Sciences, North Carolina State University. 209
 pp.

1096. North Dakota State University Cooperative Extension Service.
 1971 *Community in Change--A Curse or Challenge?* Proceedings
 of Lay-Clergy Seminar for Pastors and Church Leaders,
 Fargo, N.Dak., February 1-3, 1971. Fargo, N.Dak.: North
 Dakota State University. (various pagings)

1097. Northeast Country Church Associations.
 1909 *Proceedings of the Conference on the Problems of the Rural
 Church in New England.* Meeting held in Boston, Mass.,
 January 18-19, 1909.

1098. Nunn, Alexander.
 1954 *The New South: Its Agriculture.* Twentieth Anniversary
 Ministers' Week, Candler School of Theology, Emory
 University. Atlanta, Ga.:Emory University.

1099. Obenhaus, V.
 1961 "The Gap between the Churches and Agriculture." In
 National Farm Institute Proceedings. pp. 126-135.

1100. Ogg, W.E.
 1967 "Economic Foundations for Achieving Quality of Life."
 In *American Country Life Association Proceedings.* July 11-12,
 1967. pp 45-48.

1101. Pennsylvania Council of Churches in cooperation with
 Pennsylvania State University.
 1960 *Churches Serve the Changing Community.* Proceedings of
 the Conference on Church and Community, University
 Park, Pa., July 5-8, 1960. University Park, Pa.:
 Pennsylvania State University. 68 pp.

1102. Pennsylvania Rural Progress Association.
 1912 *Proceedings of the Pennsylvania Rural Progress Association.*
 Conference under the auspices of the Pennsylvania
 Society for Promoting Agriculture, March 14-16, 1912,
 Philadelphia, Pa. Williamsport, Pa.: Grit Press. 224 pp.

1103. Pepper, Clayton A.
    1959 *American Baptist Town and Country Sourcebook*. For use at
          the Third American Baptist Convocation on Church in
          Town and Country, Ames, Iowa, July 28-31, 1952. New
          York, N.Y.: American Baptist Home Missions Societies. 25
          pp.

1104. Randolph, Henry S.
    1956 "The Church's Interest." In *American Country Life
          Association Proceedings* 35: 33-34.

1105. Raper, Arthur Franklin.
    1948 *Land Policy and Church Stability*. Report of Commission
          Number 3 of the National Methodist Rural Life
          Conference, Lincoln, Nebr. New York, N.Y.: Department
          of Town and Country Work, Division of Home Missions
          and Church Extension, Methodist Church. 35 pp.

1106. Rapking, Aaron H.
    1943 "Implications of the Protestant Rural Convocation for the
          Methodist Church." In *The Methodist Church in Town and
          Country*. National Methodist Rural Pastors Conference,
          Columbus, Ohio, 1943. New York, N.Y.: Methodist
          Church, Department of Town and Country. pp. 52-54.

1107. Rapking, Aaron H.
    1943 "The Church and the Land." In *The People, the Land, and
          the Church in the Rural West: A Study Prepared as a Result
          of a Series of Conferences*. Chicago, Ill.: Farm Foundation.
          pp. 151-158.

1108. Rathge, Richard W. and Gary A. Goreham.
    1987 "The Influence of Economic and Demographic Factors on
          Rural Church Viability." Paper presented at the annual
          meeting of the Midwest Sociological Society, Chicago, Ill.,
          April 1987.

1109. Raven, C.E.
    1946 *Towards a Christian Community*. Rural Life Conference
          Report. 2:43-46.

1110. *Report of the First Rural Life Conference*.
    1913 Rural Life Conference held at State College of
          Washington, Pullman, Wash., June 10-18, 1913.

1111. Richardson, Harry V.
1963 "Glory Past and Present." Address to the Methodist Rural Fellowship Banquet, Quadrennial National Methodist Conference on the Church in Town and Country. Delivered July 8, 1963, Minneapolis, Minn.

1112. Quinn, Bernard, (ed.).
1968 *Ecumenical Planning for Mission in Town and Country America.* Catholic Perspectives on the Concerns of the National Consultation on the Church in Community Life, Ohio State University, September 5-8, 1967. Town and Country Report No. 3. Washington, D.C.: Center for Applied Research in the Apostolate. 83 pp.

1113. Sample, Tex.
1988 "Why Save Rural America: A Theological/Ethical Perspective." Paper presented at the annual meeting of the Rural Sociological Society, Athens, Ga., August, 1988. 17 pp.

1114. Schweitzer, H.J.
1984 "Factors Related to Discontinuing a Church Leadership Program after Fifty Years of Commitment." Paper presented at the annual meeting of the Rural Sociological Society, College Station, Tex., August 24, 1984. 9 pp.

1115. Sells, James William, (ed.).
1943 *The Methodist Church in Town and Country, Proceedings of the National Methodist Rural Pastors Conference.* Conference held in Columbus, Ohio, September 8-9, 1943. New York, N.Y.: Department of Town and Country Work, The Methodist Church. 84 pp.

1116. Sells, James William, (ed.).
1944 *The Methodist Church in Town and Country.* Proceedings of the National Methodist Rural Pastors Conference, Elgin, Illinois, November 15-17, 1944. New York, N.Y.: Department of Town and Country Work, Methodist Rural Fellowship. 60 pp.

1117. Sells, James William, (ed.).
1946 *Both Harvest and Seed, Gathered from the School for Town and Country Ministers, July, 1946.* Atlanta, Ga.: Candler School of Theology, Emory University. 127 pp.

1118. Simcoe, Mary A.
        1981   "The Rural Parish." In Mark Searle (ed.), *Parish: A Place
               for Worship*. Papers from the Ninth Annual Conference of
               the Notre Dame Center for Pastoral Liturgy, University
               of Notre Dame, June 16-19, 1980. Collegeville, Minn.:
               Liturgical Press. pp. 137-154.

1119. Smith, John Patrick.
        1985   "'Outward, Christian Soldier': The Attempted Overlay of
               Farm Modernization Upon Rural Churches in Post-
               Progressive America." Paper presented at the annual
               meeting of the Rural Sociological Society, 1985.

1120. Smith, John Patrick.
        1988   "Rural Open Country Churches: Four Decades of Change
               and Continuity." Paper presented at the annual meeting
               of the Rural Sociological Society, Athens, Ga., August 19-
               23, 1988.

1121. Smith, Rockwell C.
        1943   "A Vital Rural Church Program." In *The Methodist Church
               in Town and Country: Proceedings of the National Methodist
               Rural Pastors Conference, Columbus, Ohio, 1943*. New York,
               N.Y.: Department of Town and Country, Methodist
               Church. pp. 25-34.

1122. Southern Baptist Convention.
        1966   *Nationwide Rural Church Conference*. Atlanta, Ga.: Rural-
               Urban Missions Department, Division of Missions,
               Southern Baptist Convention.

1123. Southern Rural Life Council.
        1947   *The Church and Rural Community Living in the South*.
               Report of the Church Committee, Second Southern Rural
               Life Conference. Nashville, Tenn.: George Peabody
               College for Teachers, Southern Rural Life Council. 39 pp.

1124. Suggs, Patricia Kaylor and Vira Rodgers Kivett.
        1985   "The Significance of Perceived Importance of Religion to
               the Morale of Older Rural-Transitional Adults." Paper
               presented at the International Congress of Gerontology,
               New York, N.Y., July 1985.

1125. Taves, M.J.
       1960   "The Rural Church in 1965." In *American Country Life
              Association Proceedings* 39: 15-27.

1126. Tetreau, E.D.
       1943   "Conditions Affecting the Rural Church in Arizona." In
              *The People, the Land, and the Church in the Rural West: A
              Study Prepared as a Result of a Series of Conferences.*
              Chicago, Ill.: Farm Foundation. pp. 131-135.

1127. *The Challenge of Change for the Church in Town and Country.*
       1962   National Convocation on the Church in Town and
              Country, October 16-18, 1962. Ames, Iowa: Iowa State
              University.

1128. United Church of Christ.
       1963   *The Church and Culture in Crisis in Town and Country.*
              Report of the Town and Country Convocation of the
              United Church of Christ, Heidelberg College, Tiffin, Ohio,
              August 27-29, 1963. St. Louis, Mo.: Department of the
              Church in Town and Country, Division of Church
              Extension, United Church Board for Homeland Ministries.
              117 pp.

1129. University of Illinois Cooperative Extension Service.
       1965   *Illinois in Transition.* Proceedings of the Illinois State of
              Society Conference for Church Leaders, December 7-9,
              1965. Urbana, Ill.: Cooperative Extension Service,
              University of Illinois. 144 pp.

1130. University of Illinois Cooperative Extension Service and the
       Illinois Town and Country Church Institute Committee
       Cooperating.
       1965   *The Church Faces Poverty.* Proceedings of the Thirty-Fifth
              Rural Pastors' and Lay Leaders' Short Course, Urbana,
              Ill., February 8-10, 1965. Urbana, Ill.: Cooperative
              Extension Service, University of Illinois. 100 pp.

1131. University of Illinois Cooperative Extension Service and the
       Illinois Town and Country Church Institute Committee
       Cooperating.
       1966   *The Family in Transition.* Proceedings of the Thirty-Sixth
              Town and Country Institute, Urbana, Ill., January 31-
              February 2, 1966. Urbana, Ill.: Cooperative Extension
              Service, University of Illinois. 69 pp.

1132. University of Minnesota, Department of Agriculture.
    1947 *Rural Church Institute Papers and Discussion.* University
    Farm, St. Paul, Minn., May 5-9, 1947. St. Paul, Minn.:
    Department of Agriculture, University of Minnesota.

1133. University of Nebraska.
    1964 *Toward a Deeper Understanding of Our Town and Country
    Communities.* State of Society Conference for Church
    Leaders, November 17-19, 1964. Lincoln, Nebr.: Nebraska
    Center for Continuing Education, University of Nebraska.
    (various pagings)

1134. University of Wisconsin College of Agriculture in Cooperation
    with the National Catholic Rural Life Conference, National
    Lutheran Council, and Wisconsin Council of Churches.
    1963 *Community Development in Rural Areas.* Conference for
    Town and Country Pastors, University of Wisconsin,
    Madison, July 15-18, 1963. Madison, Wis.: University of
    Wisconsin. (various paging)

1135. University of Wisconsin College of Agriculture in Cooperation
    with the National Catholic Rural Life Conference, National
    Lutheran Council, and Wisconsin Council of Churches.
    1964 *The Role of the Church in Community Economic Development.*
    Conference for Town and Country Pastors, University of
    Wisconsin, Madison, July 13-16, 1964. Madison, Wis.:
    University of Wisconsin. 125 pp.

1136. University of Wisconsin College of Agriculture in Cooperation
    with the National Catholic Rural Life Conference, National
    Lutheran Council, and Wisconsin Council of Churches.
    1965 *The Changing Small Community.* Conference for Town and
    Country Pastors, University of Wisconsin, Madison, July
    26-30, 1965. Madison, Wis.: University of Wisconsin. 128
    pp.

1137. Virginia Polytechnic Institute.
    1961 *The Town and Country Church in an Era of Rapid Change.*
    The Lecture Series of the 1961 Virginia Summer School
    for Town and Country Ministers, Blacksburg, Va., July 3-
    7, 1961. Blacksburg, Va.: Virginia Polytechnic Institute.
    (various pagings)

1138. Vizzard, J.L.
   1958 "Mobilizing Spiritual and Philosophical Forces for Better
         Country Living." In *American Country Life Association
         Proceedings* 37: 34-40.

1139. Voelker, S.W.
   1965 "Effects of Population Trends on Churches in the
         Northern Great Plains." In *State Conference of Church
         Leaders, Proceedings, 1964.* n.p. pp. 111-123.

1140. Vogt, Paul Leroy, (ed.).
   1916 *The Church and Country Life.* Report of a Conference held
         by the Commission on Church and Country Life under
         the authority of the Federal Council of Churches of
         Christ in America, Columbus, Ohio, December 8-10, 1915.
         New York, N.Y. Missionary Education Movement of the
         United States and Canada. 273 pp.

1141. Vogt, Paul Leroy.
   1943 "Summary of Interviews." In *The People, the Land, and the
         Church in the Rural West: A Study Prepared as a Result of a
         Series of Conferences.* Chicago, Ill.: Farm Foundation. pp.
         137-149.

1142. Weber, Cheryl A. and Christopher N. Hunt.
   1985 "As Assessment of the Black Church's Role in Rural
         Development." Paper presented at the annual meeting of
         the Southern Association of Agricultural Scientists, Rural
         Sociology Section, 1985.

1143. Weber, Leonard, Bernard F. Evans, and Gregory D. Cusock,
       (eds.).
   1987 *Theology of the Land.* Papers presented at the First
         Theology of the Land Conference, St. John's University,
         Minn., 1985. Collegeville, Minn.: Liturgical Press. 126 pp.

1144. Wileden, Arthur F.
   1959 "Community Adjustment and Planning in Northern
         Wisconsin." Presented at the Trees for Tomorrow Camp,
         July 23, 1959.

1145. Wileden, Arthur F.
   1966 "Forty-Five Years of Church Leaders Conferences in
         Wisconsin". Paper presented at the Town and Country
         Church Leaders Conference, Madison, Wis., July 27, 1966.

1146. Wileden, Arthur F.
      1966   "Report of the Subcommittee on Research and Evaluation
             of the Committee on Continuing Education for Town and
             Country Pastors at Land-Grant Universities." Presented in
             Chicago, Ill., September 8, 1966.

1147. Willits, Fern K., Donald M. Crider, and E. Parfait Eloundou.
      1988   "Adolescent Participation in the Nonmetropolitan Church:
             Findings from a Pennsylvania Survey." Paper presented
             at the annual meeting of the Rural Sociological Society,
             Athens, Ga., August 19-23, 1988.

1148. Wilson, Edgar E.
      1943   "The Rural Church as an Instrument of Social
             Democracy." In *The People, the Land, and the Church in the
             Rural West: A Study Prepared as a Result of a Series of
             Conferences*. Chicago, Ill.: Farm Foundation. pp. 159-172.

1149. Young Men's Christian Associations, Country Work Department.,
      (ed.).
      1911   *The Rural Church and Community Betterment*. Minutes of
             the Rural Church Conference, New York, N.Y., December
             1, 1910. New York, N.Y.: Association Press. 136 pp.

1150. Young Men's Christian Associations.
      1912   *The Country Church and Rural Welfare*. Second conference
             in a series by the International Young Men's Christian
             Association. New York, N.Y.: Association Press. 152 pp.

Periodical,
Newspaper, and
Magazine Articles

Periodical, Magazine, and Newspaper Articles

1151. "A Chance for the Country Church."
1910 *The Presbyterian Advocate* (September 8).

1152. "A Country Church Program Developing Our Time of War Needs."
1919 *Rural Manhood* (January): 19.

1153. "A Reading List on the Town and Country Church and Related Subjects."
1947 *Town and Country Church* (February): 12-13.

1154. Abele, E.F.
1947 "The Country Church Plays Prominent Part in Life of Rural Communities." *Boonville Advertiser* (July 25): 24.

1155. Ackerman, Joseph.
1946 "The Social Values of Land Ownership." *Christian Rural Fellowship Bulletin* (111): 1-11.

1156. Ackerman, Joseph.
1948 "Practical Ideals for Rural Living." *Christian Rural Fellowship Bulletin* (134): 1-8.

1157. Ackerman, Joseph.
1951 "Rural Community Ideals." *Christian Rural Fellowship Bulletin* (159): 1-8.

1158. Ackley, C.W.
1949 "The Importance of the Individual in the Rural Church." *Town and Country Church* (May): 8.

1159. Achtemeier, A.R.
1961 "The Mission to the Church." *Town and Country Church* (September/October): 5-6, 15.

1160. "Action in the Farm Towns."
   1967 *Christian Advocate* (October 5): 2.

1161. Adams, H.B.
   1959 "The Mission of the Church." *Town and Country Church* (March): 1-4.

1162. Ahn, G.B., Jr.
   1946 "Rural Life Sunday." *Town and Country Church* (April): 4.

1163. Akers, A.
   1949 "Consolidation Saved Their Church." *Progressive Farmer* (Texas edition) (April): 70.

1164. Alexander, D.
   1950 "Warren County Group Ministry." *Garrett Biblical Institute's Rural Church* (December/January 1951): 5-6.

1165. Alexander, T.D.
   1952 "The Sharecropper's Pastor." *Town and Country Church* (March): 1-2.

1166. Allen, T.B.
   1962 "The Home Church." *Town and Country Church* (March/April): 9-10.

1167. Allen, W.S.
   1963 "Ministers Spread Stewardship Message as Conservation District Chaplains." *Soil Conservation* 28(May): 228-230.

1168. Allred, B.W.
   1949 "Conservation and the Church." *Southwestern Crop and Stock* (July): 7, 50-53.

1169. Almack, R.B. and Lawrence M. Hepple.
   1951 "Religion in Dent County, Missouri." *Town and Country Church* (December): 7-8.

1170. Alward, R.S.
   1958 "Red Barns and White Churches." *Hoard's Dairyman* (December 25): 1246-1247.

1171. Anderson, L.
   1946 "Leadership Training in South Dakota." *Town and Country Church* (December): 6-7.

1172. Anderson, W.A.
   1946 "The Challenge of Tomorrow's Rural Life." *Christian Rural Fellowship Bulletin* (114): 1-8.

1173. Anderson, W.A.
1949 "Objectives for Rural Christian Work." *Christian Rural Fellowship Bulletin* (141): 1-7.

1174. Andrew, B.
1959 "The New England Town and Country Church Commission." *Town and Country Church* (September): 10-11.

1175. Andrew, B.
1965 "The Lunenburg Concept: An Alternative to Federated, Community, and Yoked Churches." *Town and Country Church* (March/April): 5-7.

1176. Anthony, Alfred Williams.
1899 "The Problem of the New England Country Church." *Homiletic Review* (July): 23-29.

1177. Archibald, R.M.
1949 "Advertising in the Rural Church." *Town and Country Church* (October): 1-2.

1178. Armitstead, A.H.
1954 "Visual Aids in the Rural Church." *Town and Country Church* (April): 8-9.

1179. Armstrong, A.M.
1960 "Summer Service--Youth Work." *Town and Country Church* (May): 6-7.

1180. Armstrong, Harry P.
1911 "The Story of Middle Creek." *Rural Manhood* (February): 54-55.

1181. Armstrong, Robert Grenville.
1939 "The City Church's Stake in Rural Religion." *Christian Rural Fellowship Bulletin* (39): 1-4.

1182. Armstrong, Robert Grenville.
1939 "Enduring Values in Rural Life." *Christian Rural Fellowship Bulletin* (46): 1-4.

1183. Armstrong, Robert Grenville.
1945 "New Hampshire Commissions a Minister for Life Work in Rural Areas." *Town and Country Church* (15): 4.

1184. Arthur, C. Ralph.
1953 "Interdenominational Country Rural Life Institutes in Virginia." *Town and Country Church* (February): 12-13.

1185. Arterburn, Joe.
1987 "Church Activists Bring Farm Crisis to Court: Iowa Trial Highlights Plight of Small Farms." *National Catholic Reporter* 23(April 10): 24.

1186. "As We Are in the Country Church."
1952 *The Modern Churchman* 42: 343-349. (Reprint from *The Layman*, 1952.)

1187. Ash, R.J.
1965 "When is a Church Too Small?" *Christian Advocate* 9(August 12): 20.

1188. Atwater, Amy.
1937 "A Plain Farmer's Religion." *Christian Rural Fellowship Bulletin* (19): 1-2.

1189. Austin, Herbert Wendell.
1945 "The Country Church School Meets Summer." *Church School* (June).

1190. Austin, Richard C.
1964 "Mission in Rural Depressed Areas." *Town and Country Church*. (September-October): 4-7.

1191. Aylesworth, Phillip F.
1967 "The Relationship of Church and Government Programs." *Town and Country Church* (January-February): 5-6.

1192. Aylesworth, Phillip F.
1960 "In-Service Training Opportunities for Town and Country Pastors at Land-Grant Colleges." *Town and Country Church* (March): 11-13.

1193. Aylesworth, Phillip F.
1967 "The Relationship between Church and Government Problems." *Town and Country Church* (January/February): 5-6.

1194. Baepler, F.H., G. Schler, and C. Burkhardt.
1952 "Ministers Discuss Problems which Face Rural Churches of America." *Boonville Advertiser* (July 25): 2, 98.

1195. Bailey, Liberty Hyde.
1935 "The Holy Earth." *Christian Rural Fellowship Bulletin* (1): 1-4.

1196. Bailey, Liberty Hyde.
1954 "What is Democracy?" *Christian Rural Fellowship Bulletin* (191): 1-4.

1197. Bailey, R.W.G.
1948 "Types of Rural Church Cooperation." *Town and Country Church* (December): 7-9.

1198. Bailey, W.L.
1948 "'The Christian Year' in a Country Parish." *Town and Country Church* (September): 10-11.

1199. Bailey, W.L.
1948 "Wordsworth's Ideal Country Pastor: The Rev. Robert Walker, 1709-1802." *Town and Country Church* (December): 10-11.

1200. Baird, E.C.
1954 "An Adequate Program for the Rural Church." *Cumberland Seminarian* 1(Spring).

1201. Baird, E.C.
1962 "Don't Write Off the Town and Country Church!" *Town and Country Church* (September/October): 6-7, 13.

1202. Baker, O.E.
1936 "Rural and Urban Philosophies." *Christian Rural Fellowship Bulletin* (10): 1-4.

1203. Bane, Lita.
1951 "Vision and Values in Today's Rural Home Life." *Christian Rural Fellowship Bulletin* (162): 1-5.

1204. Barnes, E.W.
1957 "New Strength for the Rural Church." *Town and Country Church* (April): 1-3.

1205. Barnes, E.W.
1957 "Where Are Our Adults?" *Town and Country Church* (May): 5-6.

1206. Barnes, J.B.
1957 "Is Your Local Church 'Community Minded?'" *Town and Country Church* (October): 2-4.

1207. Barnes, J.B.
1957 "The Local Church: A Force or a Farce in Community Improvement?" *Town and Country Church* (September): 1-2.

1208. Bartholomew, A C.
        1948 "A Community Survey." *Town and Country Church*
        (February): 6.

1209. Baur, R.C.
        1949 "The Blessing of the Land." *Nature Magazine* (April): 167-
        169.

1210. Becker, Edwin L.
        1946 "How to Prepare for the Rural Ministry." *Town and Country
        Church* (February): 1-2.

1211. Becker, Edwin L.
        1949 "The Challenge of Rural America to a United Evangelistic
        Advance." *Town and Country Church* (January): 5-6.

1212. Becker, Edwin L.
        1949 "The Church and the Country." *Town and Country Church*
        (April): 2-3.

1213. Becker, Edwin L.
        1950 "The Challenge of the Rural-Nonfarm Population to the
        Churches." *Town and Country Church* (February): 3-4.

1214. Becker, Edwin L.
        1952 "Christian Faith and Community." *Christian Rural Fellowship
        Bulletin* (178): 1-4.

1215. Becker, Edwin L.
        1953 "The Rural Church and Evangelism." *Town and Country
        Church* (March): 1-2.

1216. Bedford, A. Goff.
        1980 "Social Impressions of a Country Pastor in the Kentucky
        Bluegrass Region." *Lexington Theological Quarterly*
        15(January): 6-18.

1217. Bedier, J.
        1954 "Rural Parish in Vermont." *Commonwealth* (April 23): 64-67.

1218. Bemies, Charles Otto.
        1913 "The Rural Pastor: A Community Builder." *Rural Manhood*
        4: 36-38.

1219. Bence, Evelyn.
        1986 "Assisting Hard-Hit Farm Families." *Christianity Today* 30(8):
        34-36.

1220. Bensley, Martha and Robert Bruce.
        1915 "The Church of the Fat Land." *Outlook* (March 24).

1221. Bensley, Martha and Robert Bruce.
1915 "The Church of the Lean Land." *Outlook* (April 28).

1222. Bensley, Martha and Robert Bruce.
1915 "The Church of the Other Six Days." *Outlook* (May 26).

1223. Berreth, E.O.
1952 "Fringe-Area Church." *Town and Country Church* (January): 1-2.

1224. Best, K.
1947 "'Hi, Brother Gene'" Missouri's Dynamic Extension Minister Has Found a Way to Reestablish the Rural Church as the Cornerstone of American Life." *Country Life* 117(April): 27, 108-110, 112.

1225. Betts, C.E.
1962 "Revitalizing Architecture for the Town and Country Church." *Town and Country Church* (September/October): 14-15.

1226. Bewer, Julius A.
1938 "The Significance of Land in the Old Testament." *Christian Rural Fellowship Bulletin* (35): 1-5.

1227. Beyer, R.F.
1948 "A United Church Canvass in Vermont." *Town and Country Church* (February): 7-8.

1228. Black, C.M.
1966 "Rural Youth Define the Church's Nature and Mission." *Rural Church* 28(October/December): 2-6.

1229. Biddle, W.W.
1964 "Church and Community Development." *Christian Century* 81(January 22): 106-108.

1230. Biglow, W.B.
1897 "The Country Church in America." *Scribner's Magazine* (November).

1231. "Bishops Say Farming, Land Traditions Must be Rescued."
1985 *National Catholic Reporter* 21(May 17): 7.

1232. Blizzard, S.W., Jr.
       1952 "Problems in Meeting Religious Needs in the Rural-Urban
       Fringe." *Christian Rural Fellowship Bulletin* (172): 1-8.
       Excerpts printed in *Town and Country Church* (April, 1952):
       10-11.

1233. Blizzard, Samuel W.
       1953 "The Church in the Rural-Urban Fringe." *Town and Country
       Church* (February): 3-4.

1234. Blizzard, Samuel W.
       1953 "The Religious Situation in the Rural-Urban Fringe."
       Christian Rural Fellowship Bulletin (185): 1-6.

1235. Blizzard, Samuel W.
       1953 "The Rural Church as an Integrating Institution." *Christian
       Rural Fellowship Bulletin* (183): 1-4.

1236. Blizzard, Samuel W.
       1954 "The Church and Its Community." *Shane Quarterly* 15: 153-
       168.

1237. Boaz, Roy D.
       1952 "A Rural Faith for Today." *Christian Rural Fellowship
       Bulletin* (174): 1-4.

1238. Boesch, T.L.
       1943 "The Cry of the Impoverished Farmer." *Christian Rural
       Fellowship Bulletin* (81): 1-8. Reprint from *Outlook of Missions*
       (November, 1941).

1239. Bohlman, Philip V.
       1984 "Hymnody in the Rural German-American Community in
       the Upper Midwest." *The Hymn* 35(July): 158-164.

1240. Bohanan, Luther B.
       1948 "Financing the Rural Churches of the Southern Baptist
       Convention--A Problem and Its Solution." *Christian Rural
       Fellowship Bulletin* (131): 1-7.

1241. Bole, C.
       1956 "Church Building." *Town and Country Church* (February): 12.

1242. Bonsack, Charles D.
       1937 "Agriculture as a Way of Life--The Point of View of the
       Church of the Brethren." *Christian Rural Fellowship Bulletin*
       (27, Part 4): 1-4.

1243. Bonsack, Charles D.
    1938 "Nature Speaks of God." *Christian Rural Fellowship Bulletin*
    (36): 1-4.

1244. Boycott, W.S.
    1954 "Christ and the Land: An English Farmer Speaks."
    Christian Rural Fellowship Bulletin (197): 1-7.

1245. Boycott, W.S.
    1955 "The Theology of the Land." *Christian Rural Fellowship*
    Bulletin (201): 1-6.

1246. Boyer, Gerald S.
    1945 "The Challenge of the Rural Church." *Evangelical Messenger*
    (June 2).

1247. Boyle, James E.
    1904 "The Passing of the Country Church." *The Outlook* (May
    28): 230-234.

1248. Bradshaw, J. and N. Yourchik.
    1963 "Mormons Soil-Water Stewards for More than a Century."
    Soil Conservation 28(May): 239-240.

1249. Bradshaw, V. and H. Bradshaw.
    1949 "Famous Country Churches." *Successful Farming* (May): 110-
    114.

1250. Bradshaw, V.D.
    1958 "The Dale Hollow Larger Parish." *Town and Country Church*
    (April): 1-4.

1251. Bradshaw, V.D.
    1960 "The Church in Areas of Out-Migration." *Town and Country*
    Church. (January/February): 20-21,27.

1252. Branch, H.
    1959 "The Minister and Rural Development." *Town and Country*
    Church (September): 1-2.

1253. Branyon, J.
    1949 "The Farmer and His Religion." *Alabama Farmer* (October):
    6,14.

1254. Brewer, Earl D.C.
    1959 "Research in Religion in the Southern Appalachians." *Town*
    and Country Church (September): 9.

1255. Brewer, Earl D.C.
    1964 "Religion in Relation to Southern Growth." *Agricultural Policy Review* 4(October/December): 10-11.

1256. Brewer, Earl D.C.
    1967 "Our Small Country Churches: Must They Die?" *Together: For Methodist Families* 11(September): 16-19.

1257. Bristow, W.M.
    1956 "The Church and Young Farmers' Clubs." *Rural Life* (August): 12-13.

1258. Brown, Carolyn and Stephen H. Brown.
    1983 "Myths About Education in Small Membership Churches." *Church School Today* (Summer).

1259. Brown, Sherri.
    1986 "The Farm Crisis: Harvest of Tears." *MissionsUSA* (July-August): 2-27.

1260. Browne, N.
    1954 "Catholic Action and the Rural Movement." *Rural Life* (April): 4.

1261. Brown, L. Maxwell.
    1961 "The Rural Clergy." *Christian Rural Fellowship Bulletin* (226): 1-16.

1262. Brubaker, D.L.
    1951 "Clergyman Raps Cannery Farming." *Prairie Farmer* (Illinois edition). (July 21): 5.

1263. Brunson, H.O.
    1950 "How One Farm Church Paid Off Its Debt." *Successful Farming* (June): 30, 81.

1264. Buck, Roy C.
    1958 "The Contribution of the Church to the Total Community." *Town and Country Church* (December): 5-7.

1265. Buck, Roy C.
    1960 "The Value Problem in Rural Community Development." *Christian Rural Fellowship Bulletin* (220): 1-8.

1266. Buie, T.S.
    1945 "Better Rural Churches through Wise Land Use." *Better Crops* (January): 10-16.

1267. Buie, T.S.
    1945 "Poorland Churches." *Land* 4(1): 45-48.

1268. Bull, Wilbur I.
    1954 "Democracy in Religion." *Town and Country Church* (May):
    1-3.

1269. Bullard, F. Laurison.
    1913 "A Traveling Library for Rural Ministers." *Rural Manhood* 4:
    56.

1270. Burckart, Julia.
    1985 "Plantation Christianity: Religious Practice and Moral
    Attitudes Among Louisiana Sugar Cane Workers, 1982."
    Mid-America Folklore 13(2): 12-17.

1271. Burkholder, Lawrence.
    1987 "The Mennonite Church and the Farm Crisis in Ontario."
    Conrad Grebel Review 5(Winter): 51-63. Reply by L. B.
    Siemerns. *Conrad Grebel Review* 5(Spring): 156-160.

1272. Burkholder, Lawrence.
    1987 "Trouble and Tenacity Down on the Farm." *Leadership*
    8(Summer): 36-37.

1273. Burr, Ernest W.
    1916 "Rural Religious Problems." *Rural Manhood* (January): 3-5.

1274. Burr, Walter.
    1924 "What's the Matter with the Rural Church?" *Unity
    Messenger* (December).

1275. Burroughs, B.
    1947 "Methodists Study Responsibility for Rural Church." *Town
    and Country Church* (November): 9-10.

1276. Butt, E. Dargan.
    19-- "Enriching Worship in the Rural Church." *The Pastor.*

1277. Butterfield, Kenyon Leech.
    1911 "Cooperation and Integration of Community Institutions."
    Rural Manhood (June).

1278. Butterfield, Kenyon Leech.
    1950 "The Call of the Country Parish." *Christian Rural Fellowship
    Bulletin* (152): 1-5. From *The Country Church and the Rural
    Problem*, 1911, University of Chicago Press.

1279. Cain, Benjamin H.
      1957 "The Effective Church and the Changing Countryside."
      Christian Rural Fellowship Bulletin (208): 1-6.

1280. Calhoun, Newell M.
      1900 "Federation in Winstead." *Hartford Seminary Record.*

1281. Camp, B.
      1950 "New Light for Darkened Churches." *Successful Farming*
      48(10): 34-35, 110-112.

1282. Camp, B.
      1950 "Why the Farmer Needs a Church." *Successful Farming*
      48(12): 40, 130.

1283. Campbell, Gladys L.
      1985 "People and Their Needs in Rural United States."
      Engage/Social Action 13(6): 13-19.

1284. Campbell, Gladys L.
      1988 "Building Bridges of Understanding: National Program
      Division Responds to the Rural Crisis." *Christian Social
      Action* 1(March): 28-29.

1285. Campbell, R.
      1951 "This Church Pays Its Way by Working a Farm; Its 86
      Members Support a Full-Time Pastor; A Successful Answer
      to Financial Problems of Country Churches." *Successful
      Farming* (September): 154, 156-157.

1286. Carothers, J. Edward.
      1950 "Churches Pioneer in Forestry." *Journal of Forestry* (May):
      353.

1287. Carmichael, S.T.
      1963 "Communication--A Tool of Mission." *Town and Country
      Church* (March/April): 12-14.

1288. Carr, James McLeod.
      1950 "This Way Out for the Town and Country Church."
      Christian Rural Fellowship Bulletin (155): 1-6.

1289. Carr, James McLeod.
      1951 "Who's Subsidizing Who?" *Town and Country Church*
      (March): 3-4.

1290. Carr, James McLeod.
      1954 "The Larger Parish." *Town and Country Church* (November):
      3-4.

1291. Carter, Joe H.
    1944 "The Giant of the Wastelands--A Pageant." *Christian Rural Fellowship Bulletin* (97): 1-4.

1292. Carver, Thomas Nixon.
    1913 "Ruraldom the Realm of Real Religion." *Rural Manhood* 4: 35-36.

1293. Case, J.F.
    1945 "Thirty Acres for God." *Missouri Ruralist* (December 22): 13.

1294. Case, J.F.
    1946 "Church in the Wildwood: Ozark Christians Rally 'Round and Build." *Missouri Ruralist* (June 22): 14.

1295. Cash, I.M.
    1947 "Home Lenten Services." *Town and Country Church* (April): 8.

1296. Chamberlain, R.W.
    1956 "Churching Sparsely Settled Areas." *Town and Country Church* (February): 11-12.

1297. Chapman, J.I.
    1944 "The Rural Church and the City Church." *Town and Country Church* (12): 2.

1298. Chase, Frank M.
    1926 "Shiloh, A Rural Church of Service." *The Prairie Farmer* (December 25): 1, 12.

1299. "Churches Can Help Co-ops in a Variety of Ways."
    1956 *Cooperative Consumer* (February 15).

1300. Churchill, A.C.
    1956 "Problems in the Rural South." *Town and Country Church* (April): 5-6.

1301. "City and Country Churches Together."
    1965 *Christian Advocate* 9(November 4): 2.

1302. Clark, A.W.
    1953 "Rural Life Sunday Sermonette." *Town and Country Church* (May): 1-2.

1303. Clark, Dumont.
    1943 "The Country Church with the Lord's Acre Plan." *Farmers Federation News* 24(October): 23

1304. Clark, Francis E.
      1901 "Two Decades of the Christian Endeavor Movement." *The
           Independent* 53(January 31): 263-266.

1305. Clark, Neil M.
      1954 "The Country Church Comes Back to Life." *Saturday
           Evening Post* (November 20): 32-33, 105, 108-109, 111.

1306. Clarke, D.
      1946 "The Country Church with the Lord's Acre Plan." *Farmers
           Federation News* (June): 19.

1307. Clarke, D.
      1948 "Why the Country Church Needs to Use Together
           Scripture-Prayer and the Lord's Acre Plan." *Farmers
           Federation News* (February): 8-21, 24-25.

1308. Clarke, D.
      1949 "Abundant Life for Country Churches through Daily
           Worship and Dedicated Work." *Farmers Federation News*
           (February): 6-13, 15-24, 31.

1309. Clarke, D.
      1950 "Spiritual and Financial Values in the Lord's Acre Plan."
           Rural Missions (Winter): 4-5.

1310. Clarke, D.
      1950 "The Lord's Acre--How It Can Help Your Church."
           Progressive Farmer (Georgia, Alabama, Florida edition)
           (March): 20-21. Also in *Progressive Farmer* (Mississippi,
           Arkansas, Louisiana edition) (April): 22, 48.

1311. Clarke, D.
      1956 "Co-ops Help Strengthen Rural Church Activity."
           Cooperative Digest (November): 20.

1312. Clarke, D.
      1956 "How the Farmers Federation Helps Strengthen Rural
           Churches." *American Cooperative* : 53-56.

1313. Clarkson, George E.
      1946 "Ministerial Migrants." *Town and Country Church*
           (December): 2-3.

1314. Clarkson, George E.
      1959 "New Day at the Crossroads." *Christian Rural Fellowship
           Bulletin* (215): 1-6.

1315. Clayton, C.F.
       1935 "For the Land's Sake." *Christian Rural Fellowship Bulletin* (3):
       1-4.

1316. Clingan, R.L.
       1947 "A Country Minister Views the Rural Community
       Situation." *Town and Country Church* (December): 5.

1317. Coady, M.M.
       1940 "Cooperation and Religion: The Relation between Religion
       and the Cooperative Movement Defined and Expounded."
       Christian Rural Fellowship Bulletin (50): 1-4. Also in
       Commonwealth (October 6, 1939) and in *Masters of Their
       Own Destiny*, 1939, Harper and Brothers.

1318. Cochel, W.A.
       1951 "Leadership Training--The Rural Ministry." *Quarterly of
       Alpha Zeta* (May): 8-10.

1319. Cole, W.H.
       1950 "The Church and Rural Work." *Bulletin of the General
       Theological Seminary* (November): 21.

1320. Coles, Robert.
       1972 "God and the Rural Poor." *Psychology Today* 5(8): 33-40.

1321. Collins, C.
       1954 "The Road is Our Fate." *Town and Country Church* (May): 5-
       6.

1322. Comfort, Richard O.
       1948 "The Challenge of the Rural Ministry." *Town and Country
       Church* (February): 9-11.

1323. Comfort, Richard O.
       1949 "Denominational Cooperation in a Community." *Town and
       Country Church* (October): 7-8.

1324. Comfort, Richard O.
       1951 "How to Revive the Rural Church." *Town and Country
       Church* (September): 3-4.

1325. Comfort, Richard O.
       1952 "A Theology of Rural Life." *Christian Rural Fellowship
       Bulletin* (169): 1-5.

1326. Comfort, Richard O.
       1952 "The Training of the Rural Ministry." *Town and Country
       Church* (December): 1-2.

1327. Comfort, Richard O.
      1954 "Some Qualifications for Today's Rural Minister." *Christian Rural Fellowship Bulletin* (190): 1-4.

1328. Comfort, Richard O.
      1955 "Five-Point Program in Missouri." *Town and Country Church* (October): 4.

1329. Comfort, Richard O.
      1956 "Ecumenicity at the Grass Roots." *Town and Country Church* (November): 10-11.

1330. Comfort, Richard O.
      1959 "Let's Study the Town and Country Church." *Town and Country Church* (October): 12-13.

1331. Comfort, Richard O.
      1960 "History of Relationships between Rural Churches." *Town and Country Church* (April): 3, 15.

1332. Comfort, Richard O.
      1960 "The Rural Church in Its World Perspective." *Town and Country Church* (January/February): 24-25, 27. Also in *Christian Rural Fellowship Bulletin* (219, 1960): 1-8.

1333. Compton, Edward.
      1978 "A Plea for a Theology of Nature: Consultation on Rural Society and the Church, Diocese of Hereford." *Modern Churchman* 22(1): 3-11.

1334. Conn, Harvie M.
      1984 "The Rural-Urban Myth and World Mission." *Reformed Review* 37(Spring): 125-136.

1335. Cooper, K.M.
      1947 "Rural Roads to Evangelism." *Town and Country Church* (April): 7-8.

1336. Costen, James H.
      1984 "The Black Presbyterian Church and Its Rural Ministry." *Princeton Seminary Bulletin* 5(1): 28-32.

1337. Cowling, E.
      1951 "Country Church Survey." *Town and Country Church* (January): 9.

1338. Crate, G.F.J.
1964 "Social and Spiritual Factors in the Rural Parish." *The Churchman* 78(March): 14-22.

1339. Crawford, Mary C.
1903 "Country Church Industrial." *Outlook* (February): 448-451.

1340. Crosby, P.G. III
1950 "Cooperative Work by Six Churches." *Town and Country Church* (May): 1-2.

1341. Crouch, B.
1948 "Roots in the Soil Made This Church Strong." *Successful Farming* (August): 26, 54-56.

1342. Cummins, R.
1953 "Larger Parishes in Rural Illinois." *Town and Country Church* (January): 1-2.

1343. Curtis, Doris B.
1965 "A New Dimension in Christian Mission and Service." *Christian Rural Fellowship Bulletin* (Winter): 1-16.

1344. Curtis, Doris B.
1965 "A New Dimension in Christian Mission and Service, Part II." *Christian Rural Fellowship Bulletin* (Spring): 1-16.

1345. Dailey, Charles A.
1969 "The Management of Conflict." *Chicago Theological Seminary Register* (May): 7.

1346. Dana, Malcom.
1910 "Country Village and the Church." *The Congregationalist* (August 20).

1347. Daneluk, J.P.
1949 "Farm School for Rural Clergy." *New England Homestead* (December 24): 3, 9.

1348. Daneluk, J.P.
1949 "Roanridge Operation Makes Evangelism Practical." *Indiana Farmers Guide* (September 15): 2.

1349. Danielson, Cyndee.
1988 "A Week on the Farm." *Covenant Companion* (November): 16-17.

1350. Darling, A.B.
    1947 "A Rural Minister Views the Rural Church's Task." *Town and Country Church* (December): 4.

1351. Darling, E.M.
    1949 "A Village Church and the Rural Community." *Country Journal* (Autumn): 195-197.

1352. Darling, E.M.
    1950 "Religion in the Life of the Village." *Village* 5(3): 4-7.

1353. Davidson, Gabriel.
    1937 "Agriculture as a Way of Life--The Jewish Point of View." *Christian Rural Fellowship Bulletin* (27, Part 1): 1-4.

1354. Davidson, William.
    1961 "The Church's Place in Rural Development." *Town and Country Church* (September-October): 11-13.

1355. Davison, W.S.
    1946 "The Plight of Rural Protestantism." *Religion Life* 15(Summer): 377-390.

1356. Davis, Dan R.
    1940 "A Rural Challenge to the Protestant Church." *Christian Rural Fellowship Bulletin* (51): 1-4.

1357. Davis, Dan R.
    1946 "A Community Organization Program for Small Communities." *Christian Rural Fellowship Bulletin* (110): 1-6.

1358. Davis, Harold.
    1974 "Christian Education in the Small Church." *Covenant Companion* (June).

1359. Davis, J.P.
    1945 "Solving Rural Community Problems." *Modern Farmer* 17(January): 10.

1360. Dawber, Mark A.
    1937 "Agriculture as a Way of Life--The Protestant Point of View." *Christian Rural Fellowship Bulletin* (27, Part 3): 1-4.

1361. Dawber, Mark A.
    1940 "The Place of the Rural Home and the Rural Community in American Life." *Christian Rural Fellowship Bulletin* (53): 1-4.

1362. Dawber, Mark A.
1943 "The Meaning of Christianity for Rural Life." *Christian Rural Fellowship Bulletin* (85): 1-8.

1363. Dawber, Mark A.
1944 "The Rural Way of Life: What Can the Church Contribute to It?" *Christian Rural Fellowship Bulletin* (90): 1-4.

1364. Dawber, Mark A.
1948 "Christian Education and Community." *Town and Country Church* (October): 3-4.

1365. Dawber, Mark A.
1949 "The Significance to Our Denominations of What We Have Seen and Heard." *Town and Country Church* (September): 5-6.

1366. Dawber, Mark A.
1954 "Rechurching Rural America." *Christian Rural Fellowship Bulletin* (192): 1-4.

1367. Dawson, J.M.
1946 "The Future of the Country Church." *Farm and Ranch* (May): 6, 26.

1368. Deering, F.
1946 "The Country Church, Foundation of Democracy." *Farmer-Stockman* (March): 121, 149, 169.

1369. Delaney, M.N.
1946 "The Negro Rural Church Faces the Future." *Farmers Federation News* (February): 20.

1370. Delaney, M.N.
1947 "Forward with the Lord's Acre Plan." *Town and Country Church* (November): 4.

1371. Delaney, M.N.
1948 "Christian Community Builders." *Town and Country Church* (November): 12-13.

1372. Dennis, W.V.
1945 "The Place of the Church in the Rural Community." *Town and Country Church* (February, part II): 1-4. Also in *Mountain Life and Work* 21(July, 1945): 2-5.

1373. Dettmers, H.A.
1944 "Ills of the Rural Church." *Montana Farmer* 31(July 1): 12.

1374. Dike, Samuel W.
    1885 "The Religious Problem of the Country Town, Section II."
    Andover Review (January): 38-46.

1375. "Do Farmers Go to Church?"
    1942 *Wisconsin Agriculturalist and Farmer* (October 17): 1, 17.

1376. Dorchester, Daniel.
    1894 "The Religious Situation in New England." *Methodist
    Review.* (November): 875-889.

1377. Dorsey, Frank L.
    1985 "The Churches' Response to The Rural Crisis."
    Engage/Social Action 13(6): 40-46.

1378. Doran, P.E.
    1943 "The Mountain Church." *Mountain Life and Work*
    19(Autumn): 1-3.

1379. Douglass, Harlan Paul.
    1950 "Some Protestant Churches in Rural America." *Town and
    Country Church* (January): 1-13.

1380. Douglass, T.B.
    1958 "The Church and the Rural-Urban Fringe." *Town and
    Country Church* (February): 1-3.

1381. Down, Martin.
    1984 "The Shape of the Rural Church." *Theology* 87(May): 164-
    172.

1382. Drake, F.
    1947 "The Rural Church Faces Forward." *Mountain Life and Work*
    (Winter): 10-12.

1383. Drips, W.E.
    1926 "The Devil's Half Acre Gets a New Name." *Wallace's
    Farmer* (December 17).

1384. Dudley, Carl S.
    1979 "Small Churches Are Special." *JED Share* (Spring): 4-5.

1385. Durham, B.
    1949 "The Community's Hope: Rural Churches Play a New Vital
    Role." *Grain Producer News* (May): 10, 26.

1386. Dyer, Mona.
    1984 "Make Big Plans at a Small Church Retreat." *Church School
    Today.* (Summer).

1387. Eckhardt, Betty.
1936 "Spiritual and Religious Values in Rural Art." *Christian Rural Fellowship Bulletin* (8): 1-4.

1388. Edwards, V.A.
1949 "Five-Year Plan for Rural Extension Work." *Town and Country Church* (October): 9.

1389. Ekstrom, M.H.
1954 "The Rural Church and Ministry to Migrants." *Town and Country Church* (January): 7-9.

1390. El-Arabi, M.
1963 "The Role of Religious Groups and Their Institutions." *World Food Congress* Document 6(WFC/63/CP/IVB/4b) (April 15): 4.

1391. Engebretson, O.E.
1956 "It's Town and Country Time." *Town and Country Church* (September): 1-2.

1392. English, Mrs. S.G.
1946 "The Choir in a Small Church." *Town and Country Church* (September): 5-6.

1393. English, William F.
1905 "The New Country Church." *Hartford Seminary Record*.

1394. Ensminger, Douglas.
1945 "If I Were a Rural Pastor." *Christian Rural Fellowship Bulletin* (107): 1-3.

1395. Ensminger, Douglas.
1946 "Report on the USDA Rural Church Conference." *Better Farming Methods* (July): 16, 36.

1396. Ensminger, Douglas.
1950 "Rural Issues of Concern to Rural Churchmen." *Town and Country Church* (February): 13.

1397. Erickson, H.L.
1965 "What Shall We Do?" *Covenant Companion* (December 3): 12.

1398. Erickson, T.A.
1949 "The Church and 4-H Clubs." *Town and Country Church* (September): 10-11.

1399. Eshlemann, J.R.
   1962 "Characteristics of Church Participation in the Rural
   Fringe." *Brethren Life and Thought* 7(Autumn): 24-31.

1400. Ethen, Jeff.
   1984 "New Rural Population a Challenge to U.S. Church." *Our
   Sunday Visitor.* (April 15).

1401. Evans, Bernard.
   1986 "The Rural Parish: A Just and Caring Church." *Worship*
   60(5): 399-411.

1402. Evans, Sarah Elizabeth.
   1945 "Rural Preachers Look at Their Job in the World." *World
   Outlook* (May).

1403. Faris, G.
   1946 "The Church in the Rural Community." *Farmer's Magazine*
   (February): 36.

1404. Faris, G.
   1946 "Weekday Use of Church Advocated." *Rural Co-Operative*
   (January 22): 8.

1405. Farley, Gary.
   1985 "Agricultural Crisis and the Rural Church." *Associational
   Bulletin* (June/July).

1406. Farley, Gary.
   1985 "Issues Confronting Rural Churches and Communities."
   Associational Bulletin (January).

1407. Farley, Gary.
   1985 "The Rural Church Program: 30 Years Later." *The Baptist
   Program* (November): 13, 18.

1408. Farley, Gary.
   1985 "Farm Troubles: Crisis Calls for Christian Leadership."
   Light (May).

1409. Farley, Gary.
   1986 "The Family Farm Crisis." *Home Life* (October): 18, 19.

1410. Farley, Gary.
   1986 "Understanding the Dynamics of a Small Church." *Search*
   (Fall): 40-48.

1411. Farley, Gary.
1987 "Churches and the Farm Crisis." *The Baptist Program* 9, 10, 23.

1412. Farley, Gary.
1987 "The Other Crises in Rural America." *The Baptist Program* (August).

1413. Farley, Gary.
1988 "A Dozen or So Characteristics of Smaller Churches." *The Baptist Program* (April). Also in *New Horizons* (Summer, 1988): 4.

1414. Farley, Gary.
1988 "Change in Rural America and Its Churches." *Associational Bulletin* (January/February).

1415. Farley, Gary.
1988 "Revitalizing Rural America and Her Churches." *The Baptist Program*.

1416. Farley, Gary.
1988 "Some Facts About Rural and Small Town Population/ Places." *The Baptist Program*.

1417. "Farm Pastoral From California."
1966 *America* (114, May 7): 642

1418. "Farmers-Preachers."
1947 *New Republic* 116(16, April 21): 35.

1419. Fast, H.A.
1947 "The Spiritual Values of Contributing to Relief." *Town and Country Church* (March): 12-13.

1420. Felton, Ralph Almon.
1934 "What's Right with Country Churches." *Missionary Review of the World* (December).

1421. Felton, Ralph Almon.
1943 "The Church at the Center." *Progressive Farmer* (Kentucky-Tennessee edition) 58(December): 10, 43.

1422. Felton, Ralph Almon.
1947 "The Next Great Step for Strengthening Country Churches." *Progressive Farmer* (Kentucky, Tennessee, and West Virginia edition) 62(February): 22, 86.

1423. Felton, Ralph Almon.
      1949 "How Work, Worship, Service, and Recreation Make a
      Great Country Church." *Progressive Farmer* (Mississippi,
      Arkansas, Louisiana edition) (February): 15,56.

1424. Felton, Ralph Almon.
      1950 "The Church and Its Dependence on the Soil." *Southwest
      Crop and Stock* (August): 9, 81.

1425. Felton, Ralph Almon.
      1950 "Rock Run Church (Goshen, Ind.) Develops Practical
      Christianity." *Indiana Farmers Guide* (October 15): 1-2.

1426. Felton, Ralph Almon.
      1951 "A Church Men Go To." *Farm Journal* (October): 42, 46.

1427. Felton, Ralph Almon.
      1951 "Land is the Tie that Binds." *Capper's Farmer* 62(5): 19, 76.

1428. Ferrer, C.M.
      1954 "Progress Report on Rural Missions." *Rural Missions*
      (Spring): 1-2.

1429. Ferrer, C.M.
      1959 "Points for the Rural Ministry." *Rural Missions* (Spring): 3.

1430. Fisher, E.L.
      1949 "The Transformation of Communities through Church
      Cooperation." *Town and Country Church* (February): 8-9.

1431. Fisher, E.L.
      1950 "The Town and Country Church and This Convocation."
      Town and Country Church (February): 9.

1432. Fiske, G. Walter.
      1910 "Ideals for the Country Minister." *Rural Manhood*
      (February).

1433. Fiske, G. Walter.
      1912 "The Country Church." *Rural Manhood* (February) : 35.

1434. Fjeld, Roger.
      1985 "The Rural Crisis and the Church's Ministry." *Currents in
      Theology and Mission* 12(April): 128-129.

1435. "Food and Agriculture."
    1985 "Food and Agriculture--Chapter 5 of the US Catholic
        Bishops' Pastoral Letter on Catholic Social Teaching and
        the US economy." *National Catholic Reporter* 21(May 31): 15.

1436. Forster, A.L.
    1949 "Church Life in a California Town." *Town and Country
        Church* (January): 12-13.

1437. Fortner, W.
    1962 "Church and Recreation: Relationship of the Church to
        Community Recreation Agencies." *Recreation* 55(February):
        64-65.

1438. Frederick, A.L.
    1952 "A Church Plan for the Columbia River Valley." *Town and
        Country Church* (February): 9-10.

1439. French, L.C.
    1948 "Country Church Conducts College." *Town and Country
        Church* (March): 9-10.

1440. Frerichs, Robert.
    1964 "The Future of the Disadvantaged." *Christian Rural
        Fellowship Bulletin* (235): 1-8.

1441. Fretz, J. Winfield.
    1948 "The Renaissance of a Rural Community." *Christian Rural
        Fellowship Bulletin* (132): 1-6.

1442. Fretz, J. Winfield.
    1950 "Christian Mutual Aid, A Factor in Church and
        Community Development." *Christian Rural Fellowship
        Bulletin* (158): 1-7.

1443. Galloway, T.W.
    1910 "Country Church Problem Analyzed." *The Interior* (July 23).

1444. Galpin, Charles Josiah.
    1938 "The Rural Church." *Christian Rural Fellowship Bulletin* (37):
        1-4.

1445. Galpin, Charles Josiah.
    1940 "If I Were a Rural Minister." *Christian Rural Fellowship
        Bulletin* (55): 2-3. Reprint from *The Pastors Journal* (July,
        1940).

1446. Galpin, Charles Josiah.
 1945 "My Philosophy of Rural Life." *Christian Rural Fellowship Bulletin* (101): 1-6.

1447. Gard, W.
 1949 "Horsemen for the Lord." *Cattleman* (September): 44-45.

1448. Gardiner, R.
 1954 "Husbandry, Recreation, and Worship in the Machine Age." *Rural Economics* 22(May/June): 8.

1449. Gardner, John E.
 1962 "The Small Church: Some Problems and Assets." *Cumberland Seminarian* 9(Winter): 1-6.

1450. Gardner-Smith, Percival.
 1953 "Church in the Country." *The Modern Churchman* 43(March): 44-48.

1451. "Gas Chariots and Dead Churches."
 1926 *Literary Digest* (September 11).

1452. George, E.Λ.
 1894 "Institutional Village Church." *Outlook.*

1453. Gerard, S.
 1957 "Rural People Like Rural Pastors Who Know God Knows the Soil." *Better Farming Methods* 29(4): 80-81.

1454. Gebhard, E.W.
 1950 "The Rural Church--A Fellowship of Families." *Town and Country Church* (November): 5-6.

1455. Gee, C.W.
 1949 "The Padre and His Parish." *Hoard's Dairyman* (April 10): 291, 301.

1456. Geores, C.
 1958 "Building a Strong Church in a Small Community." *Town and Country Church* (September): 1-2.

1457. Geores, C.
 1958 "The Rural Church in Declining Areas of Population." *Town and Country Church* (May): 4.

1458. Gerrard, Nathan L.
 1968 "The Serpent Handling Religious of West Virginia." *Transaction* 5: 22-28.

1459. Gilbert, C.H.
1950 "Ecumenicity in a Village." *Town and Country Church* (May): 5-6.

1460. Gilbertson, M.
1953 "A Church-Centered Community." *Town and Country Church* (May): 15-16.

1461. Gill, Charles Otis.
1910 "The Country Church and Recreation." *Auburn Seminary Record* (March).

1462. Glenn, Max E.
1986 "Oklahoma: Faith Community and Family Farm--A State in Crisis." *Christianity and Crisis* 46(16): 384-386.

1463. Goldsmith, K.
1946 "Missouri Extension Service Helps the Rural Church: Extension Minister Works with Rural Leaders to Keep Church Door Open." *Better Farming Methods* (May): 20-21.

1464. Goodenough, A.H.
1904 "How to Reach the Rural Population." *The Christian Advocate* (December 29).

1465. Goodrich, F.S.
1910 "Needs of Michigan's Rural Churches." *Rural Manhood* (May): 20-21.

1466. Gordon, E.
1949 "God's Challenge to the Rural Church." *Town and Country Church* (November): 14-15.

1467. Gould, C.B.
1945 "The Lord's Acres." *Town and Country Church* (16): 5.

1468. Gramm, Kent.
1987 "Farmers and 'Victorious Christian Living:' The Wrong End of the Stick." *Christianity and Crisis* 47(May 4): 161-162.

1469. Granberg-Michaelson, Wesley.
1983 "Farming with Justice: The Land the Lord has Loaned Us is to be Used for the Benefit of All." *Other Side* (138): 38-43.

1470. Gray, Bruce C.
1986 "Ecumenical Action in Face of the Farm Crisis." *Ecumenical Trends* 15(10): 163-164

1471. Gray, T.D.
       1949 "Church Architects Design a Rural Church." *Progressive Farmer* (Kentucky, Tennessee, West Virginia edition) (April): 130.

1472. Greene, Robert B.
       1983 "Four Priorities of the Rural Church." *Christian Ministry* 14(3): 7.

1473. Greene, Shirley E.
       1941 "A Church Program For the Rural Community." *The Christian Rural Fellowship Bulletin.* (62): 1-4.

1474. Greene, Shirley E.
       1946 "How Shall the Country Church Survive?" *Town and Country Church* (October): 3-4.

1475. Greene, Shirley E.
       1947 "Examining Protestantism's Rural Roots." *Town and Country Church* (September): 1-2.

1476. Greene, Shirley E.
       1947 "The Country Pastor Studying His Community." *Town and Country Church* (March): 5-6.

1477. Greene, Shirley E.
       1949 "Farming as a Christian Profession: A Roundtable Discussion." *Social Action* 15(December): 21-27.

1478. Greene, Shirley E.
       1949 "The Church and Agriculture." *Christian Rural Fellowship Bulletin* (143): 1-4.

1479. Greene, Shirley E.
       1950 "Christian Agricultural Relations." *Farmers Union Herald* (May 22): 7.

1480. Greene, Shirley E.
       1950 "How Shall our Resources be Saved?" *Town and Country Church* (May): 7-8.

1481. Greene, Shirley E.
       1950 "What Does It Mean to be a Christian Farmer?" *Christian Rural Fellowship Bulletin* (154): 1-6.

1482. Greene, Shirley E.
       1951 "Institutes on the Church and Family Farm." *Town and Country Church* (September): 8-9.

1483. Greene, Shirley E.
1951 "Wheat Farmers and Their Neighbors." *Town and Country Church* (November): 3-4.

1484. Greene, Shirley E.
1953 "Some Elements of Land Reform." *Christian Rural Fellowship Bulletin* (186): 1-4.

1485. Greene, Shirley E.
1960 "In-Service Training as Seen by a Denominational Executive." *Town and Country Church* (March): 14-15.

1486. Greene, Shirley E.
1960 "The Church and Agricultural Policy." *Town and Country Church.* (January/February): 17, 19.

1487. Greene, Shirley E.
1963 "Implications in Christian Theology for Human Goals and Values Affecting Rural Life." *Town and Country Church* (September/October): 3-11.

1488. Grieser, R.
1953 "The Church's R.F.D." *Town and Country Church* (May): 4.

1489. Griffeth, Ross J.
1951 "The National Rural Church Commission of the Disciples of Christ." *Shane Quarterly* 12: 155-169.

1490. Griffin, W.A.
1944 "Rural Leadership and the Clergy." *Land and Home* 7(September): 76.

1491. Griffing, J.B.
1954 "Agricultural Missions from Jesus' Point of View." *Christian Rural Fellowship Bulletin* (198): 1-8.

1492. Grindberg, Wayne.
1987 "The Church and Agriculture: Is the Church Responding to the Needs of Farm Families?" *The Farmers' Forum* Fargo, N.Dak., (May 22): 10.

1493. Grote, N.F.
1946 "Finances in the Rural Church." *Rural Church* (October/November): 2-6.

1494. Groves, Ernest R.
1915 "The Church of the Small Community." *Rural Manhood* 6: 207-210..

1495. Gwinn, Ralph W.
    1938 "Is There a Relation between the Quality of People and the
    Quality of the Land on which They Live?" *Christian Rural
    Fellowship Bulletin* (29): 1-4.

1496. Guard, S.R.
    1949 "Save Our Country Church: Get a Real Preacher and Pay
    Him Real Wages--The Lord's Livestock Plan Will Help You
    Raise Money." *Breeders' Gazette* (September): 8, 24-25.

1497. Gulinello, F.
    1947 "Before and After in Our Church School." *Town and
    Country Church* (May): 8-9.

1498. Guy, H.C.
    1947 "Soil Erosion and Soul Erosion." *Town and Country Church*
    (February): 7-8.

1499. Hafford, G.
    1947 "Catholic Youth Organization--Rural." *Land and Home*
    10(September): 67-70.

1500. Haggerty, John J.
    1952 "The United States Farmer and the World Around Him."
    Christian Rural Fellowship Bulletin (176): 1-6.

1501. Hall, Jerry A.
    1978 "Mennonite Agriculture in a Tropical Environment."
    Mennonite Quarterly Review 52(July): 266-267.

1502. Halliday, E.M.
    1947 "The Rural Church Makes Its Own Opportunity." *Town and
    Country Church* (October): 6.

1503. Halvorson, L.E.
    1963 "The Profane Priesthood: The Importance of a Secular
    Ministry." *Town and Country Church* (March/April): 10-11,
    15.

1504. Hamilton, C. Horace.
    1945 "Agriculture, Rural Life, and the Church in the Post-War
    Era." *Christian Rural Fellowship Bulletin* (103): 1-6.

1505. Hamner, E.D.
    1946 "Shifting Population: How to Plan a Church Ministry."
    Town and Country Church (January): 1-2.

1506. Hamner, E.D.
1957 "Religious Division." *Town and Country Church* (March): 1-2.

1507. Hankins, J.E.
1949 "Pilot Charges." *Town and Country Church* (March): 7-8.

1508. Hankins, J.E.
19-- "A Lay Ministry in the Tennessee Valley." *Town and Country Church* (September): 6-7.

1509. Hankins, J.E.
1952 "The Publicity Value of a Parish Newspaper." *Rural Church* (April/May): 3-5.

1510. Hanna, C. Morton.
1947 "Lost in Transit." *Town and Country Church* (October): 8.

1511. Hanna, C. Morton.
1948 "Enriching the Program of Rural Churches." *Town and Country Church* (March): 1-2.

1512. Hanna, C. Morton.
1948 "When Should a Church Come to Self-Support?" *Town and Country Church* (January): 7-8.

1513. Hanna, C. Morton.
1949 "The Church Serves the Community." *Christian Rural Fellowship Bulletin* (148): 1-6.

1514. Harbaugh, J.W.
1951 "The Long Pastorate." *Town and Country Church* (November): 1-2.

1515. Hargreaves, J. Robert.
1942 "The Significance to Rural Religion and the Rural Church of So-Called Secular Agencies Related to Agriculture, the Home, and Rural Life." *Christian Rural Fellowship Bulletin* (72): 1-8.

1516. Hargrove, Barbara.
1987 "The Church and the Rural Crisis." *Iliff Review* 44(Spring): 3-27.

1517. Harrell, D.E.
1967 "The Agrarian Myth and the Disciples of Christ in the Nineteenth Century." *Agricultural History* 42(2): 181-192.

1518. Harrelson, W.
      1955 "Biblical Faith and Rural Life." *Town and Country Church*
           (January): 1-2.

1519. Harriman, V.E.
      1944 "Training for Rural Ministers." *Mountain Life and Work*
           20(Autumn): 17-19.

1520. Harris, E.W.
      1962 "Rural Minister and Counseling." *Pastoral Psychology*
           13(October): 48-56.

1521. Harris, Marcia.
      1987 "Bucking the Trend: A Look at North Dakota Churches."
           Agweek (April 27): 57.

1522. Harris, Thomas L.
      1910 "Why Survey a Rural Community." *Rural Manhood*
           (November): 16-18.

1523. Hart, A.T.
      1962 "Country Parish Yesterday and Today." *The Modern
           Churchman* 5(January): 131-141.

1524. Hartt, Rollin Lynde.
      1889 "A New England Hill Town." *Atlantic Monthly.*

1525. Hartt, Rollin Lynde.
      1900 "Regeneration of Rural New England, III--Religious."
           Outlook (March 17): 628-632.

1526. Hartman, V.E.
      1946 "Helping the Rural Minister." *Mountain Life and Work*
           22(Spring): 15-16, 25.

1527. Hass, L.H.
      1949 "Land and the Church." *Cooperative Grain Quarterly*
           (September): 20-22.

1528. Hass, L.H.
      1957 "Rocklane Makes a Community Religious Census." *Town
           and Country Church* (May): 1-3.

1529. Hashmi, Z.A.
      1950 "Rural Church in the United States of America and Its
           Place in Agricultural Development." *Agriculture in Pakistan*
           (1): 231-237.

1530. Hatch, D. Spencer.
1944 "My Job is Village Reconstruction." *Christian Rural Fellowship Bulletin* (98): 1-8.

1531. Hatfield, S.
1945 "Landscaping Your Church." *Southern Home and Garden* 12(June): 23.

1532. Hays, Brooks.
1936 "Farm Tenancy and the Christian Conscience." *Christian Rural Fellowship Bulletin* (9): 1-4.

1533. Hays, Brooks.
1942 "The Christian's Relation to the Land." *Christian Rural Fellowship Bulletin* (68): 1-4.

1534. Hays, Brooks.
1947 "The Country Church and Public Affairs." *Town and Country Church* (December): 8.

1535. Haystead, L.
1949 "New Life for the Little Brown Church." *Country Gentleman* (April): 28, 149-151.

1536. Heckman, H.W.
1957 "Five Years in a Marginal Parish." *Town and Country Church* (March): 6-9.

1537. Heffernan, Judith B. and William D. Heffernan.
1986 "Is the Church Open to Victims of the Farm Crisis?" *Catholic Rural Life* 36(3): 5-8.

1538. Heitzman, M.
1946 "Ministers and Soil Conservation." *Town and Country Church* (November): 6-7.

1539. Henckel, Alma.
1982 "What the Small Church Does Better." *JED Share* (Fall): 8.

1540. Henderson, Charles Richmond.
1907 "Social Duties in Rural Communities." *Biblical World* (January): 23-33.

1541. Henderson, H.
1945 "An Expanding Rural Church." *Town and Country Church* (January): 5-6.

1542. Hendricks, Garland Alfred.
      1962 "The Church in the Rural Community at Home and
            Abroad." *Town and Country Church* (January/February): 11-
            14. Also in *Christian Rural Fellowship Bulletin* (227): 1-8.

1543. Hibbs, W.W.
      1948 "Financing the Country Church." *Town and Country Church*
            (December): 5-6.

1544. Hibbs, W.W.
      1955 "The Ecology of Rural Life: The Church and the Soil."
            Farmer West Virginia 2(June): 14.

1545. Higdon, H.
      1960 "The Circuit Rider." *Nation's Agriculture* 35(April): 14-16.

1546. Hillman, H.J.
      1944 "The Church and the Rural Problem." *Farmer and Settler*
            38(October 6): 11.

1547. Hobgood, P.
      1949 "A Church for Your People and a Home for Your Pastor."
            Southern Agriculture (September): 10-11, 23.

1548. Hodgdon, E.R.
      1947 "The Country Church and the Country School." *Town and
            Country Church* (December): 12.

1549. Hogge, M.
      1950 "Our Rural Churches Can Be Improved." *Missouri Ruralist*
            (April 8): 10-11.

1550. Holck, M.
      1965 "Our Parsonage is in a Pasture." *The Lutheran* (January 13):
            15.

1551. Holmes, K.L.
      1951 "New Opportunities for Rural Radio." *Town and Country
            Church* (May): 1-2.

1552. Home Missions Council, Committee on Town and Country.
      1947 "A Commitment of Advance for Rural Churches in
            America." *Town and Country Church* (March): 1-3.

1553. Hood, M.G.
      1955 "Migrant Families in California." *Town and Country Church*
            (January): 7-8.

1554. Horstick, W.W.
1958 "The Town and Country Church at Work on Her World-Wide Mission." *Town and Country Church* (February): 3-4.

1555. Hosking, J.E.
1948 "The Mechanization of Agriculture: A British Viewpoint." *Christian Rural Fellowship Bulletin* (130): 1-4.

1556. Hostetler, John A.
1954 "The Expression of Christian Community." *Christian Rural Fellowship Bulletin* (189): 1-4.

1557. Hostetler, John A. and William G. Mather.
1953 "The Rural Church: Is It Free of Class Distinctions?" *Scientific Farmer* (Summer): 5-6.

1558. Hotchkiss, Wesley A.
1955 "The Imperative of the Rural Church." *Christian Rural Fellowship Bulletin* (200): 1-6.

1559. Hotchkiss, Wesley A.
1958 "The Christian Faith and Modern Agriculture." *Town and Country Church* (January): 1-3, 15.

1560. Howard, J.T.
1959 "Some Early Roots of the Rural Church Movement." *Town and Country Church* (April): 5-9.

1561. Howard, Thomas E.
1947 "What the Church Can Do about Agriculture." *Town and Country Church* (February): 10.

1562. Hoy, R.
1945 "A Small Farm for the Pastor." *Town and Country Church* (March): 1-2.

1563. Huber, A.R.
1951 "The Church and the Resettlement of Landless Families." *Rural Missions* (Summer): 7-8.

1564. Hudgens, R.W.
1943 "Underprivileged Farm Families and the Christian Conscience." *Christian Rural Fellowship Bulletin* (81): 1-7.

1565. Huff, Harold S.
1963 "Small Church: Problem or Promise." *World Outlook* 23(July): 7.

1566. Hughes, T.J.
1954 "Extraordinary Florida Agricultural Operation Far from Civilization: Mormons Pioneer 220,000 Acre Farm." *Florida Grower and Rancher* (April): 11, 40-41.

1567. Hulteen, Bob.
1987 "Churches Called on to Save the Family Farm." *Sojourners* 16(June): 11.

1568. Hummon, S.
1967 "Hope for Small-Town Churches." *The Mennonite* (June 27): 418.

1569. Hunt, E.S. and C.E. Ploch.
1947 "Rural Ministerial Fellowship." *Town and Country Church* (September): 11.

1570. Husfloen, R.L.
1965 "Town and Country--Some Reflections." *Town and Country Church* (September/October): 9.

1571. Husfloen, R.L.
1966 "Town and Country: Last Rites for a Dying Culture?" *Dialog* 5(Spring): 136-139.

1572. Hutcheson, Richard G., Jr.
1977 "Pluralism and Consensus: Why Mainline Church Mission Budgets Are in Trouble." *The Christian Century* (July 6-13): 619-621.

1573. Hutchinson, C.R.
1950 "The Rural Church." *Ohio Farm Bureau News* (May): 10-11.

1574. Hutchinson, G.M.
1953 "Challenge to the Rural Church." *Country Guide* (March): 7, 40-41.

1575. Hyde, Mrs. S.B.
1946 "A Church Music Project." *Town and Country Church* (September): 1-2.

1576. Hyde, William DeWitt.
1892 "Impending Paganism in New England." *Forum* (June): 528.

1577. Hyde, William DeWitt.
1893 "Church Union a Necessity: The Maine Experiment." *Forum*.

1578. Igwe, G. Egemba.
      1975 "Editorial" (On Agricultural Missions). *International Review of Mission* 64(October): 341-344.

1579. Infield, H.F.
      1952 "The Campanella Community: A Study in Experimental Religion." *Cooperative Living* (Fall): 1-8.

1580. Isaac, E.
      1964 "Property in Land: A Sacred Origin? God's Acre." *Landscape* 14(Winter): 28-32.

1581. Isenhart, Charles.
      1985 "Corporate Farmers Threaten Economy, Bishop Says." *National Catholic Reporter* 21(April 12): 17.

1582. Isenhart, Charles.
      1986 "Methodists Hire Nun to Run Nation's First VISTA Program for Ailing Farm Economy." *National Catholic Reporter* 22(April 18): 1.

1583. Isenhart, Charles.
      1986 "Church, Rural Leaders Call Economic Trend Farm Threat." *National Catholic Reporter* 22(March 7): 7.

1584. Ives, Hilda L.
      1942 "The Rural Church's Task in War Time." *Christian Rural Fellowship Bulletin* (76): 1-6.

1585. James, D.H.
      1952 "Publicity for the Rural Church." *Rural Church* (April/May): 1-3. Also in *Town and Country Church* (October, 1953): 4.

1586. James, H.
      1952 "The Country Clergyman: His Field." *Town and Country Church* (January): 5-6.

1587. Jameson, Norman.
      1983 "The Power and the Promise." *Missions USA* (July-August): 55.

1588. Jameson, V.
      1960 "Range Riders' Church." *Town and Country Church* (May): 13-15.

1589. Jamison, W.G.
      1956 "Criteria for an Effective Questionnaire." *Town and Country Church* (February): 5-6.

1590. Jamison, W.G.
    1956 "Oakville's Churches." *Town and Country Church* (April): 4.

1591. Jamison, W.G.
    1956 "There's a Future in the Rural Church's Educational Program." *Town and Country Church* (May): 12-13.

1592. Jennewein, Lin.
    1986 "Hearing the Word of God Amid the Farm Crisis." *The Christian Ministry* 17(4): 20-21.

1593. Johnson, Paul C.
    1958 "A Time for Clear Thinking." *Christian Rural Fellowship Bulletin* (213): 1-6.

1594. Johnson, Paul C.
    1959 "The Greatest Need in Rural Life Today." *Town and Country Church* (December): 5.

1595. Johnstone, M.B.
    1949 "Drama in the Rural Church." *Town and Country Church* (January): 1-3. Also in *Agricultural Missions Bulletin* (Spring, 1949): 3-7.

1596. Johnstone, M.B.
    1950 "Take Off the City Blinders." *Town and Country Church* (March): 1-2.

1597. Jones, A.T.
    1957 "The Good Samaritan and the Country Church." *Town and Country Church* (April): 10-11.

1598. Jones, Thomas Jesse.
    1943 "Church and Community: Responsibility of the Church for the Community and the Social Order." *Christian Rural Fellowship Bulletin* (78): 1-6.

1599. Judy, M.T.
    1960 "The Area Ministry." *Town and Country Church* (January/February): 9-11.

1600. Judy, M.T.
    1962 "Sociological and Theological Motivations for Church and Ministry in Town and Country Areas." *Town and Country Church* (July/August): 8-10.

1601. Kaufman, Harold F.
      1946 "What Rural Church Strategy Today?" *Christian Rural Fellowship Bulletin* (112): 1-8.

1602. Kaufman, Harold F.
      1947 "Three Questions for the Mountain Church." *Mountain Life and Work* 23(Summer): 20-22.

1603. Kaufman, Harold F.
      1954 "Community Development in the Southeast." *Christian Rural Fellowship Bulletin* (193): 1-4.

1604. Kaufman, Harold F.
      1956 "A Call for Community Prophets." *Christian Rural Fellowship Bulletin* (203): 1-6.

1605. Kaufman, Harold F.
      1962 "Changing Community Types and Problems of Church Strategy." *Town and Country Church* (November/December): 3-5.

1606. Kaufman, Harold F.
      1962 "The Search for the Beloved Community." *Christian Rural Fellowship Bulletin* (230): 1-8.

1607. Keene, P.K.
      1961 "What about Penus Creek, Pennsylvania?" *Town and Country Church* (September/October): 3-4.

1608. Keilholz, F.J.
      1945 "Rebirth of the Rural Church." *Country Gentleman* 115(August): 53-54.

1609. Keim, H.H., Jr.
      1947 "Green Pastures and Still Waters." *Town and Country Church* (January): 7.

1610. Keillor, Garrison.
      1985 "Schnookered Out of the Five-Day Rural Lutheran Clergy Conference in Orlando, Florida." *Spice* 4(August): 1,2,8.

1611. Kelley, M.H.
      1955 "The Grange and Maine Churches." *Town and Country Church* (October): 1-3.

1612. Kelly, E.M.
      1950 "Church Bell Rings Again." *Kansas Farmer* (December 2): 4.

1613. Kelly, E.M.
      1951 "Kansas Ag Leaders Say the Rural Church Strengthens
      Agriculture." *Better Farming Methods* (October): 16, 18.

1614. Kelsey, G.D.
      1952 "Voluntary Service." *Town and Country Church* (January): 10-
      11.

1615. Kennedy, C.J.
      1946 "The Rural Church." *Agricultural Leaders' Digest* (May): 26,
      28.

1616. Kennedy, C.J.
      1949 "The Rural Church Needs Your Help." *Better Farming
      Methods* (June): 16, 26.

1617. Kennerly, A.B.
      1946 "Soils and Souls Sunday." *Farm and Ranch* 65(August): 10,
      11.

1618. Kester, Howard and Alice Kester.
      1942 "Ceremony of the Soil--A Service of Worship." *Christian
      Rural Fellowship Bulletin* (69): 1-4.

1619. Ketcham, J.B.
      1949 "Religious Education in the Town and Country Church."
      Town and Country Church (February): 5-6.

1620. Key, E.R.
      1953 "What a Rural Church Did in Christian Education." *Town
      and Country Church* (March): 10-11.

1621. Kime, Robert, Malachi Shaw, and A. Garrett.
      1985 "A Garden in Eden: Considerations for a Rural
      Community." *Epiphany* 3(4): 47-57.

1622. King, J.B.
      1949 "I'll Stick to My Country Pulpit: A Pastor Tells Why
      Serving Farmers Gives Him a Greater Satisfaction than He
      Could Find in a Big, City Church." *Successful Farming*
      (June): 30, 118-119.

1623. Knight, Roger D.
      19-- "A Small-Church Leadership Project." *The Christian
      Ministry*: 8-10.

1624. Kolb, John A.
      1959 "What's Happening in Rural Communities?" *Town and
      Country Church* (November): 10.

1625. Krass, Alfred C.
1980 "Strikers and Ohio Churches: In the Soup." *Christian Century* 97(August): 796-798.

1626. Krause, K.R.
1965 "The Rural Church and Rural Change." *United Church Herald* (May 15): 14.

1627. Krause, K.R.
1967 "Rural Churches Have Financial Problems." *Hoard's Dairyman* 112(15): 937.

1628. Kruger, Kathy.
1986 "Be Advocates for Family Farming, Speakers at Hearings Urge Church." *Engage/Social Action* 14(5): 37-38.

1629. Kueck, E.
1950 "The People Are Ready--Are We? An Experiment in Rural Nebraska." *Rural Church* (December/January, 1951): 2-3.

1630. Kuhlman, A.F.
1946 "Vanderbilt University Shares Books with Rural Ministers." *Library Journal* (February 1): 151-153.

1631. Kurtz, E.L.
1948 "Churches Play Important Part in Bruceton (Mo.) Life." *Boonville Advertiser* (July 30): 6.

1632. Lacy, Mary G.
1938 "Religious Significance in Rural Handicrafts." *Christian Rural Fellowship Bulletin* (30): 1-4.

1633. LaFarge, John, S.J.
1937 "Agriculture as a Way of Life--The Catholic Point of View." *Christian Rural Fellowship Bulletin* (27, Part 2): 1-4.

1634. LaFarge, John, S.J.
1938 "Agriculture and Vocation." *Christian Rural Fellowship Bulletin* (34): 1-6.

1635. "Lakeside Faith."
1955 *Life* (July 18): 89-90.

1636. Lambeth, W.O.
1951 "The Earth is the Lord's and the Fullness Thereof." *Soil Conservation* (January): 128, 130-131. Also in *Town and Country Church* (April, 1951): 3-4.

1637. Landess, W.M. and R.B. Wilson.
      1945 "Soils and Souls: A Story of the Church in the Tennessee
      Valley." *Town and Country Church* (October): 1-2.

1638. Landis, Benson Young.
      1942 "The Social Ideals of the Churches for Agriculture and
      Rural Life: Pronouncements by Official Protestant
      Agencies." *Christian Rural Fellowship Bulletin* (73): 1-6.

1639. Landis, Benson Young.
      1951 "The Antigonish Movement." *Christian Rural Fellowship
      Bulletin* (167): 1-4.

1640. Landis, Benson Young.
      1953 "Religion and Rural Welfare." *Town and Country Church*
      (October): 12-13.

1641. Landis, Benson Young.
      1956 "Warren Wilson on the Open Country Church: A Series of
      Historical Notes." *Town and Country Church* (February): 13-
      14.

1642. Landis, Benson Young.
      1958 "Notes on Recollections, VII. Are There Distinctive
      Protestant Teachings on Agriculture and Rural Life?" *Town
      and Country Church* (April): 5-6.

1643. Landis, Benson Young.
      1958 "Notes on Recollections, X. Inter-Group Cooperation." *Town
      and Country Church* (October): 8-10.

1644. Landis, Benson Young.
      1958 "Notes on Recollections, IX. Theology and Rural Life."
      Town and Country Church (September): 10-11.

1645. Landis, Benson Young.
      1959 "Cooperative Church Planning in Town and Country
      Communities." *Town and Country Church* (May): 5-7.

1646. Landis, Benson Young.
      19-- "Robert Frost on 'Frontiers of Faith.'" *Town and Country
      Church* (December): 5-6.

1647. Landis, Edward Bryant.
      19-- "A Country Minister at Work." *Rural Manhood* 1(9).

1648. Landis, Edward Bryant.
      1911 "The Reconstruction of the Country Church." *Rural
      Manhood* (February): 52-54.

1649. Landis, P.H.
1949 "Forces in Rural Life of Concern to Rural Churchmen."
Town and Country Church (February): 3-4.

1650. Landry, O.F.
1946 "Making Progress." *Town and Country Church* (April): 2-3.

1651. Langford, H.
1952 "Rural Institute on Church Music and Worship." *Town and Country Church* (March): 9-10.

1652. Laupmanis, J.
1947 "Notes from a Village Church." *Town and Country Church* (May): 7.

1653. Leadley, T.
1947 "Church Backs Soil Conservation: Methodist Rural Life Conference Sees Relation Between Soil Saving and Soul Saving." *Nebraska Farmer* 89(August 16): 5, 11.

1654. Leavenworth, Lynn.
1963 "Leadership for Small Churches." *Christian Rural Fellowship Bulletin* (232): 1-11.

1655. Lebold, K.R.
1962 "Renewal of the Church: A Growing Reality." *Town and Country Church* (September/October): 3-5, 11.

1656. Lee, C.
1956 "Serving Scattered Churches by Air." *Town and Country Church* (January): 16.

1657. Lee, R.G.
1944 "Righteous Religion and Rural Life." *Rural Life* 1(Summer): 53-63.

1658. Levy, Paul.
1986 "Study Backs German Catholic Farmers in Crisis." *Fargo Forum* (Fargo, N.Dak.) (March 30): 1, 2.

1659. Lewis, Robert.
1965 "Rural Community Development." *Town and Country Church* (183, July-August): 92-95.

1660. Lewis, T.
1947 "The Country Church, Community Builder." *Iowa Bureau Farmer* 11 (September): 12-13.

1661. Lewis, T.
       1947 "The Country Church." *Iowa Bureau Farmer* 11(October): 16-17.

1662. Lewis, T.
       1947 "The Rural Church." *Iowa Bureau Farmer* 11(May): 12-13.

1663. Linder, O.A.
       1909 "Country Life and the Church." *Outlook* (April 10): 810-811.

1664. Lindstrom, David Edgar.
       1941 "Preserving Rural Values." *Christian Rural Fellowship Bulletin* (64): 1-4.

1665. Lindstrom, David Edgar.
       1945 "Country Church Achievement." *Capper's Farmer* (December): 10, 67.

1666. Lindstrom, David Edgar.
       1946 "American Country Life and the Coming Dawn of Peace." *Christian Rural Fellowship Bulletin* (117): 1-4.

1667. Lindstrom, David Edgar.
       1946 "Country Church Leadership." *Capper's Farmer* 57(June): 11, 50, 51.

1668. Lindstrom, David Edgar.
       1947 "Country Church Obligations." *Capper's Farmer* 58(January): 23, 27-28.

1669. Lindstrom, David Edgar.
       1948 "A Christian Approach to Modern Rural Life." *Christian Rural Fellowship Bulletin* (129): 1-5.

1670. Lindstrom, David Edgar.
       1949 "Is the Rural Church Serving the Needs of the Community?" *Christian Rural Fellowship Bulletin* (142): 1-4.

1671. Lindstrom, David Edgar.
       1952 "Land Policies in Various Countries and the Church's Concern." *Christian Rural Fellowship Bulletin* (170): 1-8.

1672. Lionberger, Herbert F. and Chii-Jeng Yeh.
       1975 "The Changing Influence of Clique, Neighborhood, and Church." *Growth and Change* (January): 23-30.

1673. Lippencott, William A.
    1915 "Rural Problems and Laws of the Bible." *Rural Manhood* 6:
    83-85.

1674. Lively, Charles E.
    1958 "The Church in the Changing Rural Community." *Christian
    Rural Fellowship Bulletin* (214): 1-10.

1675. Logee, W.E.
    1916 "Regenerating the Community." *Rural Manhood* (January).

1676. Lokey, C. and R. Smith.
    1947 "The Church and Land." *Rural Church* 9(1): 5-7.

1677. Loomis, Mildred Jensen.
    1944 "Integral Rural Living and Civilization." *Christian Rural
    Fellowship Bulletin* (91): 1-8.

1678. "Lord's Acre Plan Expanded: Stewardship in Action."
    1967 *United Methodist Rural Fellowship Bulletin* 24(December): 6.

1679. "Lord's Acre Reports from States and Mission Fields."
    1944 *Farmers Federal News* 24(6): 8-16.

1680. Lorentz, A.
    1954 "Johnny's Second Crop." *Town and Country Church*
    (January): 10-11.

1681. Lovering, F.W.
    1952 "Ministry to Florida's Harvest Highway Workers: Eight
    Mission Camps Give Religious and Secular Help to Farm
    Crews in Palm Beach, Broward, Dade Counties." *Florida
    Grower* (January): 17, 32.

1682. Lovin, C.W.
    1965 "The Rural Church." *Wesleyan Methodist* (November 10): 10.

1683. Lowdermilk, Walter C.
    1942 "The 11th Commandment." *Christian Rural Fellowship
    Bulletin* (74): 1-4. Revised and reprinted from *American
    Forests* (January, 1940).

1684. Lowdermilk, Walter C.
    1959 "Down to Earth: A Plea for Soil Conservation and
    Stewardship." *Christian Rural Fellowship Bulletin* (218): 1-6.

1685. Lowe, D.L.
      1950 "Lagrange Larger Parish." *Rural Church* (December/January,
      1951): 3-4.

1686. Lutz, William B.
      1959 "A Strategy for the Church in Town and Country."
      Christian Rural Fellowship Bulletin (216): 1-6.

1687. McArthur, K.C.
      1946 "Vermont Churches Work Together." *American Agriculture*
      (March 2): 105, 127.

1688. McBride, C.R.
      1962 "On Creating the Right Image." *Town and Country Church*
      (March/April): 15, 16.

1689. McCall, Emmanuel L.
      19-- "The Small Church: Organizing for Action." *The Christian
      Ministry* : 17-18.

1690. McCanna, Henry A.
      1962 "Horizons of Hope." *Town and Country Church* (September/
      October): 8, 13.

1691. McCanna, Henry A.
      1963 "The Challenge of the Church in Transition." *Christian
      Rural Fellowship Bulletin* (233): 1-8.

1692. McCanna, Henry A.
      1963 "This Is It!--A Challenge to Local Pastors." *Town and
      Country Church* (January/February): 3.

1693. McCanna, Henry A.
      1965 "Physical and Spiritual Development in Appalachia." *Town
      and Country Church* (182, May-June): 11.

1694. McClellan, G.E.
      1961 "Vocation, Enlistment, and Ministry." *Town and Country
      Church* (November/December): 3-5.

1695. McClure, J.G.K.
      1945 "How Country Churches Can Promote Recreation."
      Progressive Farmer (Kentucky, Tennessee, West Virginia
      edition) 60(May): 24.

1696. McClure, R.G.
      1946 "Religion via a Command Car." *Mountain Life and Work*
      22(Fall): 9-12.

1697. McConnell, C.M.
1953 "All in One Country Man's Lifetime." *Town and Country Church* (February): 9-10.

1698. McCormick, M.
1948 "We Grow the Flowers for Our Church." *Farm Journal* (June): 96-99.

1699. McCormick, Naomi.
1985 "Adolescents' Values, Sexuality, and Contraception in a Rural New York County." *Adolescence* 20(78): 385-395.

1700. McConnell, C.M.
1946 "Community-Minded Churches in Town and Country." *Town and Country Church* (October): 1-2.

1701. McConnell, C.M.
1947 "The Church and Long Range Trends in Rural Life." *Town and Country Church* (January): 5-6.

1702. McDermott, William F.
1943 "Church Builds a Community." *Country Gentleman* 113(2): 13, 49-50.

1703. McDonald, Angus.
1937 "Rev. J. A. McDonald--The Soil Builder." *Christian Rural Fellowship Bulletin* (18): 1-2.

1704. MacDonald, Elizabeth.
1937 "Agriculture as a Way of Life--The Point of View of a Farm Woman." *Christian Rural Fellowship Bulletin* (27, Part 5): 1-4.

1705. McDonald, K.R.
1959 "Prefabrication--An Answer for Low Budget Churches." *Veneers and Plywood* 53(September): 22-23.

1706. McDonald, L.J.
1946 "Stewardship of the Soil." *Farm and Ranch* (July): 5.

1707. McFatridge, J.M.
1946 "More Power to Shooks Chapel." *Progressive Farmer* (Texas edition) 61(September): 13, 23.

1708. McGarrah, A.F.
1910 "Raising Money in the Country Church." *The Herald and Presbyter* (May 4).

1709. McGarrah, D.K.
      1946 "Rural Youth on the March." *Town and Country Church*
      (April): 6.

1710. McGarrah, D.K.
      1947 "The Vacation Church School." *Town and Country Church*
      (April): 5-6.

1711. McGivney, Pearl.
      1986 "Under the Citrus Trees: How Florida's Farm Workers
      Found Spiritual Renewal." *Other Side* 22(8): 15.

1712. McGrahan, A.R.F.
      1965 "The Modern Use of Timber in Churches." *Timber Plywood
      Annual*. 56, 58.

1713. McLaughlin, H.W.
      1947 "G.I.'s and the Country Church." *Town and Country Church*
      (October): 7.

1714. McLaughlin, H.W.
      1948 "Christ and the Country People." *Town and Country Church*
      (February): 4.

1715. McLaughlin, H.W.
      1948 "Southern Seminary Programs." *Town and Country Church*
      (April): 5-6.

1716. McManus, Jim.
      1987 "Churches Accused of Failing on Farm Scene." *National
      Catholic Reporter* 23(April): 19.

1717. McMullin, Stephen.
      1987 "In the Pastoral Pastorate." *Leadership* 8(Summer): 72-77.

1718. McMullin, Stephen.
      1988 "How to Grow a Rural Church." *Leadership* 9(3): 80-85.

1719. McMullin, Stephen.
      1988 "New Ways to Measure Growth." *Leadership* 9(3): 84-85.

1720. McNeel, W.
      1950 "A 4-H Sunday Service." *National 4-H News* (April): 1, 20.

1721. McNutt, Matthew B.
      1911 "Liberating the Latent Powers in a Community." *Rural
      Manhood* (February): 44-48.

1722. Magnuson, Osgood T.
1975 "Rural America: A Challenge for Churches." *Engage/Social Action* 3(August): 20-23.

1723. Magnuson, Ray F.
1948 "Soil, Sowers, and the Church." *Soil Conservation* (March): 174-176.

1724. Magnuson, Ray F.
1950 "Is Your Community 'Overchurched?'" *Nebraska Farmer* (July 15): 21.

1725. Magnuson, Ray F.
1951 "Rural Salvation." *Christian Rural Fellowship Bulletin* (161): 1-7.

1726. Mahnke, Carol.
1987 "Rural Churches Enthused." *Fargo Forum* (Fargo, N.Dak.) (May 5): A6.

1727. Mahnke, Carol.
1987 "Survival of Rural Churches: Conservative Membership Up." *Fargo Forum* (Fargo, N.Dak.) (July 10): A6.

1728. Mainelli, Vincent P.
1985 "Revolution in the Heartland." *America* (March 2): 160.

1729. Major, E.B.
1948 "A Rural Adventure in Religion." *Southern Planter* (November): 46-47, 52.

1730. Malcolm, Dana.
1929 "The State of Religion in Rural America." *Rural America* (October): 9-10.

1731. Mann, D.
1947 "How Would You Measure a Church?" *Kansas Farmer* 84(July 5): 5, 18-20.

1732. Manny, T.B.
1961 "Human Aspects of Rural Life in the Future." *Christian Rural Fellowship Bulletin* (225): 1-8.

1733. Maris, Paul V.
1949 "Highlights of 40 Years in Rural Life." *Christian Rural Fellowship Bulletin* (146): 1-8.

1734. Marriage, K.
1948 "Church Grounds." *Green Thumb* (September): 11-12.

1735. Martin, C.
        1950 "The Rural Minister and Soul and Soil Conservation."
        Missouri Farmer (April): 9.

1736. Martin, E.W.
        1949 "The Parson and the Poacher." *Village* 4(4): 15-17.

1737. Martin, Harold.
        1958 "He Works in God's Back Pastures." *Saturday Evening Post*
        (December 13): 19-21.

1738. Martin, R.
        1947 "Can the Rural Church Come Back?" *Farmer-Stockman*
        (September): 25.

1739. Martin, R.
        1947 "Strong Rural Churches Depend upon a Sound Land
        Policy." *Farmer-Stockman* 60(October): 6.

1740. Martin, R.
        1947 "Youth is the Key to Building Strong Rural Churches."
        Farmer-Stockman (October): 17,61.

1741. Martin, R.
        1948 "A Farmer-Built Church." *Farmer-Stockman* (February): 5.

1742. Martin, Bishop William C.
        1947 "Rediscovering God's Earth." *Christian Rural Fellowship
        Bulletin* (128): 1-4.

1743. Mather, William G.
        1940 "The Religious Needs of the Village Family." *Christian Rural
        Fellowship Bulletin* (58): 1-4.

1744. Mather, William G.
        1948 "Country Churches Reflect Changes in Population and
        Agriculture." *Scientific Farmer* (October): 2-3.

1745. Mather, William G.
        1948 "The Rural Church Situation as Seen by a Social Scientist."
        Town and Country Church (February): 1-4.

1746. Mather, William G.
        1950 "Country Churches Reflect Change." *Town and Country
        Church* (March): 5-6.

1747. Mather, William G.
        1950 "The Mission of the Rural Church." *Christian Rural
        Fellowship Bulletin* (149): 1-7.

1748. Mather, William G.
    1952 "The Rural Church in Pennsylvania." *Town and Country Church* (March): 13-14.

1749. Mather, William G.
    1954 "The Field is the World." *Town and Country Church* (December): 1-2. Also in *Christian Rural Fellowship Bulletin* (195): 1-6.

1750. Mather, William G.
    1966 "The Future of the Rural Church." *Scientific Farmer* 13(Winter): 2-3.

1751. Mather, William G. and Irene L. Gochnour.
    1947 "Home Valley." *Christian Rural Fellowship Bulletin* (126): 1-8.

1752. Matthew, John C.
    1966 "Town and Country Goals in Transition." *Town and Country Church* (November/December): 14.

1753. Matthews, J.
    1949 "Is Your Rural Church the Center Point of Community Interest?" *Illinois Agriculturalist* (November): 4.

1754. Maurer, B.B.
    1959 "The Church in Our Dynamic Rural Environment." *Town and Country Church* (April): 2-4.

1755. Mays, William E.
    1970 "Churches that Live and Die." *Foundations* 13(January-March): 79-92.

1756. Maynard, E. and K. McNeil.
    1947 "Two New Trends towards Better Rural Churches." *Southern Agriculture* 77(November): 11.

1757. Mease, F.R.
    1951 "The Larger Parish Plan." *Town and Country Church* (September): 1-2.

1758. Medearis, D.W.
    1952 "Toward a More Creative Observance of Rural Life Sunday." *Town and Country Church* (May): 1-2.

1759. Megill, H.R.
    1952 "The Rural Church Stabilizes the Home." *Town and Country Church* (May): 6-7.

1760. Members of the Ohio Christian Rural Fellowship with a
      Meditation by Philip H. Steinmetz.
      1958 "What The Rural Church Movement Means to Me."
           Christian Rural Fellowship Bulletin (211): 1-8.

1761. Mendenhall, H.
      1949 "The Lord's Trees." *American Forests* (December): 23, 46.

1762. "Mennonite Farmers."
      19-- *Christian Century* 102(January 16): 42.

1763. Meter, Ken.
      1985 "Church Group Likes Draft of Farm Pastoral, Urges Push
           for Fair Farm Prices." *National Catholic Reporter* 21(May 31):
           8.

1764. "Methodists Awakening to Rural Crisis."
      1947 *Christian Century* 64(August 20): 989.

1765. Miller, H.
      1946 "Lutheran Rural Life Seminar Studies Relationship of
           Church and Agriculture." *Wisconsin Farmers Union News*
           14(November 11): 1, 2.

1766. Miller, L.D.
      1946 "Extension Minister for Missouri County Churches."
           Capper's Farmer (August): 9, 19.

1767. Miller, M.C.
      1949 "Rural Churches Keep in Step with the Times." *Ohio Farmer*
           (May 21): 3, 29.

1768. Miller, Paul E.
      1949 "A Church Helps Its Members Buy Farms." *Town and
           Country Church* (October): 5-6.

1769. Miller, Paul E.
      1956 "Rural Brethren Families in Action." *Brethren Life and
           Thought* 1(4): 23-26.

1770. Mills, W.H.
      1942 "The Church and the Land." *Christian Rural Fellowship
           Bulletin* (71): 1-6. Reprint from *Union Seminary Review*,
           Richmond, Va., October, 1916.

1771. Millwood, C.E.
      1959 "Church Sponsors Pilot Forest." *Forest Farmer* (December):
           12, 14.

1772. Minkler, M.
1949 "Significant Women's Programs in Town and Country Churches." *Town and Country Church* (February): 7-8.

1773. Mitchell, J.B.
1962 "Is Rural America Losing Its Churches?" *Better Farming Methods* (February): 14-15, 24.

1774. Moberg, D.O.
1963 "The Church: Gathered and Committed." *Town and Country Church* (March/April): 4-7.

1775. Moberg, D.O.
1963 "The Church: Redeployed." *Town and Country Church* (July/August): 3-7.

1776. Moffett, Samuel H.
1951 "The Christian and Social Reform." *Christian Rural Fellowship Bulletin* (165): 1-7.

1777. Montgomery, G.A.
1946 "Serving Rural Youth." *Capper's Farmer* 57(September): 12, 62.

1778. Moomaw, Ira W.
1945 "Rural Life Objectives in the Church of the Brethren." *Christian Rural Fellowship Bulletin* (104): 1-8.

1779. Moomaw, Ira W.
1945 "The Church and the Family Farm." *Christian Rural Fellowship Bulletin* (99): 1-6.

1780. Moomaw, Ira W.
1948 "How the Rural Church Lives." *Town and Country Church* (January): 5-6.

1781. Moomaw, Ira W.
1951 "Land Reform: A Christian Challenge." *Christian Rural Fellowship Bulletin* (166): 1-10. Reprint from *Social Action* (June, 1951).

1782. Moomaw, Ira W.
1953 "Missions and Extension." *Rural Missions* (Autumn): 1-2.

1783. Moomaw, Ira W.
1953 "Training for the Rural Missionary." *Town and Country Church* (November): 13.

1784. Moomaw, Ira W.
      1956 "The Gospel and Village Life." *Town and Country Church*
      (February): 6-7.

1785. Moomaw, Ira W.
      1959 "The Present--Let's Face It." *Rural Missions* (Summer): 3-4.

1786. Moomaw, Ira W.
      1960 "Rough Roads to a New Destiny." *Christian Rural Fellowship
      Bulletin (223): 1-4.*

1787. Moomaw, Ira W.
      1962 "Handicrafts and Cottage Industries: The Church Can Help
      Achieve a Balance between Tradition and Industry." *Rural
      Missions* (Winter): 1-3.

1788. Moore, M.L.
      1949 "The Church and Conservation of the Soil." *Town and
      Country Church* (October): 4.

1789. Moore-Darling, E.
      1946 "Why Villagers Do Not Go to Church." *Countryman*
      33(Spring): 52-56.

1790. Morgan, Arthur E.
      1947 "A New Rural Pattern." *Christian Rural Fellowship Bulletin*
      (124): 1-4.

1791. Morgan, Arthur E.
      1952 "Farming by the Golden Rule." *Community Service News*
      (January/February): 20-22.

1792. Morgan, Arthur E.
      1954 "Tradition of Community Living." *Christian Rural Fellowship
      Bulletin* (194): 1-4.

1793. Morgan, Griscom.
      1950 "The Community as Person." *Christian Rural Fellowship
      Bulletin* (157): 1-4. Reprint from *Community Service News*
      (May-June, 1950).

1794. Moritz, F.L.
      1949 "God, Man, and the Land: More Hope Seen for Rural
      Churches of Missouri through New Kind of Teaching."
      Missouri Farmer (December): 3, 7.

1795. Mosher, Arthur T.
1940 "The Kingdom of God and Rural Reconstruction." *Christian Rural Fellowship Bulletin* (56): 1-10.

1796. Mosher, Arthur T.
1942 "The Spiritual Basis of a Comprehensive or 'Larger Parish' Program." *Christian Rural Fellowship Bulletin* (75): 1-6.

1797. Mosher, Arthur T.
1945 "God in the Countryside." *Christian Rural Fellowship Bulletin* (105): 1-6. Also in *Theology Today* (July, 1945).

1798. Mosher, Arthur T.
1945 "Recent Rural Missions Insights and Principles." *Christian Rural Fellowship Bulletin* (102): 1-8.

1799. Mott, Edward.
1946 "Providing Responsible Leadership in the Rural Church." *Christian Rural Fellowship Bulletin* (118): 1-4.

1800. Mott, John R.
1917 "An International Country Life Outlook." *Rural Manhood* (January): 21-22.

1801. Mueller, Elwin W.
1952 "The Rural Congregation and Community Health." *Rural Lutheran* (September): 1, 7.

1802. Mueller, Elwin W.
1958 "Eight Thousand Efficient Farmers." *Town and Country Church* (March): 12-14.

1803. Mueller, Elwin W.
1962 "Not Bigger, but Better." *Town and Country Church* (March/April): 6-7.

1804. Mueller, Elwin W.
1963 "The Impact of the Agricultural Revolution on the Religious Life of the Nation." *Christian Rural Fellowship Bulletin* (231): 1-12.

1805. Mueller, R.
1965 "World Hunger." *Limestone* 2(Sept): 12-13, 15.

1806. Muhm, D.
1952 "What's Become of our Rural Churches?" *Iowa Agriculture* (May): 4-6.

1807. Munro, H.C.
      1947 "An All-Protestant Strategy for Town and Country
      Churches: A Pattern and How to Use It." *Town and
      Country Church* (February): 1-3.

1808. Munro, H.C.
      1948 "What is Your Evangelistic 'Potential?'" *Town and Country
      Church* (January): 9-10.

1809. Murphy, R.E.
      1948 "A Laboratory Training School in Action." *Town and
      Country Church* (January): 1-4.

1810. Murphy, W.B.
      1966 "The Rural-Urban Balance." *Town and Country Church*
      (July/August): 4.

1811. Murray, C.R.
      1956 "United Effort is OK." *Town and Country Church*
      (November): 1-2.

1812. Nace, I.G.
      1950 "Rechurching Rural America." *Town and Country Church*
      (February): 1-2.

1813. Niederfrank, E.J.
      1949 "The Rural Clergyman as a Parish Leader." *Christian Rural
      Fellowship Bulletin* (144): 1-4.

1814. Niederfrank, E.J.
      1958 "Social Aspects of Church and Community Development."
      Town and Country Church (November): 1-3.

1815. Niederfrank, E.J.
      1960 "Community Development through Town and Country
      Churches." *Christian Rural Fellowship Bulletin* (Summer): 1-8.

1816. Neigh, K.G.
      1962 "The Local Church with a Worldwide Concern." *Town and
      Country Church* (May/June): 14-16.

1817. Nelson, Erland.
      1937 "Putting Culture into Agriculture." *Christian Rural Fellowship
      Bulletin* (21): 1-4.

1818. Nettleton, A.
    1952 "Caring for the Country Church." *Estate Magazine*
    (December): 499-500.

1819. Nunn, Alexander.
    1953 "Crops the Church Should Plant." *Town and Country Church*
    (May): 5-7.

1820. Nunn, Alexander.
    1955 "A Rural Church Program for the Next Fifty Years."
    Christian Rural Fellowship Bulletin (202): 1-12.

1821. Nyberg, D.E.
    1947 "Increasing Sunday School Interest with the Christian
    Year." *Town and Country Church* (October): 3-4.

1822. Obenhaus, Victor.
    1951 "Protestant Contribution to Democracy through Local
    Group Action." *Town and Country Church* (February): 3-4.

1823. Obenhaus, Victor.
    1956 "Enduring Values in Rural Life." *Christian Rural Fellowship
    Bulletin* (205): 1-6.

1824. Obenhaus, Victor.
    1959 "Christian Faith Speaks to the Farm Situation." *Social Action*
    25(February): 15-21.

1825. O'Brien, Bob.
    1973 "Growning From Harnessed Tension." *Home Missions* 43(3,
    March): 30-32.

1826. O'Cain, J.
    1953 "The Rural Church." *Agrarian* 12(Spring): 10.

1827. O'Hara, Edwin V.
    1949 "The Church Builds the Country Community." *Christian
    Rural Fellowship Bulletin* (147): 1-6.

1828. O'Hara, W.
    1947 "Farm Bureau Supports Rural Church Development
    Programs." *Hoosier Farmer* 32(March): 12.

1829. Ormond, Jesse Marvin, et al.
    1943 "Land and Human Welfare." *Christian Rural Fellowship
    Bulletin* (82): 1-6.

1830. O'Rourke, Edward W.
      1961 "The Rural Family in 1965." *Christian Rural Fellowship Bulletin* (224): 1-6.

1831. Ostendorf, David L.
      1986 "For Generations to Come: The Cost of America's Farm Crisis." *Sojourners* 15(9): 18-21.

1832. Otis, A.W.
      1915 "The Walnut Community Council." *Rural Manhood* (January).

1833. Otter, A.
      1948 "The Spiritual Life of the Village." *Village* (Spring): 12.

1834. Pankenbring, R.
      1966 "Rural Environment for the Church." *Lutheran Witness* (May): 24.

1835. "Pastoral Letter on Agriculture".
      1985 *America* (March 2): 160.

1836. Patch, C.E. (Dan).
      1952 "The Church in the Rural Community: A Challenge, A Responsibility, and an Opportunity." *Christian Rural Fellowship Bulletin* (173): 1-4.

1837. Patterson, Nancy-Lou.
      1983 "See the Vernal Landscape Glowing: The Symbolic Landscape of the Swiss-German Mennonite Settlers in Waterloo County." *Mennonite Life* 38(4): 8-16.

1838. Patton, M.H.
      1962 "The Agricultural Migrant and the Local Church." *Town and Country Church* (November/December): 6.

1839. Peck, Frank W.
      1947 "Three Measures of Farm Success." *Christian Rural Fellowship Bulletin* (127): 1-6.

1840. Pennington, J.P.
      1947 "Four Folds to Shepherd." *Town and Country Church* (September): 7-8.

1841. Pennington, J.P.
      1949 "The Church in a Four-Church Parish." *Town and Country Church* (November): 12.

1842. Pennington, J.P.
 1951 "A Parish Youth Group." *Town and Country Church*
 (October): 4.

1843. Perdue, Mrs. Calvin.
 1940 "The Kind of Rural Church I Would Like to Have in My
 Community." *Christian Rural Fellowship Bulletin* (57): 1-6.

1844. Perry, Alfred T.
 1900 "The Federation, Its Nature and Function." *Hartford
 Seminary Record.*

1845. Phillips, P.
 1946 "Land, Homes and the Church: Our Resources Work for
 the Church." *Town and Country Church* (January): 3-4.

1846. Pielstick, Don F.
 1945 "Church, Cooperative, and Adult Education." *Town and
 Country Church* (November): 1-2.

1847. Pielstick, Don F.
 1946 "Evangelism and the Lord's Acre." *Farmers Federation News*
 (January): 23.

1848. Pielstick, Don F.
 1948 "Rechurching Rural America." *Town and Country Church*
 (September): 8-9.

1849. Pielstick, Don F.
 1951 "How Can We Make a Rural Church and Community
 Study?" *Town and Country Church* (February): 10-11.

1850. Pielstick, Don F.
 1952 "In Praise and Blame." *Town and Country Church* (March):
 12-13.

1851. Pielstick, Don F.
 1952 "The Town and Country Church in the Pacific Northwest."
 Town and Country Church (February): 7.

1852. Pielstick, Don F.
 1953 "The Fields of the Spirit." *Town and Country Church* (May):
 8.

1853. Pielstick, Don F.
 1953 "The Church's Responsibility for Rural Life: An American
 Point of View." *Christian Rural Fellowship Bulletin* (187): 1-4.

1854. Pinchot, Gifford.
      1915 "Rural Religious Problems." *Rural Manhood* (January): 3-5.

1855. Pius XII.
      1948 "The Pope on the Peasant." *Cross and Plough* 15(1): 6.

1856. Plant, R.C.
      1957 "Talking the Farmers' Language." *Town and Country Church*
      (May): 10-11.

1857. Ploch, L.A.
      1962 "Social Problems in the Town and Country Church." *Town
      and Country Church* (May/June): 5-7.

1858. Poe, Clarence.
      1943 "How Can We Strengthen Country Churches?" *Progressive
      Farmer* (Mississippi, Arkansas, Louisiana edition)
      58(December): 46.

1859. Poe, Clarence.
      1945 "Churches and Recreation." *Progressive Farmer* (Mississippi,
      Arkansas, Louisiana edition) (November): 18.

1860. Poe, Clarence.
      1951 "How Can We Strengthen Country Churches?" *Progressive
      Farmer* (Texas edition) (July): 102.

1861. Pomeroy, James.
      1980 "Small Church, Big Opportunities." *The Church School*
      (March).

1862. Pope, W.
      1949 "The Rural Church Has an Answer." *Cornell Countryman*
      (March): 12, 34.

1863. Porter, Edward G.
      1893 "The Andover Band in Maine." *Andover Review* (March-
      April): 198-207.

1864. Porter, Ward F.
      1957 "Noneconomic Goals of Farming and Rural Life." *Christian
      Rural Fellowship Bulletin* (209): 1-8.

1865. Potter, Andrew.
      1944 "Let's Revive the Country Church." *Farmer-Stockman*
      57(June): 227, 251, 258.

1866. Power, Normat S.
1951 "Church in the Parish." *The Modern Churchman*
41(September): 238-243.

1867. "Prairie Church: More than Simple Survival."
1967 *Presbyterian Life* (September 1): 12.

1868. Price, C.W., Jr.
1949 "They're Near Heaven." *Farm Journal* (May): 63.

1869. Price, Frank Wilson.
1938 "The Kingdom of God in a Rural Community." *Christian Rural Fellowship Bulletin* (33): 1-4.

1870. Price, Frank Wilson.
1956 "Christian Farmers of the World--Unite!" *Christian Rural Fellowship Bulletin* (206): 1-6.

1871. Prime, W.C.
1886 "Country Churches in New England." *New Princeton Review*: 184-202.

1872. Prior, K.H.
1953 "God, Man, and the Land." *Christian Rural Fellowship Bulletin* (188): 1-4.

1873. Prunty, Kenneth G.
1983 "Growing Leaders in the Small Church." *Christian Leadership* (November).

1874. Puskarich, L.
1983 "Rural Churches Bond Communities (Ohio)." *Buckeye Farm News* (October): 34-35.

1875. Quimby, K.
1952 "New Support for the Churches!" *Town and Country Church* (November): 2-3.

1876. Quist, G.B.
1960 "Vacation Time--A Challenge to the Church." *Town and Country Church* (May): 3-5, 14-15.

1877. Ramsden, William E.
19-- "Small Church Studies: Emerging Consensus." *Christian Ministry* : 10-12.

1878. Ranck, Lee.
1967 "The Aberdeen Area Ministry." *Church and Home* 4(September): 29-34.

1879. Ranck, Lee.
       1967 "The Little Country Church--It Ain't What It Used to Be!"
       United Church Herald 10(November): 19-29.

1880. Randolph, Henry S.
       1945 "The Church in the Rural Life Movement." *Mountain Life
       and Work* 21(1): 6-10.

1881. Randolph, Henry S.
       1950 "Thy Kingdom Come in Rural America." *Christian Rural
       Fellowship Bulletin* (151): 1-4. Also in *Town and Country
       Church* (December, 1950): 1-3.

1882. Randolph, Henry S.
       1951 "An Effective Rural Church Program." *Christian Rural
       Fellowship Bulletin* (168): 1-6. Also in *Town and Country
       Church* (May, 1952): 5-6.

1883. Randolph, Henry S.
       1952 "The Christian Church and Human Integration--One
       People." *Christian Rural Fellowship Bulletin* (175): 1-7.

1884. Randolph, Henry S.
       1956 "The Rural Church Today Faces Tomorrow." *Town and
       Country Church* (February): 1-4.

1885. Randolph, Henry S.
       1960 "The Challenge of the Beckoning Seventies." *Christian Rural
       Fellowship Bulletin* (228): 1-8.

1886. Randolph, Henry S.
       1962 "The American Indian and the Church." *Town and Country
       Church* (September/October): 10-11.

1887. Randolph, Henry S. and Don F. Pielstick.
       1947 "Report for the Year 1946." *Town and Country Church*
       (February): 14.

1888. Raper, Arthur.
       1937 "Ethics of Land Tenancy." *Christian Rural Fellowship Bulletin*
       (26): 1-4.

1889. Rapking, Aaron H.
       1944 "The Rural Church of Tomorrow." *Christian Rural Fellowship
       Bulletin* (94): 1-4.

1890. Rapking, Aaron H.
       1948 "Religion and Life in the Countryside." *Town and Country
       Church* (March): 7.

1891. Rapking, Aaron H.
1949 "The Rural Minister and His Message." *Christian Rural Fellowship Bulletin* (139): 1-4.

1892. Rapking, Aaron H.
1951 "The Kingdom of God in Everyday Living." *Christian Rural Fellowship Bulletin* (164): 1-4.

1893. Rasmussen, A.O.
1949 "Face Lifting Country Churches." *Pennsylvania Farmer* (July 9): 13.

1894. Raven, C.E.
1946 "Towards a Christian Community." *Christian Rural Fellowship Bulletin* (113): 1-4.

1895. Raven, C.E.
1959 "The Earth Is the Lord's." *Christian Rural Fellowship Bulletin* (217): 1-8.

1896. Raver, P.
1952 "Developments in the Pacific Northwest." *Town and Country Church* (March): 3-4.

1897. Rawlings, J.C.
1949 "A Call to the Heroic." *Christian Rural Fellowship Bulletin* (140): 1-6.

1898. Raymond, M.
1909 "The Church of Christ in Ruralville." *Yale Divinity Quarterly* (February).

1899. Rector, F.E.
1962 "Church Planning in Town and Country." *Town and Country Church* (July/August): 11-14.

1900. Reeder, N.
1953 "Good Churches Make Good Neighbors." *Capper's Farmer* 64(3): 33, 114-115.

1901. Reitz, T.R.
1949 "Two Churches Join: Belle Plaine-Palestine Consolidation Reflects Changing Times." *Kansas Farmer* (June 4): 20-21.

1902. Renshaw, B.
1950 "Revitalized Church; The Formula is Simple, You Can Do It!" *Prairie Farmer* (General edition.) (December 2): 5.

1903. Renshaw, B.
1951 "Spiritual Harvest: God's Acre Project Encourages Good Neighbor Relations." *Prairie Farmer* (General edition) (December 15): 5.

1904. Reuss, C.F.
1944 "Church Membership and Finance in Virginia, the South, and the Nation." *Virginia University News Letter* 20(April 1): 1.

1905. Reuss, C.F.
1944 "Trends in Virginia Church Membership and Finance, 1926-1936." *Virginia University News Letter* 20(April 1): 1.

1906. Reynolds, A.G.
1944 "Values." *Christian Rural Fellowship Bulletin* (96): 1-8.

1907. Rhea, E.
1946 "Rural Laity Initiate Their Own Advance." *Town and Country Church* (December): 1-2.

1908. Rhoades, J.B.
1963 "Technical Development and the Churches." *Town and Country Church* (January/February): 11-12.

1909. Rich, Mark.
1941 "A Basic Philosophy for Promoting Cooperation among Rural Churches." *Christian Rural Fellowship Bulletin* (63): 1-6.

1910. Rich, Mark.
1947 "The Rural Church Movement." *Town and Country Church* (December): 2.

1911. Rich, Mark.
1947 "The Rural Pastoral Work of Felix Neff." *Town and Country Church* (February): 5-6.

1912. Rich, Mark.
1948 "The Minister as Evangelist." *Town and Country Church* (November): 1-3.

1913. Rich, Mark.
1953 "Ministers of the Earth." *Land* (Spring): 49-52.

1914. Rich, Mark.
1954 "Satisfaction in the Rural Ministry." *Town and Country Church* (October): 1-2.

1915. Rich, Mark.
1955 "Is Denominationalism Resurgent?" *Town and Country Church* (January): 9.

1916. Rich, Mark.
1955 "Some Impressions of the Rural Church Movement." *Town and Country Church* (December): 5-6.

1917. Rich, Mark.
1955 "Strengthening the Church's Ministry." *Town and Country Church* (November): 1-2.

1918. Rich, Mark.
1956 "Family Night in Town and Country Churches." *Town and Country Church* (May): 1-3.

1919. Rich, Mark.
1956 "The Christian Community." *Christian Rural Fellowship Bulletin* (204): 1-5.

1920. Rich, Mark.
1956 "The Minster's Role in Family Night Fellowship." *Town and Country Church* (November): 3-4.

1921. Rich, Mark.
1957 "Conferences on Cooperative Churches." *Town and Country Church* (May): 7.

1922. Rich, Mark.
1957 "Democracy and the Local Church." *Town and Country Church* (February): 9-11.

1923. Rich, Mark.
1958 "Adequacy and Trends for Rural Units." *Town and Country Church* (October): 1-3.

1924. Rich, Mark.
1958 "In-Service Training for the Rural Ministry: An Historical Analysis." *Town and Country Church* (November): 10-12.

1925. Rich, Mark.
1958 "The Bivocational Minister in Rural Society." *Town and Country Church* (September): 5-7.

1926. Rich, Mark.
1958 "Your Church Can Be Stronger through Cooperation." *Town and Country Church* (May): 5-6.

1927. Richardson, H.V.
      1947 "The Rural Church in the South." *Town and Country Church*
      (December): 6-7.

1928. Richardson, H.V.
      1953 "The Rural Church of the Negro People in the South."
      Town and Country Church (February): 14.

1929. Rickwood, Arthur S.
      1950 "The Faith of a Countryman: An English Farmer Speaks."
      Christian Rural Fellowship Bulletin (150): 1-4.

1930. Riddle, Katharine P.
      1967 "World Hunger and the Christian Conscience." *Christian
      Rural Fellowship Bulletin* (247): 1-8.

1931. Ridgeway, James.
      1986 "The Farm Belt's Far Right: A Historical Overview."
      Sojourners 15(9): 22-24.

1932. Ritschl, D.
      1962 "A Critical Look at Some Current Theses Regarding the
      Mission of the Church." *Town and Country Church*
      (March/April): 12-14.

1933. Ritchie, B.
      1949 "Wiggins Goes to Church." *Colorado Rancher and Farmer*
      (August 27): 1, 7.

1934. Roberts, Albert E.
      1911 "The Country Church Conference." *Rural Manhood*
      (January): 7-10.

1935. Roberts, Alton C.
      1917 "County Wide Community Sunday Plan." *Rural Manhood* 5:
      295-298.

1936. Robertson, James W.
      1913 "Farming in Partnership with God." *Rural Manhood* 4: 2.

1937. Rodale, J.I.
      1948 "The Church and the Farmer--A Plan!" *Organic Gardening*
      (October): 12-14.

1938. Rodehaver, M.W.
      1948 "We Need a Rural Minister." *Town and Country Church*
      (March): 12-13.

1939. Rogers, B.E.
1952 "Rural Ministers-of-the-Year Find Many Ways to Serve."
Ohio Farmer (June 7): 10-11.

1940. Rogers, Clyde N.
1946 "Adventures in Home-Grown Religion." *Successful Farming*
(April): 32, 52.

1941. Rogers, Clyde N.
1946 Rural Church at the Cross-Roads." *Nebraska Farmer* (May
11): 1, 30, 31.

1942. Rogers, Clyde N.
1948 "The Ways of the Creator in the Natural World." *Christian
Rural Fellowship Bulletin* (136): 1-6.

1943. Rogers, Everett M.
1962 "Social Change in Rural Society." *Christian Rural Fellowship
Bulletin* (228): 1-8.

1944. Root, E. Talmadge.
1906 "Progress of Church Federation in New England." *Church
Federation.*

1945. Root, E. Talmadge.
1909 "What's the Matter with the Churches?" *Delineator*
(December).

1946. Rose, Royce A.
1983 "The Rural Church: Not Gone, But Forgotten." *Baptist
History and Heritage* 18(October): 44-46.

1947. Roush, W.
1946 "Cortland Community Churches' Office." *Town and Country
Church* (November): 3-4.

1948. Runnells, D.
1945 "Dynamic Kernels." *Farm Journal* 69(September): 18.

1949. "Rural Churches: Teaming Up, Pulling Together."
1965 *Together* 9(September): 3-4.

1950. Russell, Connie.
1964 "Church and a Community Work in Town and Country."
Methodist Rural Fellowship Bulletin 21(3, September): 14.

1951. Russell, D.
     1949 "A Broad Program of Rural Church Organization." *Town and Country Church* (September): 12-13.

1952. Russell, George W.
     1915 "The Rural Community." *Rural Manhood.*

1953. Russell, H.L.
     1945 "Success Gained in Iowa Church with the Lord's Acre Plan." *Farmers Federation News* 25(May): 18.

1954. Ryan, R.H.
     1963 "Program Planning in the Rural Parish." *Church School* 16(June): 18-19.

1955. Ryter, Rene A.
     1964 "Give Us a Vision." *Christian Rural Fellowship Bulletin* (237): 1-10.

1956. Ryter, Rene A.
     1967 "Where Does Our Fellowship Stand in the Critical Fight Against World Hunger?" *Christian Rural Fellowship Bulletin* (248): 1-8.

1957. Sala, J.P.
     1950 "From Big City to Country Lane." *Town and Country Church* (January): 14-15.

1958. Samuelson, Clifford L.
     1955 "Spiritual Resources for Today's Rural Life." *Christian Rural Fellowship Bulletin* (199): 1-7.

1959. Sanders, Irwin T. and T.W. Spicer.
     1941 "The Social and Religious Significance of the Rural Neighborhood." *Christian Rural Fellowship Bulletin* (65): 1-6.

1960. Sanderson, Dwight.
     1939 "Disadvantaged Classes in Rural Life." *Christian Rural Fellowship Bulletin* (38): 1-7. Reprint from *Rural America* (December, 1938).

1961. Sanderson, R.W.
     1949 "The Responsibility of the Town and Country Church for the Rural Community." *Town and Country Church* (February): 1-2.

1962. Sanderson, R.W.
    1952 "Cooperatively Churching the Columbia Valley." *Town and Country Church* (February): 3-4.

1963. Sanger, Florence Z.
    1957 "Pastorale Farm Life." *Brethren Life and Thought* 2(1): 67-74.

1964. Sass, H.R.
    1946 "Lord's Auction." *Saturday Evening Post* 219(November 23): 30-31, 82, 85, 87.

1965. Saunders, C.C.
    1954 "More Power to Our Rural Churches." *Town and Country Church* (February): 7-8.

1966. Saunders, C.W.
    1950 "The 4-Square Life." *Town and Country Church* (March): 4.

1967. Sayre, Ruth Buxton.
    1948 "A Country Woman Looks at the World." *Christian Rural Fellowship Bulletin* (138): 1-5.

1968. Saywell, C.W.
    1946 "The Church Goes to the Fair." *Town and Country Church* (November): 1-2.

1969. Schaller, Lyle E.
    1965 "Can We Afford So Many Small Churches?" *Christian Advocate* 9(March 25): 11-12.

1970. Schiefele, Theodore C.
    1949 "Study of Closed Rural Pennsylvania Churches." *Lutheran Quarterly* 1(May): 200-205.

1971. Schilling, W.E.
    1947 "Making the Church Building Serve." *Rural Church* (December/January 1948): 1-3.

1972. Schimek, W.
    1946 "Retreats for Farmers." *Land and Home* (March): 5-7.

1973. Schnucker, Calvin T.
    1944 "The Pulpit and the Plow." *Christian Rural Fellowship Bulletin* (89): 1-4.

1974. Schnucker, Calvin T.
    1947 "The Iowa Religious Census." *Town and Country Church* (January): 4.

1975. Schnucker, Calvin T.
      1952 "What Should We Emphasize in Our Programs?" *Town and Country Church* (February): 1-2.

1976. Schores, D.M.
      1958 "This Holy Earth." *Town and Country Church* (February): 13, 15.

1977. Schores, D.M.
      1959 "Methodist Rural Adjustment Policy." *Town and Country Church* (March): 7-8.

1978. Schores, D.M.
      1966 "The Leisure Revolution Has Strengthened This Church." *Town and Country Church* (July/August): 12-13.

1979. Schroedel, M.P.
      1947 "Church Buildings and Programs." *Rural Church* 9(February/March): 1-4.

1980. Schroeder, Martin.
      1940 "Ministering to the Dispossessed in Rural Communities." *Christian Rural Fellowship Bulletin* (52): 1-4.

1981. Schroeder, Martin.
      1940 "The Rural Minister and the Country Church: The Country Church is Different." *Christian Rural Fellowship Bulletin* (55): 1-3. Reprint from *The Christian Century Pulpit* (June, 1940).

1982. Schroeder, Martin.
      1944 "The Church's Part in Building the Rural Parish." *Christian Rural Fellowship Bulletin* (88): 1-8.

1983. Scott, David L.
      1951 "Century Ago in a Country Parish." *The Modern Churchman* 41(June): 104-109.

1984. Searson, C.M.
      1944 "The Church and the Rural Community." *Christian Rural Fellowship Bulletin* (92): 1-6.

1985. Seaton, H.
      1947 "Let Gay Flowers Adorn Your Churchyards." *Guild Gardener* 22(June): 10.

1986. Seaton, H.
      1947 "Your Church Set in a Garden." *Guild Gardener* 22(August): 2.

1987. Selcraig-Furlow, Elain.
    1973 "Search for a Better Way." *Home Missions* 43(3, March): 26-29.

1988. Sells, J.W.
    1948 "An Experiment Station for Your Church." *Progressive Farmer* (Texas edition) (August): 41.

1989. Sells, J.W.
    1949 "A Rural Church Harvest; Recognition for Work Well Done Leads to Ideas for Future Labors." *Progressive Farmer* (Texas edition) (October): 18, 113.

1990. Sells, J.W.
    1950 "Better Rural Churches Bring a Better Rural Life." *Progressive Farmer* (Georgia, Alabama, Florida edition) (September): 22, 117.

1991. Sells, J.W.
    1950 "Prettier Church Grounds." *Progressive Farmer* (Georgia, Alabama, Florida edition) (April): 17.

1992. Sells, J.W.
    1953 "Mississippi's Egypt Methodist Church Believes in a Better Church, Community, and World." *Progressive Farmer* (Texas edition) (October): 53-54.

1993. Selvamoney, C.
    1962 "Theological College in a Rural Community." *Christian Rural Fellowship Bulletin* (229): 1-6.

1994. Severson, H.
    1946 "The Country Church that Found Itself." *Southern Agriculture* (April): 11.

1995. Seymour, B.
    1950 "Thanksgiving Church Did It: Maybe Your Church Could." *Progressive Farmer* (Texas edition.). (November): 70, 79.

1996. Shane, G.
    1951 "Church Finds Farming Profitable." *Town and Country Church* (October): 3.

1997. Shaw, William.
    1910 "The Christian Endeavor Society as a Factor in Village Life." *Rural Manhood* (February): 9-11.

1998. Sheldon, Frank M.
      1926 "What We Can Do to Help the Country Church."
      Oklahoma Farmer-Stockman (December 15).

1999. Sheldon, Frank M.
      1927 "One Strong Church Instead of Two Weak Ones."
      Oklahoma Farmer-Stockman (January 1).

2000. Sheridan, George.
      1973 "Hard Times to Hoe." *Home Missions* 43(3, March): 17-19.

2001. Sherman, J.K.
      1956 "To What Extent Can the Traditional Institutional Church
      Serve an Area?" *Town and Country Church* (February): 10-11.

2002. Shipley, Anthony J.
      1976 "Everybody Wants to Go to Heaven, But Nobody Wants to
      Die." *Christian Century* 93(April 7): 326-327.

2003. Showalter, C.
      1954 "Raising the Crop." *Town and Country Church* (April): 4.

2004. Singh, J.C.B.
      1948 "The Place of the Church in Rural Work." *The Christian
      Rural Fellowship Bulletin* (137): 1-4.

2005. Skelley, G.
      1946 "Rural Church--Community Spirit." *Iowa Bur. Farmer* (May):
      10.

2006. Skinner, Stanley E.
      1941 "The Characteristics of a Christian Rural Community: The
      Hubbardsville-East Hamilton Community, New York."
      Christian Rural Fellowship Bulletin (59): 1-6.

2007. Slack, Kenneth.
      1985 "Death of the Country Church?" *Christian Century* (October
      2): 854-855.

2008. "Small-Town America Still Has Great Appeal."
      1966 *Town and Country Church* (September-October): 8.

2009. Smathers, Eugene.
      1941 "A Rural Church Program that Makes Religion the
      Qualifying Factor in Every Experience in Life." *Christian
      Rural Fellowship Bulletin* (66): 1-8.

2010. Smathers, Eugene.
1941 "The Characteristics of a Christian Rural Community: The Big Lick Community, Texas." *Christian Rural Fellowship Bulletin* (61): 1-6.

2011. Smathers, Eugene.
1943 "The Church and Rural Security." *Christian Rural Fellowship Bulletin* (86): 1-8.

2012. Smathers, Eugene.
1946 "The Church in Rural Reconstruction." *Christian Rural Fellowship Bulletin* (116): 1-6. Also in *Soil Conservation* 12(October): 55-59.

2013. Smathers, Eugene.
1949 "The Function of the Minister in Relation to Rural Culture." *Christian Rural Fellowship Bulletin* (145): 1-8.

2014. Smathers, Eugene.
1953 "The Church Moves the Community." *Christian Rural Fellowship Bulletin* (179): 1-7.

2015. Smathers, Eugene.
1957 "The Christian Faith and Community Concern." *Christian Rural Fellowship Bulletin* (210): 1-6.

2016. Smathers, Eugene.
1965 "How to Be a Successful Pastor." *Town and Country Church* (November/December): 10-15.

2017. Smith, Mrs. G.
1945 "The Useful Garden as a Church Instrument." *Town and Country Church* (October): 5.

2018. Smith, Hilary.
1966 "Main Street: A Job for the Church." *America* 114(May 14): 689-691.

2019. Smith, Mervin G. and John B. Mitchell.
1963 "The Rural Nonfarm Population." *Christian Rural Fellowship Bulletin* (234): 1-12.

2020. Smith, J.M.
1948 "Rural Life and the Church." *Farmer's Advocate and Home Magazine* (May 13): 356-357.

2021. Smith, Rockwell Carter.
1943 "Some Basic Implications in the Development of a Vital Rural Church Program." *Christian Rural Fellowship Bulletin* (84): 1-6.

2022. Smith, Rockwell Carter.
1945 "The Rural Church and International Cooperation." *Christian Rural Fellowship Bulletin* (100): 106.

2023. Smith, Rockwell Carter.
1950 "The County Seat Church and Rural Life." *Town and Country Church* (February): 5-6.

2024. Smith, Rockwell Carter.
1959 "The Church in Rapidly Growing Rural Communities." *Town and Country Church* (May): 1-3.

2025. Smith, Rockwell Carter.
1960 "In-Service Training for the Town and Country Pastor." *Town and Country Church* (March): 13-14.

2026. Smith, Rockwell Carter.
1960 "The Work in the Great Plains Area." *Town and Country Church* (March): 3-4.

2027. Smithson, J.T.
1967 "Building a Religious Home through Work, Play, Worship, and Love." *American Coop* (September): 101-104.

2028. Snyder, C.
1948 "Help for Rural Churches." *Mountain Life and Work* (Winter): 24-25.

2029. Snyder, C.
1948 "The Church Sets the Pattern for Community Living." *Mountain Life and Work* (Fall): 18-19.

2030. Snyder, C.J.
1951 "Town and Country Church and this Convocation." *Town and Country Church* (February): 13.

2031. Snyder, C.J.
1953 "The Town and Country Church and Convocation." *Town and Country Church* (February): 5-6.

2032. Southern Baptist Convention.
1987 "Cooperative Program Support Comes from All Sizes of SBC Churches." *RD Digest* 8(7): 1-2. Research Division of the Home Mission Board, Southern Baptist Convention.

2033. Spicer, William C.
  1908 "Modern Problem of the American Church in Rural Communities." *Auburn Seminary Record.*

2034. Spickler, E.A.
  1947 "Building the Rural Church: A Bibliography." *Rural Church* (December): 5-6.

2035. Stacy, William H.
  1948 "Things that Are Right with Churches." *Town and Country Church* (September): 13.

2036. Stacy, William H.
  1952 "Recognizing Church-Community Relationships." *Town and Country Church* (January): 3.

2037. Stacy, William H.
  1955 "Extension and 3-D Programs of Churches." *Town and Country Church* (January): 5-6.

2038. Stacy, William H.
  1958 "Spotlighting Church-Community Relations." *Town and Country Church* (January): 7-10.

2039. Stacy, William H.
  1958 "Spotlighting Church-Community Programs." *Iowa Farm Science* (March): 723-724.

2040. Stacy, William H.
  1964 "Rural Life Sunday and Churches in Rural Development. *Town and Country Church* (175, March-April): 10.

2041. Stafford, Garland Reid.
  1937 "The Rural Church and the Tenant Farmer." *Christian Rural Fellowship Bulletin* (22): 1-4. Reprint from *The Christian Advocate* (May 21, 1927).

2042. Stark, C.H., Jr.
  1947 "Raising the Sights." *Town and Country Church* (September): 3-4.

2043. Steinmetz, P.H.
  1949 "Growing Grassroots: Opportunities for the Rural Ministry." *Town and Country Church* (October): 11.

2044. Stewart, W. and G. Crenshaw.
  1947 "Extending the Vacation School." *Town and Country Church* (May): 1-2.

2045. Stockman, Ralph W.
   1950 "God's Garden Spot." *Christian Rural Fellowship Bulletin*
   (153): 1-5.

2046. Stoerker, C.F.
   1960 "Ecumenical Voluntary Service Projects." *Town and Country
   Church* (May): 8-9.

2047. Stone, A.M.
   1951 "Rural Gospel Schools." *Rural Missions* (Autumn): 6.

2048. Stotts, Herbert E.
   1954 "Protestantism in Montana." *Town and Country Church*
   (January): 5-6.

2049. Stotts, Herbert E.
   1954 "Ties Bind Rural Churches and Cooperatives." *News of
   Farmer Cooperatives* (September): 7, 14.

2050. Stotts, Herbert E.
   1958 "The Role of the Town and Country Church in the Light
   of Today's Needs." *Christian Rural Fellowship Bulletin* (212):
   1-8.

2051. Stotts, Herbert E.
   1962 "An Overview of the Northeast." *Town and Country Church*
   (May/June): 3-4, 10.

2052. "Strangers and Guests: Toward Community in the Heartland."
   1982 *Bishop's Bulletin Special Supplement* (February).

2053. Struckman, R.P.
   1945 "The Holland Settlement Rural Church in Gallatin County,
   Montana is Large and Healthy." *Montana Farmer* (December
   15): 1.

2054. Stubbings, Leslie.
   1945 "Community." *Christian Rural Fellowship Bulletin* (106): 1-4.

2055. Sturm, R.A.
   1947 "A Church Orients Itself to Its Rural Task." *Rural Church*
   (October/November): 1-3.

2056. Stuenkel, W.W.
   1951 "Rural Life and the Church." *Concordia Theological Monthly*
   22(January): 33-45.

2057. Sweeney, G.R.
    1947 "The Pastor's Office." *Rural Church* (December/January 1948): 3-4.

2058. Sydnor, C.S.
    1960 "The Church and the Rural Industrial Community." *Town and Country Church* (January/February): 28-30.

2059. Talmage, N.A.
    1954 "A Farmer Talks to His Son." *Town and Country Church* (December): 5-6.

2060. Taylor, B.M.
    1948 "The Alpine Parish." *Town and Country Church* (February): 8.

2061. Taylor, Carl C.
    1925 "The Task of the Rural Church." *Rural America* (September): 3-4.

2062. Taylor, Carl C.
    1925 "The Program in the Rural Church." *Rural America* (October): 7, 10.

2063. Taylor, Carl C.
    1951 "Some Rural Situations and the Responsibilities of Rural Churches." *Town and Country Church* (February): 7, 16.

2064. Taylor, Graham.
    1902 "The Civic Function of the Country Church." *The Chautauquan* (December).

2065. Taylor, Henry C.
    1941 "Rural People and World Peace." *Christian Rural Fellowship Bulletin* (60): 1-8.

2066. Taylor, Henry C.
    1946 "Economic Groupism and the Church." *Christian Rural Fellowship Bulletin* (115): 1-6. Reprint of Chapter 5 of *The Faith of the Free*. Chicago, Ill.: University Church of the Disciples of Christ.

2067. Taylor, Robert Joseph.
    1986 "Religious Participation Among Elderly Blacks." *Gerontologist* 26(6): 630-636.

2068. Teed, F.S.
    1950 "The Pastor: Public Relations Agent." *Town and Country Church* (May): 3-4.

2069. Tellis-Nayak, V.
1982 "The Transcendent Standard: The Religious Ethos of the Rural Elderly." *Gerontologist* 22(4): 359-363.

2070. "The Church as a Center of Rural Organization."
1902 *Michigan Political Science Association Publications* Vol. 4.

2071. "The Country Church."
1910 *The Westminster* (February 12).

2072. "The Problem of the Country Church."
1888 *Andover Review* (October).

2073. "The Rural Church Problem."
1910 *Wallace's Farmer* (December).

2074. Thiessen, Walter.
1986 "Farmers in Crisis: A Pastoral Response." *The Christian Ministry* 17(4): 19-22.

2075. Thomas, R.B.
1949 "Promoting Christian Unity in the Rural Community." *Town and Country Church* (April): 1-2.

2076. Thomas, R.B.
1949 "The Peru, New York Plan." *Town and Country Church* (November): 3-4.

2077. Thompson, Dennis.
1986 "Meeting Human Needs During the Rural Crisis." *Engage/Social Action* 14(9): 26-33.

2078. Thompson, J.J.
1974 "Southern Baptist City and Country Churches." *Foundations* 17(October-December): 351-363.

2079. Thompson, W.H.
1948 "Recruiting by the Rural Ministry." *Town and Country Church* (January): 11.

2080. Tindall, C.
1947 "We Do Need Rural Churches." *Missouri Ruralist* 88(April 26): 6, 14-15.

2081. Torkelson, Willmar.
1985 "Rural Life Ministers Urge Respect for Environment...New Politics, Economics for Land and Resources." *National Catholic Reporter* 21(September 27): 26.

2082. Torkelson, Willmar.
1985 "Churches Map Program for Farmers' Troubles." *National Catholic Reporter* 21 (February 1): 7.

2083. Townsend, H.E., Jr.
1947 "A Church that Practices Forestry." *Farm and Ranch* 66(March): 18.

2084. Townsend, T.H.
1945 "Farmer-Preacher Tackles Rural Church Problems: Rev. Laurence K. Pickard Divides Time between Tilling Soil and Carrying on Rural Church Work in Schuyler County Parish." *Dairymen's League News* (December 4): 10. Also in *Town and Country Church* (March 1946): 6-7.)

2085. Tripp, Thomas Alfred.
1945 "Rural Culture Needs the Church." *Town and Country Church* (February): 4.

2086. Tripp, Thomas Alfred.
1945 "Shall Ministers Farm?" *Town and Country Church* (December): 5.

2087. Tripp, Thomas Alfred.
1945 "What is the Rural Church?" *Town and Country Church* (October): 4.

2088. Tripp, Thomas Alfred.
1946 "Some Advantages of Circuits." *Town and Country Church* (October): 6.

2089. Tripp, Thomas Alfred.
1947 "In Search of a Philosophy of Rural Life." *Christian Rural Fellowship Bulletin* (125): 1-4.

2090. Tripp, Thomas Alfred.
1948 "Rebuilding the Rural Church." *Town and Country Church* (March): 4.

2091. Tripp, Thomas Alfred.
1948 "The Rural Church and the City Church." *Town and Country Church* (April): 9.

2092. Tripp, Thomas Alfred.
1949 "Renewal at the Roots." *Town and Country Church* (November): 1-2.

2093. Tripp, Thomas Alfred.
      1951 "A Cooperative Rural Home Missionary Service." *Town and Country Church* (December): 1-2.

2094. Tripp, Thomas Alfred.
      1951 "Evangelism: A Basic Problem of the Church." *Town and Country Church* (October): 5-7.

2095. Tripp, Thomas Alfred.
      1951 "Making 'Great' Rural Churches." *Christian Century* 68(January 24): 109-110.

2096. Tripp, Thomas Alfred.
      1951 "Rural Congregationalism in America." *Congregational Quarterly* 29(April): 128-133.

2097. Tripp, Thomas Alfred.
      1951 "Witness of the Rural Church." *Town and Country Church* (March): 1-2.

2098. Tripp, Thomas Alfred.
      1952 "Challenge of the Rural Nonfarm Population to the Churches." *Town and Country Church* (May): 9-10.

2099. Tripp, Thomas Alfred.
      1952 "Life Ministry to Town and Country Churches." *Town and Country Church* (October): 1-2.

2100. Tripp, Thomas Alfred.
      1953 "Denominational Town and Country Church Departments." *Town and Country Church* (November): 12.

2101. Tripp, Thomas Alfred.
      1954 "The Theology of Arthur E. Holt." *Town and Country Church* (February): 1-4.

2102. Trott, N.L.
      1948 "How the United Church Canvass (Plan) Improved a Town's Religion." *Town and Country Church* (February): 5-6.

2103. Trotter, Ide P.
      1947 "Soils and Souls." *Christian Rural Fellowship Bulletin* (121): 1-4.

2104. Tunis, John.
      1888 "The Practical Treatment of the Problem of the Country Church." *Andover Review*.

2105. "Two Country Church Numbers."
      1904 *The Congregationalist and Christian World* (July).

2106. Ulrey, O.
      1947 "Articles on Religion and Church in Farm Journals: Sixty
      Farm Journals During Period January to July 1946." *Town
      and Country Church* (February): 9.

2107. Underwood, Bruce.
      1950 "A Strong Church Needs a Strong People." *Christian Rural
      Fellowship Bulletin* (156): 1-8.

2108. Upton, W.H.
      1945 "The Town and Country Meet at Church." *Town and
      Country Church* (February): 1-2.

2109. Urbain, J.V.
      1945 "Rural Communities of Tomorrow." *Land and Home* 8(1): 2-
      4.

2110. Vandermyde, J.B.
      1948 "Midland Goes to Churches." *News of Farmer Cooperatives*
      (April): 10, 18.

2111. Van Horn, G.A.
      1962 "The Church's Concern for Rural Nonfarm People." *Town
      and Country Church* (March/April): 3-5.

2112. Vernon, Matt.
      1943 "Bibles-Bulletins, Get Together." *Arkansas Farmer* 45(8): 6,
      14.

2113. Vetters, Kenneth and Cindy Vetters Lanning.
      1984 "Evangelism in a Small Town." *Leadership* (Spring): 74-78.

2114. Voelker, S.W.
      1959 "Mileage and Travel-Expense Records." *Town and Country
      Church* (October): 1-3.

2115. Vogt, Paul Leroy.
      1943 "The Resources of the Country Church." *Christian Rural
      Fellowship Bulletin* (87): 1-6.

2116. Wagner, P.W.
      1962 "The Rural Minister and His Preparation." *Rural Missions*
      (Fall): 1-2.

2117. Wakely, R.E.
       1950 "The Development of the Resources of the Missouri Valley
            in Relation to Rural Life and the Rural Church." *Town and
            Country Church* (February): 10-11.

2118. Waldo, W.P.
       1947 "United Church in Wooded Hills." *Town and Country
            Church* (April): 3.

2119. Wallace, Henry.
       1945 "My Ideal Rural Civilization." *Christian Rural Fellowship
            Bulletin* (108): 1-4.

2120. Wammer, O.M.
       1959 "The Church and Rural Youth." *Town and Country Church*
            (November): 1-2.

2121. Warburg, J.P.
       1958 "The Role of the Town and Country Church in a Changing
            World." *Town and Country Church* (February): 5-9.

2122. Watermulder, G.A.
       1946 "Native (Indian) Leadership Training." *Town and Country
            Church* (April): 5.

2123. Watson, Doris and George Watson.
       1951 "A Lost Generation." *United Seminary Quarterly*
            7(November): 23-29.

2124. Watts, David.
       1983 "The Work of the Hertforshire Baptist Union: A Case
            Study in Rural Mission." *Baptist Quarterly* 30(April): 67-73.

2125. Watts, R.L.
       1946 "An Amazing Country Church." *Pennsylvania Farmer*
            (February 23): 126.

2126. Webb, J.E.
       1949 "Family Farm Opportunities through the Methodist
            Church." *Rural Church* (April/May): 3-4.

2127. Webster, Norman C.
       1926 "Opportunities for the Country Minister." *The New England
            Homestead* (December 4).

2128. Weeks, Nathan A.
       1900 "The Regeneration of Rural Iowa." *Outlook* 65.

2129. Wells, George Frederick.
1906 "The Country Church and Its Social Problem." *Outlook* (August 18): 893-895.

2130. Wells, George Frederick.
1907 "An Answer to the New England Country Church Question." *Bibliotheca Sacra* (April): 314-330. Reprinted in *Christian Rural Fellowship Bulletin* (182, 1953): 1-8.

2131. Wells, George Frederick.
1907 "The Country Church and the Making of Manhood." *Rural Manhood* (August): 102-107. Also in *Homiletic Review* (August, 1907): 102-107.

2132. Wells, George Frederick.
1907 "What Our Country Churches Need." *Methodist Review* (July): 540-550.

2133. Wells, George Frederick.
1910 "How Two Country Churches Became One." *The Watchman* (March 17).

2134. Wells, George Frederick.
1910 "The Institutional Country Church." *Rural Manhood* (February): 11-13.

2135. Wells, George Frederick.
1953 "Origin of the Country Life Movement." *Town and Country Church* (May): 7.

2136. Wentworth, B.F.
1946 "The Church Helps to Build the Community." *Town and Country Church* (September): 7.

2137. Westrom, B.
1954 "The Church and the Rural-Urban Fringe." *Town and Country Church* (April): 14-15.

2138. Wetherell, G.W.
1953 "Training Rural Ministers." *American Coop* (25): 83-84.

2139. Whitaker, J.B.
1962 "Ministry with Migrants." *Town and Country Church* (September/October): 12-13.

2140. White, E.S.
1943 "Report of a Panel Discussion on the Effects of War on Religion and the Church in the Southern Highlands." *Mountain Life and Work* 19(2): 15-18.

2141. Whitehead, R. Don.
      1983 "Why Rural Churches Decline." *The Christian Ministry*
      14(September): 27-28.

2142. Whitman, Lauris Burchard.
      1947 "Signs for Town and Country Churches: How to Use
      Them." *Town and Country Church* (March): 8-9.

2143. Whitman, Lauris Burchard.
      1951 "Ministerial Candidates." *Town and Country Church*
      (December): 5-6.

2144. Whitman, Lauris Burchard.
      1952 "The Mission of the Church in Training Pastors for Rural
      Leadership." *Town and Country Church* (April): 5-6.

2145. Whitney, W.J.
      1947 "Cooperation with a Local Library." *Town and Country
      Church* (February): 4.

2146. "Why the Country Church Needs the Lord's Acre Plan."
      1944 *Farmers Federal News* 24(6): 6-8.

2147. Wiesen, G.W.
      1945 "The Lord's Acre Method in a New England Church."
      Town and Country Church (March): 3.

2148. Wileden, Arthur F.
      1958 "Church-Community Relationships in the World-Wide
      Mission." *Town and Country Church* (February): 9-13.

2149. Wiley, Bob.
      1983 "Portrait of a Small Town." *MissionUSA* (July-August): 47-
      54.

2150. Wiley, Bob.
      1983 "Small Town Churches: Entering an Era of Challenge."
      MissionUSA (July-August): 72.

2151. Williamson, Ralph L.
      1939 "The Christian Rural Fellowship Looks Ahead." *Christian
      Rural Fellowship Bulletin* (47): 1-4.

2152. Williamson, Ralph L.
      1943 "Spiritual Development through Neighborhood Fellowship
      Groups." *Christian Rural Fellowship Bulletin* (79): 1-7.

2153. Williamson, Ralph L.
    1944 "We Need a Rural Philosophy." *Christian Rural Fellowship Bulletin* (95): 1-8.

2154. Williamson, Ralph L.
    1948 "Amsterdam and the Rural Churches." *Christian Rural Fellowship Bulletin* (133): 1-6.

2155. Williamson, Ralph L.
    1951 "The Rural Church Institute." *Town and Country Church* (October).

2156. Williamson, Ralph L.
    1952 "Some Common Concerns and the Cooperative Approach." *Christian Rural Fellowship Bulletin* (177): 1-8.

2157. Williamson, Ralph L.
    1953 "Common Concerns and the Cooperative Approach." *Town and Country Church* (February): 1-2.

2158. Williamson, Ralph L.
    1953 "Federated Churches." *Town and Country Church* (November): 1-2.

2159. Wilson, Warren Hugh.
    1930 "The Rural Church Volunteers." *Missionary Review of the World* 53(August).

2160. Wilson, Warren Hugh.
    1936 "National Protestant Rural Life Departments." *Rural America* (February): 40.

2161. Willson, Warren Hugh.
    1942 "The Second Missionary Adventure." *Christian Rural Fellowship Bulletin* (77): 1-8.

2162. Wilson, Warren Hugh.
    1946 "The Sexton's Holy Calling." *Christian Rural Fellowship Bulletin* (109): 1-4. Reprint from *Rural Religion and the Country Church*, 1927, New York, N.Y.: Fleming H. Revell Company.

2163. Wilson, Warren Hugh.
    1951 "The Rural Church as a Vitalizing Agent. (excerpts)" *Town and Country Church* (December): 3-4.

2164. Wilson, (Mrs.) Warren Hugh.
    1913 "Boys and Girls in the Country Church." *Rural Manhood* 4: 330.

2165. Winters, R.L.
       1947 "A Synodical Rural Church Program." *Town and Country
            Church* (November): 5-6.

2166. Wolcott, D.K.
       1955 "The Function of the Commission on Education in the
            Rural Church." *Rural Church* 16(December/January): 2-6.

2167. Work, P.
       1951 "A Bell Rings Out; The New Rural Church Emerges from
            the Old." *American Agriculture* (March 17): 178, 181.

2168. Work, P.
       1953 "The Rural Church Institute." *Town and Country Church*
            (November): 3-4.

2169. Wyker, J.D.
       1945 "The Church and Rural Agencies." *Mountain Life and Work*
            21(July): 29.

2170. Wyker, J.D.
       1947 "Green Valley." *Town and Country Church* (September): 5-6.

2171. Wyker, J.D.
       1947 "The Group Approach to Rural Church Work." *Town and
            Country Church* (February): 3-4.

2172. Wyker, J.D.
       1950 "Redemptive, Creative, Christian." *Town and Country Church*
            (April): 13-14.

2173. Wyker, J.D.
       1956 "You Can Do It Too." *Town and Country Church* (January):
            5-6.

2174. Wyker, Mrs. J.D.
       1952 "Contributions of Women's Organizations." *Town and
            Country Church* (February): 5-6.

2175. Yates, H. Wilson.
       1969 "Social Change and the Church in Nonmetropolitan
            Society." *Worship* 43(June-July): 318-338. Also in Victor J.
            Klimoski and Bernard Quinn (eds.) (1970) *Church and
            Community: Nonmetropolitan America in Transition.*
            Washington, D.C.: Center for Applied Research in the
            Apostolate. pp. 1-22.

2176. Yergin, Vernon N.
1905 "The Social Services of the Church in the Country."
Auburn Seminary Record.

2177. Zellers, Harry K., Jr.
1947 "'Plowboy' Religion." *Christian Rural Fellowship Bulletin*
(123): 1-4.

2178. Ziegler, Edward Krusen.
1941 "A Christian Rural Life Philosophy." *Christian Rural
Fellowship Bulletin* (67): 1-8.

2179. Ziegler, Edward Krusen.
1942 "Guidance in Worship in the Rural Church." *Christian Rural
Fellowship Bulletin* (70): 1-6.

2180. Ziegler, Edward Krusen.
1947 "The Bible as a Rural Book." *Christian Rural Fellowship
Bulletin* (120): 1-8.

2181. Ziegler, Edward Krusen.
1947 "The Church with Wide Horizons." *Christian Rural
Fellowship Bulletin* (123): 1-5.

2182. Ziegler, Edward Krusen.
1948 "A Bibliography on Worship for the Rural Church."
Agricultural Missions (Spring): 1-10.

2183. Ziegler, Edward Krusen.
1951 "Worship Methods in the Rural Church." *Town and
Country Church* (February): 1-2. Also in *Christian Rural
Fellowship Bulletin* (163, May 1951): 1-6.

2184. Ziegler, Edward Krusen.
1955 "Church Loans for Farm Ownership." *Town and Country
Church* (March): 3-4.

2185. Zimmerman, Donald W.
1948 "Church Cooperation in Ashfield, Massachusetts." *Town and
Country Church* (September): 1-2.

2186. Zimmerman, Donald W.
1952 "The Task of the Rural Church." *Town and Country Church*
(May): 14.

2187. Zimmerman, Donald W.
1958 "The Church in Rural America." *McCormick Speaking*
12(December): 20-23.

2188. Zimmerman, Donald W. and A. Kelley.
       1967 "Religious Value Structures in Non-Metropolitan Society."
       Town and Country Church (September/October): 7-12.

Soli Deo Gloria.

Indexes

Author Index

A & M College of Texas
986-988
Abele, E.F. 1154
Abell, Troy D. 1
Achtemeier, A.R. 1159
Ackerman, Joseph 2, 263, 517,
1155-1157
Ackley, C.W. 1158
Adams, H.B. 1161
Adams, Rachel S. 3
Agricultural Missions, Inc. 4-6
Ahn, G.B., Jr. 1162
Aiton, E.W. 349
Akers, A. 1163
Alexander, D. 1164
Alexander, J. 356
Alexander, John L. 7
Alexander, T.D. 1165
Alison, W.H. 8
All New England Conference on
the Rural Church 989
Alldredge, Eugene P. 9
Alleger, D.E. 990
Allen, T.B. 1166
Allen, W.S. 1167

Allred, B.W. 1168
Allred, Thurman W. 10
Almack, R.B. 1169
Alward, R.S. 1170
American Lutheran Church 11
American Unitarian Association
12
Anderson, Dwight E. 13
Anderson, L. 1171
Anderson, Loren E. 14
Anderson, W.A. 707, 708, 1172,
1173
Andrew, B. 1174, 1175
Andrews, David G. 15
Anthony, Alfred W. 1176
Archibald, R.M. 1177
Armitstead, A.H. 1178
Armstrong, A.M. 1179
Armstrong, Harry P. 1180
Armstrong, Robert G. 1181-1183
Arrington, Leonard J. 709, 710
Arterburn, Joe 1185
Arthur, C. Ralph 1184
Arvold, Alfred G. 860
Ash, R.J. 1187

Cain, Benjamin H. 89-93, 1279
Calhoun, Newell M. 1280
Callahan, Kennon L. 997
Camp, B. 1281, 1282
Campbell, Gladys L. 1283, 1284
Campbell, R. 1285
Cantrell, Randolph L. 728-730,
    867, 868, 882, 928-930, 971,
    998
Carlson, William E. 94
Carmichael, S.T. 1287
Carothers, J. Edward 95, 1286
Carr, James M. 96-99, 208,
    1288-1290
Carroll, Jackson W. 100
Carter, Joe H. 1291
Carter, Michael V. 101, 731-734,
    883, 999
Carver, Thomas N. 102, 1292
Cascini, William 38
Case, J.F. 1293, 1294
Cash, I.M. 1295
Catholic Church 103
Catholic Rural Life Conference
    104
Caudill, Harry M. 105
Chadwick, B.A. 711
Chamberlain, R.W. 1296
Chambers, Martin R. 106
Chapin, Stuart F. 107
Chapman, J.I. 1297
Chase, Frank M. 1298
Childs, Alan W. 295
Choate, Norman 108
Christensen, John R. 735
Christiano, Kevin 697
Church of the Brethren 109
Churchill, A.C. 1300
Cisin, Ira H. 742, 736

Clark, A.W. 1302
Clark, Carl A. 110, 737
Clark, Dumont 1303
Clark, Elmer T. 111
Clark, Francis E. 1304
Clark, Neil M. 1305
Clarke, D. 1306-1312
Clarkson, George E. 1313, 1314
Clawson, M. 738
Clayton, C.F. 1315
Cleland, Charles L. 739, 1000
Cleveland, Philip J. 112, 113
Clingan, R.L. 1316
Coady, M.M. 1317
Cobb, A.L. 114
Cobb, Stephen G. 589
Cochel, W.A. 1318
Cofell, William L. 115
Cogswell, James A. 116, 147,
    250, 501, 572, 648
Cole, W.H. 1319
Coles, Robert 117, 1320
Collins, C. 1321
Colliver, McGuire C. 1001
Comfort, Richard O. 118, 740,
    741, 1322-1332
Commission on Religion in
    Appalachia 1002
Committee on Continuing
    Education for Clergy at
    Land-grant and State
    Universities 1003
Committee on Town and
    Country 1004, 1552
Compton, Edward 1333
Congregational Christian Church
    119
Congregational Christian
    Churches in the U.S.A 120

United Christian Youth
  Movement 627
United Church of Christ 628,
  629, 1128
United Methodist Church 630,
  631
United Presbyterian Church in
  the U.S.A. 632
United Presbyterian Church
  U.S.A. 633
United States Department of
  Agriculture 976, 977
University of Illinois Cooperative
  Extension Service 1129-1131
University of Minnesota,
  Department of Agriculture
  1132
University of Nebraska 1133
University of Virginia, Extension
  Division 978
University of Wisconsin College
  of Agriculture 1134-1136
Upjohn, Richard 634
Upton, W.H. 2108
Urbain, J.V. 417, 478, 635, 636,
  693, 2109

Van Horn, G.A. 2111
Van Saun, Arthur C. 637
Vance, Rupert 638
Vandermyde, J.B. 2110
Vangerud, Richard D. 851
Vernon, Matt 2112
Vetters, Cindy V. 2113
Vetters, Kenneth 2113
Vezina, Jacqueline P. 979
Vidich, Arthur 639
Vier, Lester B. 640

Virginia Council of Churches
  641
Virginia Polytechnic Institute
  1137
Vizzard, J.L. 1138
Voelker, Stanley W. 642, 1139,
  2114
Vogt, Paul L. 643, 1140, 1141,
  2115

Wagner, James E. 644
Wagner, P.W. 2116
Wakeley, Ray E. 980
Wakely, R.E. 2117
Waldo, W.P. 2118
Walker, J. Marshall 645
Wallace, Henry 2119
Walrath, Douglas A. 157, 646
Walter, Oliver 762
Waltner, Sherman K. 647
Wammer, O.M. 2120
Warburg, J.P. 2121
Warehime, Hal M. 648
Warner, Paul D. 1009
Warner, R. Stephen 649
Warren, Gertrude L. 981
Wasserman, Ira M. 852
Watson, Doris 2123
Watson, George 2123
Watts, David 2124
Watts, R.L. 2125
Weatherford, W.D. 58, 650
Webb, Charles G. 982
Webb, J. E. 2126
Webber, Frederick R. 651
Weber, Cheryl A. 1142
Weber, Leonard 1143
Webster, Norman C. 2127
Weeks, Nathan A. 2128

Subject Index

Appalachia (cont'd)
  mission(s) 241, 297, 550, 1002
  mountaineers 652
  pastors' views 341
  pastors 277
  poverty and the church 233
  Presbyterians 633, 799, 948
  psychological perspectives 1,
    494
  religion 59, 323, 463, 496, 650,
    732, 754, 778, 818, 961 1253
  religiosity 342
  role of the church 1093
  sects 781
  snake handlers 780
  social forces 143
  social ministries 654
  sociological perspectives 1,
    494, 495
  spiritual development 1693
  surveys 57
  suspicion 582
  textbook censorship 743
  theological perspectives 1, 494
  values 1001
  voluntarism 999
Architecture 634, 952, 1225, 1471
Arizona 1126
Art 1387
Attendance 697, 1426
Attitudes 754, 811, 917, 979
  morals 1270
  religion 949
  seminary courses 835
Autonomy 730

Back-to-the-land movement 722
Baptist churches 26 141
Baptist General Conference 213
Beliefs 361, 545, 593, 727, 754,
  776, 1054
Bible 1673
  as a rural book 2180
Bible colleges 1913, 1993
Bible readings 25

Bibliographies 87, 311, 314, 429,
  540, 546
  Appalachia 949
  on religion and church 2106
  rural churches 1153, 2034
  worship 703, 2182
Black churches 202, 535, 760,
  788, 823-825, 857, 1142, 1928
  future 1369
  Presbyterian 1336
  religious attitudes 318
Black farmers 1359
Blacks 2067
Blue Ridge Mountains 336
Bulletins 2112
Bus 193, 1422

Cain, Benjamin H. 93
California 78, 761, 1019, 1417,
  1436, 1553
Care 1401
Cascades 1088
Case studies 88, 108, 112, 149,
  248, 442, 573, 618, 995, 1180,
  1379
  Appalachia 336, 695
  Black pastors 204
  church conflict 167
  church finance 1263
  Elmtown 294
  pastors 206
  Protestant churches 185
  rural churches 160, 198
  rural missions 2124
  soil conservation 203
Catholic churches 81, 130, 215,
  337, 351, 355, 417, 444-446,
  478, 544, 636, 693, 696, 808,
  856, 955, 970, 1062, 1112,
  1231, 1261, 1435, 1499, 1633,
  1658, 2052, 2109
  fertility 809
  theology 103
Catholic Rural Life Conference
  104
Census 876-880

Intermarriage 723
International cooperation 2022
International outlook 1800, 1816
Iowa 151, 357, 604, 972, 1083,
    1164, 1185, 1281, 1427, 1953,
    1974, 2128
Iowa Christian Rural Fellowship
    972
Irrigation 78
Israel 762

Jewish Agricultural Society 138
Jews 138, 142, 832, 1353
Johnny Appleseed 1680
Justice 239, 1401, 1469
Juvenile delinquency 1063

Kansas 71, 405, 856, 864, 893,
    894, 1613, 2108
Kentucky 723, 869, 873, 923,
    924, 956, 1001, 1216, 1696
Kingdom of God 524, 1795,
    1869, 1881, 1892
  and agriculture 219
  stewardship 700

Labor 35
Laity 343, 1907
  theological perspectives 348
Land 2, 20, 21, 29, 47, 49, 178,
    179, 392, 580, 587, 767, 1427
  and Christ 1244
  and Christianity 721
  and human welfare 1829
  and hunger 53
  and the church 2, 50, 197,
    266, 724, 759, 1018, 1107,
    1527, 1676, 1770
  biblical perspectives 53, 66,
    814, 1226
  bibliographies 311
  church work 1845
  management 222
  misuse 1315
  moral directives 750
  Native Americans 847

ownership 203, 1155, 1580
philosophical perspectives
    1209
policy 525, 1105, 1671, 1739
quality of life 1495
reform 1484, 1781
stewardship 432, 449, 1049,
    1248
tenancy 1532, 1888
tenure 1021
theological perspectives 66,
    109, 265, 896, 1143, 1195,
    1245, 1533, 1742, 1794, 1872,
    1895, 1976
use 186, 1266
values 774
way of life 839
Land reform 264
Land-grant universities 841,
    1003, 1016, 1024, 1146, 1192
Landless people 985
Landlessness 1563
Landscaping 865, 909, 952
Law 767
Lay ministry 1508
Leaders 626, 627, 857, 861, 905,
    976, 1145, 1463, 1873
  education 939
  problems 1055
Leadership 13, 442, 598, 826,
    944, 978, 1054, 1114, 1490,
    1667, 1799, 1813
  and farm crisis 1408
  and pastors 2144
  projects 1623
Leadership training 1171, 1318,
    2122
Leisure 1978
Lenten services 1295
Liberals 649
Libraries 612, 1630, 2145
  for pastors 1269
Life cycles of churches 770
Lord's Acre Plan 180, 195, 1303,
    1306, 1307, 1309, 1310, 1370,
    1467, 1678, 1679, 1847, 1902,